Scribe Publications
THE WORDS TO REMEMBER IT

The contributors to this book are all members of the Sydney Child Holocaust Survivors Group. The group was formed in 1987, following a visit by Sarah Moskovitz, a child psychologist and educator from the US. Sarah has specifically researched children under 12 who survived the Czechoslovakian concentration camp Theresienstadt during the Second World War, and who then went to a Jewish orphanage called Lingfield House in Surrey, England.

Sarah coined the term 'child survivor', and published her findings in a book called *Love Despite Hate*. She started a support group in Los Angeles, and from there other groups quickly followed.

In Sydney, Eva Engel, a skilled community networker, was responsible for initiating the formation of the group, recruiting Litzi Lemberg to help her. A newly identified child survivor, Litzi became the spokesperson for the fledgling support group.

With steady prodding and encouragement from Eva, the group grew and prospered. Members met regularly to talk to each other, and then became increasingly involved with the survivor, and wider, community.

Members of the Sydney Child Holocaust Survivors Group have been together now for 22 years. The group is now part of the World Federation of Jewish Child Survivors of the Holocaust.

The Words to Remember it

MEMOIRS OF CHILD HOLOCAUST SURVIVORS

SCRIBE
Melbourne

Scribe Publications Pty Ltd
PO Box 523
Carlton North, Victoria, Australia 3054
Email: info@scribepub.com.au

First published by Scribe 2009

Copyright © this collection Scribe Publications 2009.
Text and photographs © retained by the individual authors, except where otherwise acknowledged.

All rights reserved. Without limiting the rights under copyright reserved above, no part of this publication may be reproduced, stored in or introduced into a retrieval system, or transmitted, in any form or by any means (electronic, mechanical, photocopying, recording or otherwise) without the prior written permission of the publishers of this book.

Typeset in 12/15.6 pt Adobe Garamond by the publishers
Jacket design by Miriam Rosenbloom
Printed and bound in Australia by Griffin Press. Only wood grown from sustainable regrowth forests is used in the manufacture of paper found in this book.

National Library of Australia
Cataloguing-in-Publication data

The words to remember it: memoirs of child Holocaust survivors

9781921372636 (pbk.)

Holocaust, Jewish (1939-1945)–Personal narratives; Jewish children in the Holocaust; Holocaust survivors.

940.5318

www.scribepublications.com.au

Contents

Introduction: Caroline Jones, AO	1
Litzi Lemberg	9
Peter Rössler	19
Mark Spigelmam	47
Paul Kornmehl	69
Ruth Leiser	81
Lexie Keston	115
Eva Grant	132
Elizabeth Levy	144
Cesha Glazer	160
Charles Feldman	168
Naomi Goldrei	176
Pierre Meyer	185
Jozef Vissel	197
Maria Lachs	205
Paul Drexler	218
Walter Lachs	227
Peter Nash	232
Ruth Rack	240
Eva Engel, OAM	253
Charles Kessler	261
Magdalena Langer	265
Nora M. Huppert	273
Halina Robinson	291
Dasha Caminer	305

Cella Baruch	316
Jenine Cibulka	321
Greta Silvers	327
Shulamit Ullmann	330
Kathy Valer Gordon	337
Judy Bahar	343
Acknowledgements	345

CAROLINE JONES, AO

Introduction

This book will be a gift to all who read it, for what can be more precious to us than our life stories, the record of who we are, where we've come from, what trials we've met on our journeys, where we've found courage, and how we've kept our hope in life?

The writers of this book are my contemporaries; we were children of the Second World War. But our experiences stand in sharp contrast. The book places my own childhood into a wider perspective, deepens my sense of gratitude — and fills me with sadness and horror that little children suffered as they did.

When I was born in Sydney, Australia, in 1938, Ruth Rack (then Landesberg) was ten years old and living in Leipzig, Germany, with her father, Bernhard, her mother, Anna, three siblings, and a large extended family. She remembers a home filled with love. But, in November of that year, all but one of Leipzig's nine synagogues were destroyed by Nazi mobs in the pogroms of *Kristallnacht*. Ruth's father was taken to the Sachsenhausen concentration camp; her mother was forced into slave labour for three years, then transported with 245 men, women, and children to Belzyce in Poland, where they were all murdered. In the meantime, Ruth was sent to England, where she lived all through the war with terrible uncertainty about the fate of her parents. It was not until after her visit to Leipzig in 2001 — recounted in this book — that she learned what had happened to them.

When I was born, Peter Rössler was eight years old and living with his elder brother, Honza, and his parents, in the centre of Prague, Czechoslovakia. Peter cherishes memories of his mother, Lilly, playing the piano: 'The Blue Danube' reverberates in his mind to this day. He was proud to see how other men would greet his father, Karel, when they walked together in the street.

When war broke out in 1939, my father, Brian, enlisted immediately in the Australian Military Forces. My mother and I moved to the country to live with my grandmother and aunt in a weatherboard cottage in Murrurundi, New South Wales. In March 1942, my father came home briefly on leave and made me a little wooden table and two chairs. At that same time, after five months of deprivation and malnutrition in the squalid, overcrowded Lodz Ghetto in southern Poland, Peter Rössler, aged 11, watched helplessly as his father fell ill and died, aged 46. Only a few months later, his mother also died. Lilly Rössler was 36, the same age as my mother, Nancy.

Safe in Australia, I was three years old and walking down to the shops on Mayne Street with my grandmother. I noticed that everyone addressed her warmly and respectfully: 'Good morning, Mrs Pountney.'

On the other side of the world, another three-year-old, Lexie Keston, was trying to stay alive in the Krakow Ghetto in Poland. Lexie remembers her grandmother, Mrs Silberman, being hidden from the Nazis under a pile of doonas. Her grandmother was elderly, frail, and blind. Lexie does not remember the day the Nazis found her and took her away forever.

In early April 1945, I was excited by learning and playing with my friends under the spreading shade trees of Murrurundi Central School. Each afternoon, I walked home to the cottage on Mayne Street, with its violets and hollyhocks in the front garden. We had afternoon tea with homemade biscuits, often with visitors who had brought us fresh eggs and cream from their farms.

On 6 April 1945, Lexie was forcibly crammed onto one of three trains with her parents and 2500 other prisoners from the Bergen-Belsen concentration camp in north-western Germany. They had already spent nearly two years in Bergen-Belsen, suffering starvation, epidemics, appalling sanitary conditions, and uncertainty about what would happen to them next. After seven days on the train, the Nazi guards suddenly fled from the approaching US 743rd Tank Battalion. The prisoners spilled off the trains, and gaunt, sick men, women, and children stumbled up the embankment to their liberators, who were shocked to see people in such a wretched plight.

Anne Frank was not on the train. She had died in Bergen-Belsen a month earlier.

Apart from their parents, nine close relatives of Peter and Honza Rössler also perished in the Lodz Ghetto, or were deported to death camps or labour camps. The two boys had to fend for themselves. They spent nearly four years in Nazi internment, surviving Auschwitz-Birkenau, Kaufering Lager IV, and a 50-kilometre death march almost to Dachau, on the outskirts of Munich. On 30 April 1945, they were liberated by the 42nd 'Rainbow' Division of the US army.

On the same day, Hitler committed suicide in his Berlin bunker, and I, aged seven and a half, was excited about my father coming home from our own war in the Pacific.

Ruth, Peter, and Lexie's stories are three of the stories you will read in this book. The families of most of the other writers were also cruelly separated, scattered, and decimated. They were forced to flee from their homes; their possessions and symbols of belonging, treasured by every family, were stolen or desecrated. It is difficult to encompass the extent of their losses. The imagination baulks at the prospect of leaving behind one's dolls and toys, all the treasures collected in a child's cubbyhouse; of leaving behind warm jumpers, coats, socks, singlets, dresses, and shirts, shaving brushes and soap, sanitary articles, tweezers, hairbrushes, mirrors, combs, sewing baskets, scissors, cups and saucers, glasses, tablecloths, flower vases, wedding presents, photographs, pictures, musical instruments, tools, personal papers, and identification documents. Many of their parents would never again sit at their own dining tables, or use their own plates and knives and forks, in homes furnished with cushions and curtains at the windows; would never again sleep in their own nightclothes, in their own sheets on their own beds, with pillows in pillowcases, under warm blankets; never again have any personal privacy; never again be in control of the welfare of their own children, or have access to their savings.

For some of the writers, it's been a long process to realise that they are, in fact, child survivors of the Holocaust. Litzi Lemberg says that for the first 18 years of her life, she didn't even know that she was a survivor. She carried memories that were a mystery to her — memories of getting into trucks, of a man dressed in striped pyjamas, of wooden floors, bare feet, shaven heads, of a railway journey. But they were 'disembodied memories with no time frame or place to park them'. Sometimes she wondered about them, but mostly she denied them, or in some way diverted them. Later, being a survivor meant being an outsider looking in, wondering who she was, feeling invisible.

In 1985, the American researcher Sarah Moskovitz came to Australia to speak, on the 40th anniversary of the liberation of Auschwitz-Birkenau. Her lecture concerned a group of children who had been in the Theresienstadt concentration camp in Czechoslovakia. As Sarah Moskovitz unfolded the facts of what had happened to these children, Litzi was shocked to recognise that this stranger was telling *her* story. So, her mysterious memories were given a context and a meaning. Her connectedness with the

Holocaust began that day. She was 45. In 1987, as other child survivors came to their own realisations, a Sydney child survivors group was formed. Gradually, in this safe environment, the painful stories began to be shared, compared, further researched, and validated.

For those in the group, it has been a long, difficult, and continuing journey of discovering, in some cases, just who they are and what they endured, and of adding dates, names, places, and clarifying details to their often blurred memories. Information on the internet is still helping to put some of the elusive pieces into place.

Now, with this book, members of the group have taken the significant step of sending their stories out into the world. They are publishing these accounts so that the facts of their history are recorded for their families and for students; so that this chapter of human history will not be forgotten or denied or distorted; and in the hope that their experiences will never be suffered by children in the future. For these are not only eyewitness accounts of twentieth-century history — they also have urgent relevance today. Like the canary in the mine, they warn of potential danger; they remind us of the worst depravity of human behaviour. They set alarm bells ringing when any group in society becomes the subject of rumours or is made a scapegoat. They alert us to the terrible things that can happen when good people do and say nothing. Regrettably, these are reminders that we still need today, and perhaps there will always be such a need, given the potential for evil, as well as good, in the human psyche.

These stories of survival also illuminate the best of human nature. They tell of kindness and compassion, and of the readiness to risk personal safety for the sake of strangers in trouble. This book illustrates the particular tenderness, duty, and complexity of family relationships from the trusting and dependent viewpoint of little children. The 'children' write of their parents, grandparents, aunts, uncles, and cousins with a poignant love and longing, all the more affecting because of the shocking losses that they suffered at such early ages. While many people take their family connections for granted, these children have only a few precious years of memories to treasure. They enshrine the smallest fragments of recollection like icons, in order to give some reality to long-dead beloved family members, to restore their dignity, to afford them their rightful places of respect and affection in the communities from which they were so disgracefully and unforgivably wrenched.

The child survivors are now in their sixties, seventies, and eighties. Over recent years, I have had the privilege of coming to know some of them. Three of the writers in this book told me something of their stories on 'The Search for Meaning' program (which ran from 1987–94 on ABC Radio National), where they struggled to select suitable words to describe the terrifying incidents of their childhood.

It is a miracle that any of these child survivors are alive. Most came perilously close to death when they were very young. I could so easily have missed knowing them. Australia could have missed their deep loyalty and their rich contributions as citizens. Although they are now mature people, gifted and qualified in many fields, I sense an unusual child-like quality in them — perhaps because I encountered them first through their childhood stories, rather than through meeting them as my doctor, physiotherapist, taxidriver, salesperson, or golfing partner. Or perhaps because, even though they are mothers, fathers, grandparents, accomplished professionals, artists, tradespeople, and businesspeople, when telling their life stories they have the gentle dreaminess of children still awaking, not yet quite disentangled from the remnants of their nightmares, speaking too calmly and with an odd detachment about fearful events that no child should ever have been permitted to witness. Sometimes they seem to me like rare butterflies, beautifully fragile in their unlikely survival, and yet possessing an essence of spiritual strength forged through their own suffering and refined by the enduring grief of their losses, a grief held in dignified reserve.

A number of the writers of this book consider it their mission to relate their Holocaust experiences as guides at the Sydney Jewish Museum, particularly to groups of schoolchildren. They find it rewarding to do so. With this publication, these stories take their place in the wider Australian story. They become part of the rich weave of our national identity, of who we are as a people. And, beyond that, they go out into the world to document a shameful chapter in the history of humankind, from which something of value was won, like opal sparkling in the rock face. For, although these are chronicles of imprisonment, cruelty, and death, they have a liberating quality, because they also tell of love and self-sacrifice. They demonstrate that, no matter how fearful our circumstances, we have one precious freedom remaining — the freedom to choose our response to what happens to us, a hard-won insight from Viktor Frankl in his classic book *Man's Search for Meaning*.

The authors of this book lost almost everything that was most essential, dear, and precious to them; yet, they chose life and hope; they chose to have children in a new country that they love, and to which they belong and contribute with generosity, compassion, humour, and purpose; and they managed to give back much that was stolen from them in the impressionable vulnerability of childhood.

These are stories to move the heart profoundly; to elicit gratitude for all that we have; powerful stories to make us determined to speak out and take action against prejudice or hateful gossip; stories to encourage a vigorous, constructive questioning of authority; stories to remind us always that the price of liberty is, indeed, eternal vigilance, by all the people, on behalf of all the people.

LITZI LEMBERG

What it means to be a Holocaust survivor

In 1997, Tom Kramer of the Sydney Jewish Museum asked me to give a 20-minute talk on what it means to be a Holocaust survivor. That request started me on a path of thought that I had not consciously trodden before — perhaps because for the first 18 years of my life, being a survivor meant absolutely nothing to me. In those 18 years, I didn't even know I was a survivor. The memories I carried within me were a mystery to me. Sometimes I wondered, tentatively, why I had them. But mostly, I denied them to myself, or in some way diverted them.

They were memories of getting onto trucks; of travelling between different places; of holes in the ground with wooden seats over them, and of a fear of falling in; of wondering, 'Whose shoe is that in there, and how did it get there?' Memories of other children; of walking with faceless adults over crunchy leaves, of knowing to be quiet, of seeing a man dressed in striped pyjamas leading the way; of arriving in a place with wooden bunks and being greeted by a stern, grey woman; a special memory of a urine puddle on the ground. 'Who did that?' demanded the iron-grey lady. 'He did,' said I, pointing to a boy. There was a slap for him, and a slap for me. I knew that you mustn't cry, whatever you do.

And then memories of wooden floors, bare feet, a splinter in my foot, an infirmary … what were they going to do to me? Memories of walks outside — cobblestones, tall buildings, a faceless 'someone' looking after us; and memories of shaven heads, of parcels of clothing. A vivid memory: 'Choose one item.' I made my choice, an apron pinafore with frills — until I saw the sparkling necklace with blue and orange beads. I couldn't take my eyes off it. How I had to beg to exchange the pinafore for that necklace!

'Can you speak any English?' asked our carer, with an unexpected friendliness. Memories of injections in the arm; of extreme resistance to this; of three or six pairs of arms and hands (or so it seemed) restraining my efforts to escape. Memories of a railway journey to a big city, of a fun park with huge slippery slides, and of eating pink ice cream. Laughing. Then a plane trip, lying down with my head on someone's lap. So sick and tired. Who was pulling my hair?

They were disembodied memories, with no time frame or place to park them. Then clearer memories of coming to a very large country house in a very large garden with a large pool; being welcomed by a lady in a black dress with a white collar and cuffs; settling in with other children, playing, learning Jewish stories told by a nice man who came regularly.

Going to school. Meeting other children who spoke differently, but somehow understanding them. A vivid memory of a pretty, smiling, welcoming girl who said, 'Hullo.' My answer was a hearty kick to her knee, making it bleed profusely. Her stunned look of puzzlement. Why did I do that and when would I be punished? I waited all day for punishment. Nothing happened.

Memories of meeting a young lady with flaming-red hair. Then the lady came again, this time with a tall, dark-haired man. 'I'm your father,' he said. I accepted this statement. Then a visit from him and a short, plump, pretty lady wearing a tall black hat. 'This is your mother,' said he. Confusion. 'Was the red-haired lady my mother before this lady?' I asked. I don't remember the answer.

Then, some time later, a visit to London to stay for the weekend. Then a move to stay permanently with my 'parents'. Meeting other family members, an uncle and aunt and numerous cousins, feeling the warmth and kindness from them. Then going to Jewish Day School, settling in, making friends with Stanley and Monica.

Then … we're going to Australia to join my three aunts, Rosl, Jeanette, and Eva, and their families. Torn away from friends, family, and the increasingly familiar life of England, in 1948 we came to Sydney to start a new life. I remember the feeling of loss and sadness at that time. But, being young and resilient, I tried to settle into a new school in a strange place with strange children — children who were not so welcoming. I remember being asked by my new teacher, who was filling in a form, 'What religion are you?' I shook my head. She assumed I did not understand, so she drew a church. I steadfastly continued to shake my head in spite of her continuing frustrated efforts to make me understand. I was very relieved when she gave up.

I grew up into a fairly turbulent teenager, and, in one of those turbulent periods, as a first-year physiotherapy student, I found out from my 'father' that I was a Holocaust survivor. By then, I was 18.

I already knew that I was born in Vienna in 1939. Now I learned that my 'father', Bume Sonnenschein, was in fact my uncle. My real father, his brother David, had died in Buchenwald in 1940. My mother, Stephanie Sonnenschein, had died somewhere in Vienna. I had had an older brother, Hershl, but no one knew what had happened to him. And I had never been sent to the English countryside to escape the bombing of London. That was the answer I had been given years before when I asked about my memories. In fact, I had been in Czechoslovakia, in the concentration camp Theresienstadt. But I should think myself lucky, because Theresienstadt was one the 'less severe' camps.

So, what did being a survivor mean then? Shock, numbness,

complete and utter confusion at having my life as I knew it turned upside down. And yet, there was also relief. 'Ah, that was what those memories were about.' But how could I find out more? For all those years, my true parents hadn't existed for me, because of a well-meaning conspiracy of silence by the whole family. My tentative questions were so difficult. How could I ask about such a painful subject after all those years of silence? Perhaps it would be best to leave it alone and get on with life. Maybe I wouldn't get the right answers anyway.

What did being a survivor mean to me? As long as I can remember, it meant being an outsider looking in, being alone. It meant feeling invisible, not being one of the girls, having a poor sense of myself and of my lack of connection with my past. After all, who was I, and why was I so alone? It meant needing to talk ... but to whom? A psychiatrist? Psychiatrists seemed inaccessible and unattainable in the 1950s. A certain amount of self-pity came with these half-thoughts. My communication with my adoptive parents was quite fragile, and no doubt they were also at a loss.

In my mid-teens, I had joined the Zionist youth group Habonim, where I finally met other teenagers — ones I felt at home with. There was something about their company that filled the lonely gap in my life. For me, the aims and philosophy of Habonim were very much secondary; it was the newfound friends that meant everything to me. It was only many years later that I realised many of them were also Holocaust survivors — child survivors, like myself. But, at that time, we knew so little about each other, and I knew so little about myself. And I knew nothing about my Holocaust past.

As I entered my twenties, I put the 'Holocaust thing' on the backburner. I told myself I was not really part of 'all that', because I hadn't really suffered and I'd been too young to remember anything terrible, hadn't I? And it had happened so long ago. The memories faded as I married, was widowed 14 months later, and eventually married again and had three wonderful children.

Talk of my personal Holocaust was something to be avoided, something private — not something to be discussed over a cup of tea or coffee with politely interested or prying friends and extended family.

And so family life continued. My adoptive parents died relatively young, and the past receded even further. Family duties took priority ... until 1985, when my past came suddenly and squarely to meet me. The year was the 40th anniversary of the liberation of Auschwitz-Birkenau, and the Australian Association of Jewish Holocaust Survivors held a week's commemoration, inviting guests from overseas to speak. My very best friend ever since I was 15 was my friend Eva (who has since passed away). She was a Holocaust survivor, but with none of the hang-ups about it that I endured. She was keen to hear a lecture on children in the Holocaust, and she asked me if I would like to come. I might find it interesting, she said, and I might 'find something out'.

I had no plans that day, and I said I would go. I sat in a packed room, relaxed, and listened to a tall, gentle, white-haired but youthful lady called Sarah Moskovitz talk about research she had conducted into a group of children. These children had been in the Theresienstadt concentration camp. After their liberation they were taken to Prague, and then to England, where they were eventually transported to an orphanage called Lingfield House in Surrey. She had interviewed 25 of these children as adults, and had written a book about them called *Love Despite Hate*.*

By the time she finished speaking, I was physically doubled up in my comfortable chair. I realised with disbelief that she was talking about me! I was one of those children. How was it possible? For the first time in my life, this stranger was telling my story —

---

* Sarah Moskovitz, *Love Despite Hate: child survivors of the Holocaust and their adult lives*, Schocken Books, New York, 1983. Professor Moskovitz is now Emeritus Professor of Educational Psychology at California State University, Northridge, USA.

or rather, the story of the children I had been with. After all those years …

Of course, I spoke to Sarah after the lecture. She had heard of me and knew me by name. She gave me her copy of her book, and I showed her my photo, printed inside it. I had the same picture at home, and, in younger years, I had often wondered about the story behind it.

What did being a survivor mean to me at that point? Huge, heaving tears and waves of pure emotion, followed once again by a stunned relief. Then, Sarah interviewed me, and, in that interview, for the first time in my life, I verbalised my memories, the blurred margins of my memory expanding and coming into focus. Being a survivor, a 'child survivor', as Sarah called it, took on a whole new feeling for me. My memories were validated: I really had been there, in the camp, in the orphanage. My connectedness with the Holocaust began there.

It was Mother's Day, and I will never forget the effort my children put in to make it as special as they could. They saw how emotionally drained I was, and their support and concern was touching. That was the time to talk to them and tell them more about myself and my family. I was 45 years old.

So, what next? Through Sarah, I met other child survivors, including Tanja Kessler (née Muench) who had been in Theresienstadt with me, and her husband, Charles, who had been in the orphanage in Surrey. Their stories were in Sarah's book, and they had been living in Sydney all this time.

Some time later, I was approached by a very persistent lady called Eva Engel (all the Evas in my life have played very significant parts, including my Aunt Eva and, of course, my late friend Eva) to ask if I would like to help her take this further and get other child survivors together, as Sarah's visit had created so much interest. In 1987, Sarah returned to Australia to address a large gathering of child survivors, and from this gathering we started the Sydney Child Survivors Group.

From Theresienstadt to the Lake District: After their liberation from Theresienstadt in 1945, many child survivors were accommodated in hostels in Windermere, northern England. Litzi Lemberg (above, third from left; below, second from left) learned only many years later that she was received in Windermere prior to moving to Lingfield House in Surrey.

Helping to found the Child Survivors Group was not an easy process for me. It took an enormous amount of energy. What kept me going was the knowledge that if having a chance to talk about the past was so beneficial for me, then it would be for others who had been too young to talk in the past, but who could talk now, given a safe environment. So our group grew and prospered. We helped the Melbourne Child Survivors Group get started, and made contact with other child survivor groups in Britain and the United States.

So, what did being a survivor come to mean to me? As I read more books on the Holocaust and learnt about the enormity of the bigger picture, I found a new perspective of myself in that picture. As I learned more, I realised how hard it must have been for my adoptive parents, and the enormous task they faced in raising me. It meant the beginnings of coming to terms with my past. It meant that I was one of an emerging family; that I was reunited with many of my former Habonim friends; and that I met so many new friends. It also meant that I widened my horizons in the Jewish community. My new friend Eva introduced me to her extensive circle of friends in our community, and I met wonderful people in the older survivor community.

Most importantly, I learnt that I could begin to talk about myself to other people more openly, and even in public — something I had never been able to do before, on any level. This release of energy was not without anxiety, as I was often asked, 'Why are you doing this?' Doing this has helped me to come to terms with who I am, where I come from, and who my family were and are. As I asked more questions, I received more information from my aunts in Sydney, and my mother's sister and my cousins in London. I also had help from willing, generous people in our survivor community.

I found out that my father, David Sonnenschein, had indeed died in Buchenwald. His ashes were sent to my family with the explanation, 'shot while trying to escape'. According to an eyewitness, my mother, Stephanie, had committed suicide — or was pushed — from a high terrace at Hartheim Castle in the Austrian town of Alkoven, where thousands of physically and mentally handicapped people were gassed to death. She died within a week of my father's death. My brother, Hershl, had been sent, with me, to Theresienstadt. He was sent to Auschwitz on the last transport in October 1944, and there he perished.

I have built, and continue to build, quite a dossier of photographs, letters, and facts about my family in an attempt to find the missing pieces in the puzzle of my life. As I get a more detailed picture, I find it easier to speak from a stronger sense of identity, to talk to others — Jews and Gentiles — about my story. I am always amazed at how much they want to hear it.

And now, what does being a Holocaust survivor mean to me? It has been a process of

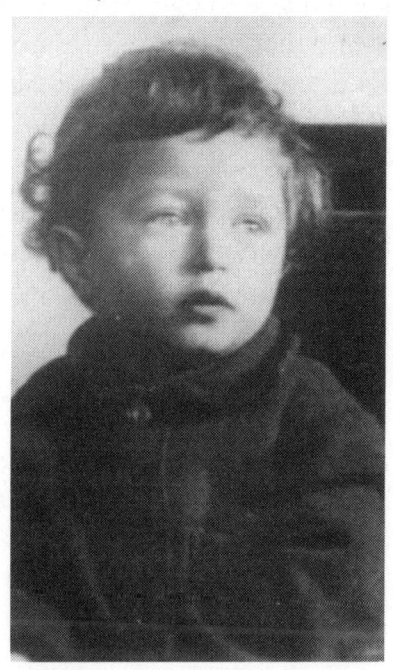

Hershl, the lost brother: On the last transport from Theresienstadt to Auschwitz.

peeling off layers, layer by layer. Like peeling an onion, if you like. With the tears.

Perhaps my last protective layer of secrecy was peeled off in 1995. I am a Feldenkrais practitioner and also a physiotherapist. Every five years, the physiotherapists I trained with have a reunion. The 1995 reunion was our seventh, marking 35 years in the field. After lunch, over 30 of us each stood to say a few words about where we were in our lives, and how our lives had changed over the years. I was prepared to talk about my work with the Feldenkrais method; but, as I listened to each speaker, I slowly realised that I was finally going to tell them about myself. I also realised that I would be the last speaker!

And so, my turn eventually came, and, with a pounding heart and a strangled voice, I started. I told them I had discovered in the first year of our training that I was a Holocaust survivor. I told them a short version of my story: about the Child Survivors Group, about the Holocaust Association,* about the Jewish Museum (where I am a guide), and about the Spielberg Project.† And I told them about the personal growth I had experienced through all of this. As I bared my soul, there was stunned silence, followed by disbelief, and then a sincere appreciation and gratitude that I found very warming.

For the last time, I ask, 'What does it mean to be a survivor?' Somebody once said to me: 'It just means bad luck.' And perhaps it does; but the dictionary defines 'survivor' as one who lives through a time, event, or disaster, and is marked by the deaths of others. So, as one of the 150 children who survived Theresienstadt, I can only think of my good luck. To give that some meaning, it's important to come out of hiding and stand in the light.

---

* The Australian Association of Jewish Holocaust Survivors was formed in 1980. In 1985 the association organised a gathering of survivors to commemorate 40 years since liberation, to which they invited international speakers, including Sarah Moskovitz.

† When Steven Spielberg made the film *Schindler's List*, he was inspired to set up a foundation to enable Holocaust survivors throughout the world to give their testimony on archival film, which would then be, and is now, available as an educational resource and as irrefutable evidence of the most terrible genocide of all time. I was an interviewer, as well as an interviewee, for this project.

PETER RÖSSLER

Memorable experiences in the Lodz Ghetto and Auschwitz-Birkenau, 1941–45

I was born to Jewish parents, Karel and Lilly Rössler, in Prague in 1930. I had an older brother, Honza; much later, in Australia, he took the name of Henry. We lived in the family home at 15 Bredovská Street, in the centre of Prague. Honza and I were fortunate that, even as young children, we had tuition in German and English. In time, for very different reasons, each of these languages was to prove invaluable.

Our home had four storeys. Grandmother Karolina lived on the first floor, and on the floors above lived three branches of our extended family: Uncle Fritz and his family; my own family; and my father's identical twin brother, Uncle Josef, with his wife, Aunt Anny — all of us in our own apartments. The building had a flat roof where we children had a sandpit and the adults enjoyed taking in the sun in summertime. The ground floor was given over to offices and, at the back, a goods store. It too had a flat roof, but this one was covered in grass. That was where my cousin Herbert Brumlik kept his pet white rabbit in its hutch.

My father and Uncle Josef were wholesale merchants in spices, tea, and similar goods in the family firm Rössler & Fischer, which my grandfather Ludvík had founded in 1890. The firm's spice mill was at Osadní Street, in the industrial suburb of Holešovice, but the stock was kept on the ground floor of our home. To this day, I have fond memories of the wonderful characteristic aromas of paprika, pepper, cinnamon, marjoram, and other spices that wafted through it.

Some of my early memories of my father go back to when I was very young, before I started school. I always looked forward to hearing the rattle of keys around midday. That sound meant he was unlocking the front door after coming up from the office for lunch and a little rest. He used to tell me stories about horse-drawn trams running on tracks (*koňka* in Czech) on Wenceslas Square; or how he used to read and study at night by the light of a kerosene lamp; or how he used to play football with Uncle Josef in Krakovská Street, where they used to live; and about the mix-ups at school when the teacher couldn't tell the identical twins apart. Later, I loved Father telling me about the origins of the game of chess and explaining its basic moves to me. At other times, we had fun together as he gave me puzzles in simple arithmetic; much later, I became quite proficient at mathematics and chose to become a scientist. Everybody seemed to like Father, and when I walked with him on the streets of Prague I was proud to see how frequently men would greet him, calling out, 'Poklona, pane Rössler!' and raising their hats, as he would likewise greet them.

Both my parents used to visit the fashionable spa town of Karlovy Vary, widely known by its German name as Karlsbad, in Western Bohemia. There, Father took the cure for his chronically unsettled stomach, a condition I was told was due to the time he spent in Italy as prisoner-of-war during the First World War. He had served as an officer in the Austro-Hungarian army.

Our family was not overly religious. We did not keep a kosher home, but I remember attending services with the family on High

Holidays at the nearby Jubilee Synagogue in Jeruzalémská Street. My last visit before the Holocaust was as a seven-year-old in 1937. Mother, Honza and I sat upstairs in a morning Shabbat service and watched Father downstairs, where, as was customary, the men were sitting separately from the women and children. Upon being called up to the Torah — by his Hebrew name, Meyr ben Leib — Father read the blessings. I am certain that it was in this same synagogue that Father and Uncle Josef (always called 'Pepa' in the family) celebrated their bar mitzvahs.

In our primary school, at 6 Panská Street, there were only four Jewish boys in a class of 30, and every week we had one hour of Jewish religious tuition from a rabbi. For this we went to a separate room, while the rest of the boys had their Catholic Scripture. I never experienced anti-Semitism there or anywhere else in pre-war Czechoslovakia.

I have happy memories of family summer holidays by the lake

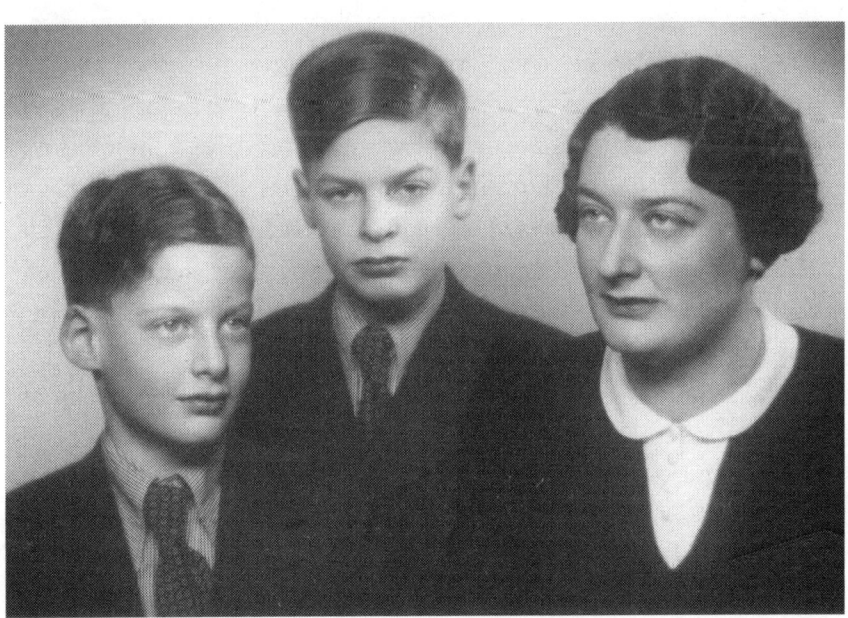

Peter Rössler, his brother, Honza, and their mother, Lilly, in January 1938.

in Radošovice, near Prague, where I learned to swim. I remember winter holidays in Špindlerův Mlýn in the Krkonoše Mountains, the 'giant' mountains near the Polish border, where we enjoyed tobogganing and skiing, accompanied by our governess, Miss Brünerová. I cherish memories of my mother playing the grand piano at home, sometimes with her friend Mrs Fischl, who came to accompany her in four-handed playing. The tune of 'The Blue Danube' still reverberates in my mind from that time. I owe my love of classical music to her.

When Mother was in her early twenties, she lost a series of family members. Her father, Daniel Schulz, a glove manufacturer, died in the 1920s. So did her mother, Hermína. And my mother's only sibling, her sister Ilka, died shortly after giving birth to my cousin Hanna Pick — Hanička, as we always called her. They were all buried in the one grave, with a common headstone, in the little Jewish cemetery in the suburb of Malvazinky. It wasn't far from the suburb of Smíchov, where Mother lived before her marriage, in Zborovská. I am certain that their deaths, coming one after another, saddened her deeply, and left their mark on her.

I never knew my paternal grandfather either. Grandfather Ludvík died in 1929, shortly before I was born. But I used to love visiting Grandmother Karolina. We went to see her on Sundays for lunch in her apartment. She was hard of hearing by then, and I remember talking loudly into an ear-trumpet that she held to her ear. She passed away in November 1939, and so was spared the horrors to come.

In September 1938, Hitler demanded that Czechoslovakia hand over its northern border areas, the so-called Sudetenland, or face war. The British and French, hoping to secure 'peace in our time', naively signed the Munich Pact to appease him. Within weeks, the Germans had occupied the Sudetenland. Less than six months later, on 15 March 1939, they marched into Prague and occupied all the rest of the Czech part of the country. That day, Hitler, in person,

Two generations: (Left to right) Peter Rössler's parents, Karel and Lilly Rössler; paternal grandparents, Karolina and Ludvík Rössler; and Karel's brother Josef, in 1927.

Karel Rössler: A portait of Peter Rössler's father from July 1937.

came to Prague Castle and declared Czechoslovakia abolished; the Czech lands were now the 'Protectorate of Bohemia and Moravia'. Our street, renamed Bredauergasse, became the unwilling host of Gestapo headquarters in Petschek Palace, opposite us on the next block.* It became a byword for incarceration and torture.

I remember sensing the sadness and pessimism of my parents, which, naturally, affected me. Mother would come in the evenings and sit on the side of my bed, telling me not to worry, that things would be all right again soon. But my parents were trying desperately to get us all out of Czechoslovakia — to Argentina, to Venezuela, to Uruguay — in order to escape Hitler. I clearly remember them having Spanish lessons for that very reason. But their efforts to leave proved unsuccessful.

We now faced the full force of Hitler's anti-Semitic Nuremberg Laws. Our personal freedom and our rights as citizens were restricted, and we were gradually isolated from the rest of the Czechoslovak community. Jews were no longer allowed to go to parks, theatres, cinemas, libraries, or swimming pools. On public transport, we were allowed to stand only on the rear platform of trams, and we had to travel in the rear compartment of the last carriage on a train. On top of the food rationing, which applied to everyone, Jews were only allowed to go shopping from 3 p.m. to 5 p.m., and their allocation of food was smaller. In February 1940, Jews were issued with identity cards stamped with the letter 'J', and, by order of the Gestapo, were forbidden to leave their homes after 8 p.m. It was also forbidden for Jews to have radio sets (or later, even telephones), but I remember listening to broadcasts of Hitler's hysterical anti-Semitic tirades.

Father's business was taken over by the Nazis, and he and Uncle were no longer allowed to work in it. Jewish men were still required to work, however, and Father and Uncle Josef found a job in some

---

* Bredovská Street is known today as Třída politických vězňů, the Street of Political Prisoners.

vegetable gardens at Troja, a suburb near the Prague Zoo. They were employed by two kind Gentiles, Mr and Mrs Jandera, who were growing lettuce, tomatoes, and carrots that needed watering by hand. They did not work Father very hard. Uncle Josef later found work at the Office of the Jewish Community.

In 1940, an edict came out that Jews were no longer allowed to attend the public schools, and my brother and I had to stop going. Then our family — as well as the families of Uncle Josef and Uncle Fritz — were thrown out of our house. We all had to move to one of several designated suburbs in Prague. My parents, Honza, and I moved to 29 Mánesova Street in the suburb of Vinohrady. There we had no choice but to live in a single room, as sub-tenants in an apartment belonging to another Jewish family, the Bondys. Uncle Josef and Aunt Anny moved nearby, into the apartment of their friends Mr and Mrs Fischl, in Na Smetánce Street.

About that time, Honza and I started going for some open-air exercise to the Hagibor sports ground, which was then still owned by the Jewish community. There the well-known Jewish youth leader Freddy Hirsch organised games and sports activities for Jewish children. He later became an active youth leader in the Theresienstadt (Terezín) Ghetto; but, sadly, he perished in Auschwitz.

Another open-air area that was still available to us was the Jewish section of Prague's Strašnice Cemetery. It became popular for outings. It had a strangely peaceful atmosphere, with its overgrown graves, walkways, and paths lined with shady shrubs and trees. Franz Kafka is buried there.

For the next five years, Honza and I had no formal schooling, although for a while we attended classes arranged illegally by the Jewish community. Known as *kroužky* (circles), they were held in Jewish apartments to give Jewish children at least some basic tuition. I went to classes at Nekázanka Street, a short walk from Bredovská, where about ten of us were taught several subjects by an attractive young lady teacher who made a big impression on me. We had to leave unobtrusively, only two at a time, so as not to attract attention.

My parents and other Jewish parents tried their best to give their children some alternative entertainment to the movies and drama that they had been shut out of. I recall watching black-and-white adventure and cartoon film with friends invited to our home in 1940. My parents probably hired the films, together with the projector, from a lending library. We also used a nineteenth-century magic lantern that projected glass slides onto a screen. We called it the *Laterna Magica*. Then there was my friend Pavel Kummerman, who attended the *kroužky* classes with me. He used to invite me and other friends to his apartment in the Smichov district, where his father had a puppet theatre that he had built himself. We sat in rows of chairs, like we were in a real theatre, watched the show, and then had afternoon tea. We all thoroughly enjoyed it.

But things were going from bad to worse. From September 1941, Czechoslovakia's Jews had to wear a Star of David. Cut from yellow cloth and carrying the word *Jude* ('Jew') in black, it had to be sewn onto the left breast of one's outer garment. The idea was to stigmatise the Jews. But it also meant that you could tell who your friends were: when they saw you on the street, they would make a point of showing their solidarity by coming to shake your hand.

The Lodz Ghetto

In October 1941, deportations 'to the East' began. Uncle Josef and Aunt Anny were among the thousand Prague Jews who received a letter requiring them to assemble, on October 16, at the Exhibition Building in Letná, Prague 7, for the very first transport. They were then living near us, as sub-tenants at Vinohrady. They duly went to the assembly point with their luggage, and I remember how terribly upset Father was when he came home after bidding them goodbye. Yet, the very next evening, to our great surprise, Josef and Anny turned up on our own doorstep. A tearful and joyous reunion with Father followed.

It appears that a number of extra 'reserve' people were commonly called up in addition to the required thousand, and the excess people would be released if the quota was filled. I also believe that Uncle Josef and Aunt Anny may have been spared on this occasion because he had been working at the Jewish Community Office. The Germans may have thought he could be useful to them in setting up the Theresienstadt Ghetto. He was sent there shortly afterwards.

The euphoria at Josef and Anny's reprieve was short-lived. Only five days later, on 21 October, it was our turn for deportation. In the second of five transports — each of which took a thousand Czech Jews — Mother, Father, Honza, and I were sent to the ghetto that the Germans had established in Lodz ('Litzmannstadt') in southern Poland.

Our parents must have been suffering a degree of anguish and trauma that we boys — Honza was 13, and I was 11 — could not imagine. Their worst nightmare was now unfolding. Even so, I believe they knew little of the full horrors that lay ahead, or even of the true destinations of those early transports from Prague. After all, our transport was an ordinary passenger train, and we were permitted 50 kilos of luggage each. No one knew the truth. The Nazis kept things vague, referring euphemistically to the deportation process as 'resettlement'.

The ghetto we were heading for was established in February 1940, when Jews from Lodz and its environs were forced into an area of four square kilometres in the notorious Baluty district, a slum quarter that had previously been home to thieves and the underworld. Two major roads belonging to the 'free' city, Zgierska Street and Limanowski Street, divided the ghetto into three parts that were linked by massive wooden footbridges. Underneath the bridges, the two roads were busy with trams and cars proceeding on their normal business. I remember crossing the bridge on a cold December evening and seeing the lights of Christmas decorations in 'free' Lodz.

When we arrived in the ghetto, we were accommodated in a large building in Lagiewnicka Street — or, to the Germans, Hanseatenstrasse. It was a former school that had been specially vacated for us. There were large rooms with some two-storey bunks that were claimed by some of the luckier people, but the four of us had to sleep on straw mattresses laid side by side on the floor. The youth leaders and educators organised a few sessions of supervised tuition for the younger children. But the atmosphere was depressing, the rooms overcrowded. The little food we got was prepared for us. For a few days we were able to supplement this with items that we had brought with us, such as tins of sardines and dry salami.

I remember that Father had brought several practical personal items, which he may have remembered from his army days: a manual razorblade sharpener that incorporated a leather strap and extended the useful life of the blades, and also several battery-free long-lasting hand-torches. These were called *kočka* (cat) in Czech because you repeatedly squeezed the dynamo of the torch to generate current, and it made a miaowing noise.

I also remember hearing Mr Freund, a friend of Father's, playing the violin. He had given me violin lessons once a week till just before we were deported. Dvořák's 'Humoresque' was one of his favourite tunes, but he also practised a lot, playing finger exercises. And there was a boy called Paul Seideman, who was a couple of years older than me; he played chess with me, and always beat me. Our destinies were strangely linked. He was with us in the ghetto orphanages, he survived the war, as we did, and he too immigrated to Australia.

The conditions in the ghetto were terrible, even at the outset. Most of the buildings had no running water or flushing toilets. Water had to be fetched in buckets from outdoor hand-operated pumps; the latrines were planks of wood with circular holes. The primitive conditions were aggravated by overcrowding, a severe shortage of food (estimated to be only one-tenth of the minimum daily requirement), lack of hygiene, lack of medicine, substandard accommodation, and bitterly cold winters. The food was not only in short supply; it was also nutritionally poor. It consisted mainly of cabbage, turnip, sometimes beetroot, potatoes (mostly frozen), margarine, bread, brown sugar, and *ersatz* coffee — a coffee substitute, probably ground chicory root. We never saw milk, fruit, or eggs. Of meat, all we had was a ration of horseflesh, and that was only once.

For the arrivals from Central Europe, the shock of the sudden transition to ghetto conditions was such that the Czechs, Germans, and Austrians quickly lost weight, suffered from malnutrition and disease, and began to die. Father soon became very ill; he was unable to tolerate the diet, and just lay on the mattress on the floor. There was almost no medication available. The Czech doctor attending to him prescribed potato peels, a precious commodity, probably for their vitamin content. They were to be washed and made into soup.

I found Father's suffering very upsetting. On his birthday, late in January 1942, I didn't know what to say to him, nor could I bring myself to congratulate him. In March, only five months after our arrival, he died. He was 46.

Miraculous survival during the September 1942 *Sperre*

Honza and I were in Nazi internment for nearly four years. We found that one had to be extremely lucky to survive the crucial moments — events that, in a split second, decided whether one lived or died. We each had several narrow escapes from moments like these. One of them came during the notorious September 1942 *Sperre* (curfew and ban on all movement), when people were rounded up for deportation.

The day-to-day running of the ghetto was in the hands of the *Judenrat* (Jewish Council), chaired by Chaim Rumkowski, the *Judenälteste* (Jewish Elder), under the orders and supervision of the Gestapo. Among other duties, the members of the *Judenrat* had one unenviable task: drawing up lists of people to be sent when the Nazis asked for a number of people, usually 1000, to be ready for deportation the next day. As a general rule, the old, the sick, or children of 11 or younger were chosen, perhaps on the rationalisation that these groups had a lesser chance of survival. It was these groups that were chosen in the wave of deportations that took place in September 1942.

At the time, Mother, Honza, and I, as well as Uncle Fritz, Aunt Fritzi, and my cousin Herbert, were living in a dilapidated wooden house at 9 Braune Gasse.† 'Existing' would be a better word than 'living'. Mother was very sick; she was bedridden and suffering from

Before the Holocaust (1930): Left, Peter's uncle, Pavel Pick, with Peter's cousin Hanička; right, Peter's father, Karel Rössler, with Peter's brother, Honza. Of the four, only Honza survived the Holocaust.

---

† 'Braune Gasse' was the street's German name. We knew it by the pre-ghetto name of 'Lwowska'. It was recently renamed 'Skury-Skaczynskiego'.

malnutrition, loss of weight, and diarrhoea. There was a curfew. Jewish police, accompanied by wooden carts pulled and pushed by male inmates, were rounding people up. Those who could stand up had to stand in the street, and the police then entered the building looking for others.

The police took Mother and put her on the cart, where there were already other sick people. Honza and I insisted on accompanying her, and we followed the cart to a large building that had been converted into a sort of hospital. We entered it with Mother, helping her to walk. There were already hundreds of old, sick, and very young people there crying, screaming, and moaning.

And then, one of a number of incredible strokes of fate took place. A lady, possibly a Jewish nurse, approached the three of us.

Before the Holocaust (1930): (Standing, left to right): Peter's father, Karel, Peter's uncle Fritz Brumlik and his son Herbert; seated, Lilly Rössler, Peter's great-aunt Amalie and great-uncle Dr Adolf Schulz; governess Miss Gabrielová, with Peter on her lap; and Fritzi Brumlik. By 1941, the Schulzes had passed away; all of the others, except for Peter and Miss Gabrielová, perished either in the Lodz Ghetto or in camps such as Chelmno.

She must have noticed the two young boys — we were now aged 12 and 14 — with their mother, and taken pity on us. She may have known the fate awaiting the wretches gathered in the building. This lady directed us to a door leading to the outside and let us leave by it. With our help, Mother managed to drag herself back to our house, and so we survived for another day.

We found out later the destination of the transport that we had narrowly escaped joining. It went to the Chelmno extermination camp, which was nearby, and everyone on it, without exception, was gassed.

Sadly, soon after surviving that ordeal, Mother died. She was only 36. Nine other close relatives from Prague — including Hanička, and her father, Pavel — also perished in Lodz, or were deported elsewhere, probably to the Chelmno extermination camp or to Auschwitz-Birkenau. Of the 5000 people who were deported to the ghetto from Prague, only 277 survived long enough to be liberated.

My most unforgettable birthday

With Mother's death, the atmosphere in our little cottage became more and more depressing. Uncle Fritz became ill, and so did Aunt Fritzi. Both of them died late in the year. Our cousin Herbert, who was 18, had managed to get himself the highly valued job of ghetto fireman, which had the wonderful privilege of qualifying for an extra bowl of watery soup. This meant that he was not home much during the day, and then he disappeared altogether. We concluded that he must have been removed from the ghetto in one of the waves of deportations. Only recently I found out from surviving Lodz Ghetto records that he was sent to Chelmno.

Honza and I tried to fend for ourselves, often standing in long queues to collect our fortnightly rations of raw food and coal, fetching water in a bucket or a jug from the hand-operated outdoor pump, and attempting to cook as best we could. It was difficult to keep warm in winter; we often went to bed fully clothed. This was one of the saddest periods of our stay in the ghetto.

A black market existed in the ghetto, and small items of food could sometimes be bought without ration coupons for a large amount of 'ghetto money': specially printed ghetto Marks that were dubbed 'rumkies', after Rumkowski, whose signature appeared on the notes. This currency, useless outside the ghetto, was meant to be used for the purchase of rations. The barter system — whereby one could trade, say, an item of scarce clothing for food, mostly bread — also flourished. The Polish Jews had gradually got used to the small food rations, and their families were somehow able to forego some of their bread in exchange for good-quality clothing items brought in by the more affluent Central European Jews.

Honza's birthday and my own being just two days apart, on the second and the fourth of June, we decided to celebrate both on the middle day, 3 June 1943, by treating ourselves to a bowl of soup. We would trade a pair of winter boots that we still had from Prague for it. The transaction took place in one of the ghetto's communal gas-kitchens, where people went to cook, using ingredients they had brought with them. Soup was the most common dish. We bought a cabbage soup, thick with pieces of potatoes, hot, and delicious — it was the best meal we had had in a long time, and a truly memorable birthday treat.

Around that time, a ghetto social worker found us in the deserted house, and we were taken to live in a ghetto orphanage in Gnieznienska Street. The orphanage was a three-storey building near the western boundary of the ghetto, and there our lives took on a degree of normality. There were boys and girls aged about 12 to 17, we slept in proper beds, and food was prepared for us and served in a dining room. On Fridays, Shabbat Eve was celebrated in the same room, and the children were encouraged to sing and recite poetry. There was even a library, mostly with Polish books, which by now I was able to read. Paul Seideman was there, as well as three other Czech boys. The orphanage was professionally run by

Pani Tabakowa and her husband. I believe that Chaim Rumkowski, the friend of the Lodz orphanages, protected the children at Gnieznienska Street from early deportation.

Most inhabitants of the ghetto who were considered well enough now had jobs, usually in one of the many small factories that produced goods for export to the Reich. This gave them some protection from early deportation and, as a bonus, they earned an extra bowl of watery soup. Jobs were found for us, too: first, in a German army-uniform factory known as the Schneider Resort; later, in a metal-parts processing factory, the Metall Resort; and, lastly, in a clog or shoe factory, the Schuh Resort. The Schuh Resort made clogs with canvas uppers nailed to wooden soles, to be worn by Jews.

At its peak, the Lodz Ghetto had a population of 165,000; but, as we found out later, it was really only a transit camp. Transports from Czechoslovakia, Germany, Austria, and Luxembourg, totalling about 20,000 people, arrived in late 1941. Tens of thousands of people were also deported from the ghetto, mainly to death camps and labour camps, particularly after the middle of 1942. These deportations gradually reduced the ghetto's population to just 70,000 at the end of July 1944.

The miracle of the loaf

After staying for some months at Gnieznienska Street, Honza and I moved to the single-floor Marysin Orphanage, located near the Schuh Resort, the railway station, and the cemetery. About 5000 gypsies were incarcerated in an isolated area not far away from the orphanage. It was run by a caring *opiekunka* (social worker), Miss Stawówna, who kept in touch with Paul Seideman after the war.

By now, Honza and I could both speak Polish, a Slav language similar to Czech, as well as Yiddish, which we thought at first was a dialect of German.

Honza and I were still in the Marysin Orphanage when, in

March 1944, we were permitted to write a short note on a Lodz Ghetto postcard, with Hitler's portrait on the stamp. We were to write in German (no doubt to facilitate censorship) to relatives or friends in the 'Protectorate of Bohemia and Moravia'. We sent our postcard to Uncle Josef in the Sudetenkaserne barrack of the Theresienstadt Ghetto. We knew he'd been deported there in late 1941, because Aunt Anny had written to Father from Prague at the time, sending him money and informing him of what had happened. In the meantime, she too had been deported to Theresienstadt.‡ We informed Uncle Josef that both our parents had died, that we were living in an orphanage, and that we were working.

This Star of David was worn by Peter's Aunt Anny in Prague 1941–42 and in Terezin (or Theresienstadt) Ghetto 1942–45, sown onto the left breast of her outer garment.

---

‡ I learned much later that Uncle Josef was sent to Theresienstadt as a part of Transport Ak (for *aufbaukomando*, construction brigade). There he was appointed to the senior position of supervisor of the *proviantlager*, the provisions warehouse. Anny was sent to Theresienstadt about six months later, and worked in *kinderfürsorge*, childcare.

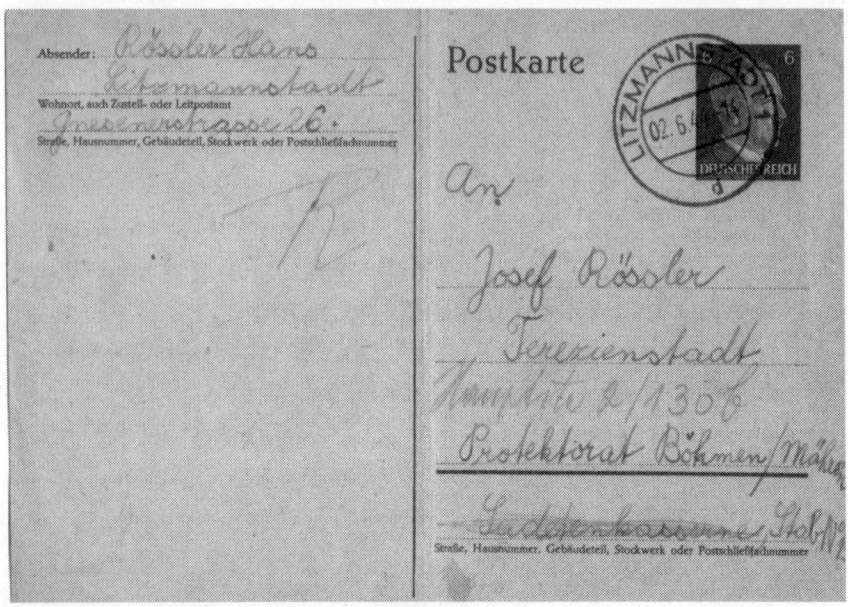

From ghetto to ghetto: This postcard, written in German and using the German forms of names, was sent from the Lodz Ghetto (German Litzmannstadt), in Poland, to Peter's uncle Josef, in the Terezin Ghetto (German Theresienstadt) in Czechoslovakia in May 1944.

The postcard reads in part:

Dear Uncle and Aunt,
How glad we are to be able to write to you again after such a long time. It's awful for us to inform you that both our parents are dead, we are both living in an orphanage. We are well and are working, Hans as a draughtsman, Peter as an electrical engineer …

To our amazement, in about June 1944, we unexpectedly received a parcel from Prague. It was wrapped in brown paper. When we tore it open, a miracle was revealed: a loaf of stale rye bread covered in green mould! Of course, we attacked it without hesitation, and gobbled it up as if it were the finest delicacy. We learned later that it had been sent by a Prague baker, Mr Husák, who was a friend and business customer of our father. Somehow, after receiving our postcard, Josef or Anny had sent him word of our whereabouts, and the kindly Mr Husák had wrapped the loaf up, still warm from baking, and posted it to us.

By August 1944, the Soviet army was approaching, and the ghetto — the longest surviving of all the ghettoes in Poland — was finally being closed down. Its remaining inhabitants were deported on daily transports to Auschwitz-Birkenau. Not even the orphanages, which Chaim Rumkowski had protected till the end, were spared. Honza and I were taken to the Marysin railway station, where, with hundreds of others, we were herded into overcrowded cattle trucks for transportation to an unknown destination.

Auschwitz-Birkenau: lottery of life and death

The railway line at Auschwitz had, by then, been extended an extra three kilometres, from Auschwitz I to the extermination camp Auschwitz II at Birkenau. When the train stopped at the ramp, the doors of the wagons were opened, and we were chased out to abuse and yelling by SS men holding Alsatian dogs on short leashes. Ordered to leave our meagre belongings on the ground ('You will get it back later!'), we were marched off to be separated into two groups: men, and women with children. Honza and I joined the column of men of all ages on the ramp, and moved slowly through the nightmarish landscape. I noticed a strange, acrid smell. The next day, a 'veteran' prisoner explained to us what it was: the smell of burning human flesh and bones.

Walking beside Honza in the column, I saw we were

approaching a table where an SS officer was sitting. As the column moved forward, we saw that one man at a time had to briefly face the table to be inspected and spoken to. Then he was directed to walk to the left or to the right.

The moment arrived, and it was my brother's turn. He was asked his age — he was 16 at the time — and was briefly inspected by the uniformed man. He was directed to proceed to the right. Next it was my turn. I said I was 14. That could have been fatal. The man, who I later found out may have been the notorious Dr Mengele, the 'Angel of Death', looked at my undeveloped, starved body, and pointed me to the left. Without hesitation, I turned round and followed my brother to the right … and nobody stopped me.

As I found out later, I had escaped the gas chamber to live another day. The left meant death; the right, survival. I had once again won the lottery to live and tell the story.

I joined Honza in the depleted file of men, and we were directed to the shower complex. We had to strip naked, everyone's hair was shaved off and, after showering, we were issued with striped uniforms, a belt, cap, clogs, and a metal plate and spoon.

We were then taken to barracks inside one of the many camps in Birkenau. Like all the rest, our camp was enclosed by an electrified barbed-wire fence and guarded by armed soldiers in high towers. Our camp was referred to as the *Zigeunerlager*, the gypsy camp, after the thousands of gypsy families that had been murdered there. The barracks were overcrowded, and Honza and I slept on the concrete floor.

Honza and I survived the next six weeks on a daily starvation diet of a piece of bread, thin soup, and *ersatz* coffee. We spent most of the time on the Appelplatz, where we stood to be counted for many hours every day. By then we had no names, only a number that was issued to us: mine was 112,027. I have no tattoo on my arm, as this procedure had been discontinued by then.

Later a fellow prisoner told me that the only way out of the Birkenau extermination camp was to be selected for a labour camp, and that one had to be at least 16 years old to qualify. Fortunately, on 29 September 1944, Honza and I both got ourselves selected for labour. When asked my age, I made myself two years older, saying I was 16. Honza boosted his age by one year, to 17.

Over 50 years later, in 2001, I returned to the camp as a visitor, accompanied by my family. Records in the Auschwitz Museum archives confirmed the exaggerated ages that Honza and I had given. They probably saved our lives.

Auschwitz: Peter Rössler revisits the camp in 2001.

Labour Camp Kaufering

From Birkenau, a railway cattle-truck took us to Kaufering Lager IV (Hurlach), near Landsberg in Bavaria. This was what passed for a *krankenlager* (a camp for the sick), or, more accurately, a *sterblager* (a camp for the dying).§ There we both spent about seven months. On arrival at the camp, we were surprised to hear a man in a striped prisoner-uniform calling out in Czech, 'Are there any Czechs?' We responded immediately, 'Yes, yes!' We followed the man, who was called Poldie, through the gates into the camp, and he took us to a small barrack to meet another prisoner, Dr Leon Halpern. It was Dr Halpern who had sent Poldie to meet the train; he turned out to be a Jewish doctor from Prague, and was the medical supervisor in the camp.

In Kaufering Lager IV, the wooden barracks or bunkhouses were set about 1.5 metres deep in the ground. Each barrack had a central aisle, with two wooden shelves about 1.5 metres wide on each side. We slept on these shelves, without mattresses, and with only thin blankets as a covering.

I was suffering from a severe leg injury sustained when an SS man had kicked me to the ground at Birkenau. The kindly Dr Halpern took me to stay with the other doctors in their barrack, cared for me till the leg wound healed, and then arranged for me to have the job of messenger-boy, or runner (*läufer*). This was considered a cushy job, as it had the bonus of a daily extra bowl of soup. It involved me standing in or near a sentry box near the camp entrance, and waiting for the order '*Läufer zum Tor!*' (Messenger to the gate!) At the gate, or even outside it, I would be told whom to fetch or what message I was to pass on.

On one memorable occasion, Dr Halpern even produced a particular delicacy — a single raw egg! I pierced the shell and half-drank, half-sucked it dry.

Honza was assigned to another barrack, and had to go to work outside the camp every day. Some time later, he was moved to another of the 11 Kaufering camps, and I became very worried at not hearing from him. Again, Dr Halpern came to the rescue with

---

§ Raim, Edith, *Überlebende von Kaufering*, Metropol, Germany, 2008, p. 17.

his apparent influence and, after a few weeks, somehow managed to arrange for Honza to be moved back to Kaufering Lager IV. Then, late in 1944, lice and lack of hygiene led to an epidemic of typhus in the camp, causing many deaths. Honza came down with typhus but, miraculously, he survived. I was spared, because the doctors in my barrack generously shared their doses of vaccine with me.

Another remarkable event was an achievement of one of the doctors in my barrack. Sometime in early 1945, I developed a severe toothache. To my amazement, the Hungarian Dr Elekesz — who was a medical doctor, not a dentist — took me to one of the huts in the camp, produced a foot-operated dental drill and, as far as I remember, fairly painlessly drilled and filled the cavity, saved the tooth, and cured the ache. Whatever the filling material was, it lasted till I had it looked at by our dentist, Dr Neumann, on my return to Prague, and he was surprised at the quality of Dr Elekesz's work.

Thinking back to what helped sustain me throughout these years of uncertainty and incarceration, I know that I only lived from day to day, dreaming of food, especially juicy bunches of grapes. Each day, I tried to survive to another day, not thinking too much about the future. I am not religious but, in early childhood, our non-Jewish governess, Miss Brünerová, who was probably a Catholic, taught me a prayer about a Guardian Angel, which we recited with her every night before going to sleep.

> Andělíčku můj strážníčku
> opatruj mi mou dušičku
> opatruj ji ve dne v noci
> od všeho zlého a zlé moci.

Loosely translated, it goes:

> Little angel, my little guardian,
> care for my little soul,

protect it by day and by night,
from all evil and evil might.

From the time I learned it, I have said this prayer to myself every night, sometimes more than once. I said it throughout those years of horror, supplementing the verses by asking for protection for all my closest relatives and loved ones, naming each one.

Death march and liberation

In April 1945, with the Americans approaching, Kaufering Lager IV was liquidated. Those who could walk were forced to march out of the camp with an escort of cruel SS men; those who couldn't walk were evacuated by a train that, we later discovered, was mistakenly bombed by Allied aircraft.

The column that left the camp on foot was made up of hundreds of prisoners marching five abreast. Honza and I were part of it. We endured a 50-kilometre death march to Camp Allach, near the Dachau concentration camp, on the outskirts of Munich. There, along the barbed wire fence, we found piles of corpses. The barracks were filthy and full of emaciated, skin-and-bone prisoners who were barely able to move. For some reason, they were called *Muselman*, German for 'Muslim'. The stench was terrible. But it was there, a few days after our arrival, that we were liberated by the 42nd 'Rainbow' Division of the United States army. It was 30 April 1945.

For many years, I didn't know the exact date of our liberation — I only learned it recently from the internet. It was the same day that Hitler committed suicide in his Berlin bunker.

After liberation, we were deloused with DDT powder, our filthy striped prisoner-uniforms were burnt, and we were issued with new, clean uniforms. For lack of any alternative, they were German army uniforms. And, after all my narrow escapes, these new clothes nearly cost me my life. I wore them to return to Prague and, as

I was walking across Wenceslas Square, a Russian soldier pulled a gun on me. He had mistaken me for a German.

After the war

Honza and I returned to Prague on 10 May 1945. We found our way back to our house on Bredovská Street, and there we found a loyal employee, Mr Doubrava, still working in the old business. Amazed to see us, he told us that Uncle Josef and Aunt Anny, our only other relatives, had survived the Theresienstadt Ghetto. We also met up again with Dr Halpern, who had been reunited with his wife in Prague.

We lived with Uncle Josef and Aunt Anny, who had no children of their own, in our old family house, and I attended the Dušní Street high school, near the Old Town Square. When I first got back, I weighed about 30 kilos, my voice had still not broken, and

Return to Prague: Peter Rössler (left) with his Uncle Josef and Aunt Anny, and his brother Honza (right), in August 1945.

I hadn't begun to shave. That worried me at the time.

I remember the impression my first decent meal of bread made on me: it was a very large, thick slice, cut from a fresh 'peasant loaf', a huge, circular loaf of rye. I spread it with just a thick layer of strawberry jam, and consumed it with great relish. My first meal of Czech apricot fruit dumplings, together with a roast goose that Uncle miraculously managed to obtain, was also incredibly memorable. So were my first visits to Czech, American, and French movies, to concerts, and to the operas that my aunt encouraged me to go and see. I absorbed it all like a sponge. At the same time, I had to work hard at school to catch up on the years I had missed. There was a lot of catching up to do all round, but gradually life returned to normal.

In 1948, the Jewish Welfare Guardian Society made it possible for Honza and me to come to Australia. We were both sent to

Passport photo: Peter Rössler at the time of his coming to Australia in 1948.

Brisbane, where Jewish guardians were appointed for us, and the local Jewish community helped us settle in the new country.

I was fortunate in that I was allowed to continue my studies as a boarder at Brisbane Grammar School. I matriculated there, and qualified for a Commonwealth Scholarship, which enabled me to study at the University of New South Wales in Sydney. I graduated in science, and later became a research chemist. Honza became a successful architect in Sydney. Sadly, he died in 1992.

Uncle Josef and Aunt Anny managed to get out of Communist Czechoslovakia, and arrived in Sydney in 1949. Both have since passed away.

Mr Doubrava remained a wonderful, loyal friend to our family. He kept writing to us, even in Australia, which was risky under the Communist regime, and he kept sending us the uniquely flavoursome wild dried mushrooms that he loved picking on his walks in the Czech forests.

One of my most treasured possessions is a pre-war photo album of my family. Uncle Josef remembered it had been hidden and stored for us in Prague through the war years by our Gentile friends Mr and Mrs Jandera, at great risk to themselves. They returned it to us after the war.

I met my future wife, Pauline, while skiing in the Australian Alps in the winter of 1965, and we married two years later. I have a married daughter, Carolyn Anne — named after my grandmother Karolina and Aunt Anny — and two granddaughters and a grandson. Sadly, my wife died in February 2007 after a long battle with cancer.

Today, on special occasions, services are held once again in the Jubilee Synagogue in Prague. It has been beautifully renovated, inside and out, after years of devastating neglect during the Communist regime, from 1948–89. In October 2007, I happened to be visiting Prague and, on a Saturday morning, I decided to go and see if the synagogue was open. To my amazement, a service attended by about 30 worshippers was being conducted upstairs in the smaller hall, where I'd sat with Mother 70 years earlier. I arranged to have myself called up to the Torah. Shrouded in a *talit*, or prayer shawl, that I had only just bought in Old Jerusalem, I felt quite sad as I thought of my parents. That service had a very special meaning for me ... it completed another chapter in my life.

I am now retired from work and serve as a guide at the Sydney Jewish Museum. I consider it my duty to relate my Holocaust experiences, particularly to groups of visiting school students, to whom I also try to convey the importance of racial and religious tolerance.

The Jubilee Synagogue, Prague: The restored interior.

MARK SPIGELMAN
And you shall dream all the days of your life

My birth — adjacent to the German border in southern Poland, in November 1940 — was not well timed for a Jewish child. My survival during the Holocaust is a testimony to the remarkable courage, perseverance, dedication, and love of my parents, Majloch and Gustava Szpigelman. I did not survive because I was smart — or at least, I do not accept that I survived because I was smart; I maintain that I survived because I had smart parents. From my childhood, I have memories; but, in reality, my memories are partly my nightmares and partly the stories I heard from my parents.

My memories from the first four years of my life are short picture-postcards of traumatic events with no chronological order. Over time, I have tried to place them into some sort of order in my mind. I divide them into two types. The first and most important are the ones that have terrorised my sleep and still wake me on occasion, even now. These, I know, are moments in my childhood where I feared for my life or was somehow threatened. Second, there are the stories recounted numerous times by my

Mark Spigelman with his parents, late 1941: His mother has rolled down her armband bearing the yellow star with the word *Jude* ('Jew'); his father's armband has been torn out of the picture.

parents — never to me, but in conversation with their friends and other Holocaust survivors. I now realise that I was allowed to sit and listen to these conversations because I was a survivor myself; usually, they would meet and discuss the events from the time of the war, but only if there was no other person around. Thus, if a non-survivor was in the group, the conversation became topical, but the sensitive stories of their survival were never mentioned. These were only talked about when a few friends (say, four to six) got together and sat down quietly in a room, and one would say, 'Do you or I remember …?' Then there would be several hours of going over stories of events, experiences, and long-lost friends and relatives.

In our early days in Australia, many a Saturday night was passed this way. Only I could sit in on these sessions: my brothers were always asleep by the time the conversation reached this point. In retrospect, I realise that they often repeated their stories to the same people over and over, and vice versa. Interestingly, I never thought this was strange behaviour, but I did notice that if there was one non-Holocaust person present, a different conversation ensued.

The earliest story I can recall from my childhood is a story my mother told to boast about how smart I was as a child. Apparently, I would blackmail my grandmother (we were living with the Brauners in the town of Bendzin) to get an extra piece of cheesecake by saying to her, 'If you do not give me the extra piece I will tell the Germans where you hide the onions.' Mum would say that Mark thought the Germans needed onions to make explosives. Naturally, I have no memory of this and, as my grandmother was murdered before my third birthday, it had to be very early in my life. I do not know why I thought this was a threat — but I still do love cheesecake.

Mark Spigelman as a little girl, mid-1942: With him are his grandfather Jacob and his cousin Pucek. Both of them died in Auschwitz within months of this photo being taken.

I spent the war dressed as a girl, and I was a pretty little girl, with nice blue eyes and long blond hair. The reason I was a girl is very simple: in Poland, a boy could be easily identified as Jewish — you just pulled his pants down. You do not pull pants down on girls. So, that is how I spent the war; because, of course, blue-eyed and blond is not exactly the way the anti-Semites thought of us Jews — though if you go to Israel today, you find there's a hell of a lot of them. King David was redheaded (so was my grandfather) and blue-eyed. So, I had blond hair, my mother had dyed blonde hair, and we travelled in the streets without papers, on the basis that my mother spoke German. She would always travel in the compartment of the tram reserved for Germans, because they never checked papers in there — and with a blond, blue-eyed kid, she had a chance to get away with it ... but not all the time.

At one stage, there was a round-up of Jews in our town. Every now and then the Germans would have a round-up, gather hundreds of people, put them on a train, and ship them off to Auschwitz. My mother got caught in this round-up. There was a selection done by the Polish police, and she noticed all the women, children, and the old were going to the queue on the left; the young workers were going to the queue on the right. So this Polish policeman said to her, 'Go to the left.' My mother instantly went to the right. The guy grabbed her, pushed her, and said, 'Go to the left.' She just kept going to the right, so he started beating her. At this stage, the German officer in charge came over and said, 'What's going on?' And the Pole said, 'This Jewess, she wants to go to the right and I want her to go to the left. She's to go to Auschwitz.' And the German looked at us, and looked at me, and the story is, he belted the Pole, and he said, 'Do not touch this woman; let her go to the right! Look at this lovely little girl — she reminds me of my little daughter.' And we went to the right, and we were saved. Everybody who went to the left was dead within 24 hours; they were gassed and burnt in Auschwitz.

I believe that this event is the source of a recurring dream that

I have. I recall that I am in my mother's arms, and somebody is beating me with a stick. I am trying to smile, and just as the stick is about to hit me, I wake up in a sweat. I do know that my instructions from early childhood were, 'Never talk, never cry. If anybody comes and is doing something to you or talking to you, just open your eyes and smile.'

Many times, this story was retold by my parents, and we always used to say, 'Weren't we lucky?' Now, when they introduced war crimes legislation to Australia, I remember thinking about this story, and I thought of it, probably for the first time ever, in a different light. I said, 'You know, there was this German. What was his job? His job was to send women and children to their deaths; and look, let us not kid ourselves, they knew what they were doing. They were very efficient. They knew the trains were going 30 kilometres, day after day, to "re-settle" people, and you never saw them again, and the camp isn't that big — those people were not exactly being squashed into the same building. So they knew they were dying. And there's this guy — he was not an inhuman monster, he was not a thoughtless, mindless automaton who did what he was told. This man actually cared enough for his little child to think about letting another child have a chance at life. So, while he was sitting there saying, "You go to death; you go to death; you live," he was not filled with rage or even hatred; because I reminded him of his child, he said, "Let them live." That's what he said to my mother. He said, "I'm going to let you live, because your child reminds me of my child."'

The Hollywood model of the Nazis is wrong. Hollywood determines that either they were buffoons, like those on the TV series *Hogan's Heroes*, or maybe thoughtless, mindless, automatic robot-types whom, eventually, the clever Americans fool and defeat in the war. But that's wrong: they were ordinary people, like the man who gave us a chance at life. And they were the sort of people who live in Adelaide, in Sydney, all over — because, after the war, we imported some of them to Australia. And I'm sure they were very nice people — it's just that they had this little bad habit: they killed a few people here or a few thousand there. They are anti-Semites, but that is a secondary problem of their first disease, which is racism. They are racists. The reason they were anti-Semites is because in the Ukraine, in Poland, in Lithuania, in all these countries, the group that was different from the usual inhabitants were the Jews.

One of the stories we used to be told is that my mother went out, and for three days she did not come back, and my father went into despair and said, 'Look, we cannot go on. I cannot support you. We are going to throw ourselves under a train.' (I sort of remember this, and every now and then I forget it, and people who heard the story from my parents remind me.) I do have a recurring nightmare in which I am standing next to a railway line with my father, and I am hearing a train and tasting fear. For 60 years, that taste woke me, and I have never gone beyond this stage of my dream; indeed, it took many years before I realised what woke me. I had developed a defence mechanism whereby, no matter what the dream, soon after waking I forgot it completely, went back to sleep, and had a normal day, with no recollection of a disturbed night. The story goes that, apparently, I said to my father (I must have been between three and four), 'Look, if you want to die, jump. I want to live. I'm not jumping!' And, in fact, Dad decided at that stage, so the story goes, that he'd give it one more try. We went back, and Mum had come back; she'd been caught up in an *Aktion*. That was about the only contribution I could really make to my parents' survival.

Bendzin was captured the day after the war began. Our part of Poland was then annexed to Germany, so there were some laws that indirectly protected us, in contrast to the part of German-occupied Poland called the 'General Government'. Nonetheless, in the first atrocity, the Germans rounded up over a hundred Jews, and burned them in the synagogue and nearby houses.

We had to wear the yellow star, but, otherwise, we were

Mark Spigelman's Star of David: Worn until the family went into hiding, then hidden until after the war.

more or less left alone at first, except that every now and then they would kill somebody, or send them off for 'resettlement'. But then we were rounded up and put into the Srodula Ghetto, which was set up early in 1943. In the ghetto, the horror started.

My father survived, and my family survived, because my father was a socialist. In those days, he was a real socialist; he believed in workers' rights and all the tenets of socialism when it really mattered. In fact, he was responsible for delivering the socialist paper to our district on his motorbike. And he really believed in it; when the fascists came, he just had the view that they were fascists, and that you do not believe fascists, they are liars. So whatever the Germans said, resettlement or anything else, my father would say, 'They are fascists, they lie. Do not believe a word they say.'

By the time the ghetto was formed, they had already taken a lot of people off to various concentration camps. They did not allow children into the ghetto — most of the children were killed in the streets of the town, and there are well-recorded stories of kids just being bashed against the wall. I was hidden, and smuggled into the ghetto. Once more, this is anecdotal, but my cousin Art Spiegelman's book *Maus* does graphically show this, as well.* I do have a number of recurring nightmares from this period.

In the ghetto, my father was in charge of the shoe store that repaired boots for the German army. The moment we went into the ghetto, he started digging a hole under our barrack ... and he dug and dug and, when it was big enough, he smuggled me into the ghetto. This period was the only time I was not with one or both of my parents during the war. Apparently, they gave me to some Poles to look after until they could take me into the ghetto. He smuggled me in inside a sack. I must have been just a bit under three.

The story is (and I have no personal knowledge of this): I was smuggled in, and we were caught by a German guard who was known as 'the Shooter', because every now and then he would shoot somebody. And my father and mother always used to say, 'Well, he found us, took you out of the sack; said to your father, "Stand aside".' He was going to shoot me, but Dad picked me up and said, 'If you're going to shoot my son, you must shoot me.' People told me that the German said, 'You are such a brave Jew, take the child. If I see him again, you are both dead.'

And that's why, in the next few months, until the ghetto was cleared, I was in hiding underground; I never came up. When the ghetto was cleared, my father and 20-odd people hid in this bunker for three or four days, and all those people survived. We walked out of the ghetto, as all the guards were gone. Everybody else from the ghetto went straight to Auschwitz, where they were killed. One of my most vivid and terrifying dreams could be from this event: I suddenly feel something cold and metallic pushed into my mouth. I feel such a burst of fear that I wake up. I am

---

* Art Spiegelman's *Maus* (Pantheon Books, New York, 1986) tells the story of the Holocaust in comic-book form, with Jews depicted as mice, and Nazis as cats.

sweating, sitting up, and my heart is racing. Could this be the guard's gun?

I now believe that another of my dreams also comes from this period. I am alone in an attic, against some tiles. It is dark. I am huddling as far as I can get from a grate that is throwing up light into the space of the attic. I hear German voices, and something that looks like a knife is poked through the grate. I wake, sweating. Another dream that may be from this period is this one: I am walking along a creek with my father, and asking him, 'Why did you take me away from those people?' His reply is, 'They were going to tell the Germans about Mother and me and you. They were going to put you into a sack and throw you into the river.'

I accept that for a three-year-old child to spend days on end in a hollowed-out sort of hole in the ground is unusual. Although I was never told how long it was, apparently I stayed there for something like three months, without seeing the sun, playing with rats. But I had been warned that if I heard a voice I had to be quiet, and I knew that, if I heard a German voice and they found me, I would be killed. One of the recurring nightmares I have always had is being in this dark room, all on my own, and hearing a German voice; and somehow I wake. I still wake once in a while with this terrible dream of hearing a voice and saying, 'I am going to be killed,' and then lying perfectly still, and not moving.

When we left the ghetto, we had to go into hiding until the liberation, which was still over a year away. First, it was in the town garbage dump. My father built a shelter there, and we stayed there for a period. It must have been a period when I was not threatened, as I have no memories of this at all. But it could be from this time that other vivid nightmares come to me.

Before the war, Mum had studied at the Hebrew University in Jerusalem. Ironically, she studied High German there, under teachers who had been forced to flee Nazi Germany. As a result, when she went out to get food, she would travel with her blond, blue-eyed 'girl' in a section of the local trams reserved for Germans, as nobody ever checked one's identity papers there. It must be one such trip that I remember in a dream in which I am sitting between Mum and a German dressed in a black uniform. The dream is so vivid that I can recall all the features of his face. A sudden fear runs through me, and I wake.

A story I often heard (but I have no memory of it actually happening) is that we were in a similar tram when, suddenly, a Polish woman in the street yelled, pointing at Mum, 'That woman is a Jew!' Mum turned to a German soldier in the tram and, in her High German, said, 'Are you going to let that woman insult me like that?' With that, the German got off and gave the woman a beating. German propaganda saved us — no Jew spoke High German and had a blond, blue-eyed child!

We found our final shelter in a farmhouse with a lady called Mrs Matoniowa. Her husband was a German collaborator, and he was going to be in trouble when the war ended — for, by Christmas 1944, everybody knew that the Germans' days were numbered. Apparently, she decided to hide a Jewish family in her farmhouse, so that we would be witnesses to how good she was. In fact, it worked bloody well, because my father stood up and said, 'Yes, she hid us.' And every month until the day she died, we'd send her a parcel of food or clothing from Australia. Dad made a point of taking us to the post office to see him doing it.

From the farm, I have several memories which are more vivid and, because I was older, I remember them without the benefit of dreams. I do remember a Christmas present, and I can date it to the day, because it was Christmas Eve, 1944. Mrs Matoniowa walked into the room, and she had two big slices of black bread with cream cheese and sugar, and two sweets, one in a grey wrapper, one in a blue wrapper. And I'm quite certain that this is the first time in my life I remember eating anything sweet. In life-events from which you can make comparisons, you say, 'Is it better than this or worse than this?' Well, since that day, any meal I have is a percentage of how good those two bits of bread and those sweets tasted. I've been to some great restaurants in my life, some of them have even come up to 75 per cent of that! It was the greatest meal I've ever had in my life ... I'll never forget it. You know, I was four; there were several things I had not done in life. One of them, obviously, was eating sugar. Another one was that I had never played with another child — that was to come later. I was pretty street-wise, but socially I was quite backward.

Two vivid memories stand out from this period. One is of Mum, Dad, and myself standing in a wardrobe in the Matoniowas' bedroom, while in the next room Mrs Matoniowa was entertaining some German soldiers (I heard the voices) who were apparently stationed near the farm. I wasn't scared, but I was dying for a pee. Mum was squeezing my hand to get me to hold on — it was agony.

Then, I recall that I had been warned never to look out of the window. The curtains in our room were always drawn. Naturally, I did look out one day. On drawing the curtain back, there, to my horror, I saw a German soldier with his back to me. He was working on what must have been a mobile field kitchen. I can still remember seeing the pots hanging off the cart, and feeling the cold sweat as I quickly drew the curtain.

I know that, towards the end, I knew there would be a time when the war would be over, because I kept asking my parents, 'When will the war be over?' Then, one day, I got impatient and looked out of the window again. There on the snow were several men crawling along with guns pointing out. The Russians! As soon as I was told by Dad, 'It's over!' my first words were, 'So now can I pee in public?' 'Yes,' said Dad. With that, I ran outside and peed in the snow, almost causing myself a severe injury.

A week or so after we were liberated, a platoon of Russian tanks and armoured cars pulled up, and the Russians said to us, 'Come with us.' We went with them. I remember my parents were very concerned; they were talking as we drove. When we got to the Russian headquarters, I saw a huge man. I was only a little kid, so he was probably only 5 feet 2 inches, but he looked huge, standing there with lots of medals and surrounded by dozens of officers. We were pushed along to him, and he asked, 'Is this the Jewish child?' The soldier said, '*Da,*' and he grabbed me and started hugging me. I still remember his beard (it hurt me a lot), and I remember also looking at my father. I remember I raised my eyes, and my father looked at me, you know, like, 'Who the hell is this guy?'

Anyway, he turned round to my parents and he said (and this, I'm sure, is my parents dramatising), he said, 'For a thousand days, through a thousand villages I've taken my troops and everywhere I've looked for a Jewish child, because my wife is Jewish and I promised her that when I saw a Jewish child who could play with my children, I would let her know. And you're the first Jewish child I have seen since Moscow.' Now, I'm sure he was exaggerating. But, anyway, for the next two weeks, I lived the life of a lord, because I had a Russian platoon. I drove everywhere on a tank, and apparently the platoon commander was told that if anything happened to me, he was dead. And so, until the war moved on, I was the safest kid in Poland. And the reason I mention that is: a man actually was searching for children from one religion for such a long time and he could not find any ... Maybe this is a story that will tell you something about what the Holocaust really was, because, you know, you get these figures thrown at you ... 'six million people' ... that's beyond human comprehension. Two Sydneys; how can you think of two Sydneys? If you get a coffee-jar full of sand, that's six million grains. That story may give you an idea of what the devastation of the Holocaust really meant.

After the war, I finally got to play with children, but it was difficult. I had ingrained in me a paranoia and mistrust of all but my immediate family, so conversation was difficult. The children I first associated with were all survivors, and they had a similar outlook to mine, so making contact was very hard. It took us a long time to even start communicating at a very superficial level. My parents did try to put me into a local school, but there I met with so much hatred from my peers — I recall well standing in a playground, surrounded by Polish kids, and being hit and pushed and accused, 'You Jews started the war! You killed Jesus!' I had no idea what they were talking about. I saw a teacher and looked to him for help, and I can still see him turning his back and walking away. And the worst thing was, all I could do was stand there and look at them. I didn't know how to cry. I was never going to cringe, because that was a show of weakness, and weakness meant death. So the only thing I could do was to stand there and look, and I still have not learnt how to cry.

As a result of incidents like this, the remnants of the Jewish community took the decision to start a Jewish school for the surviving children. It was named in memory of the Warsaw Ghetto Fighters. All of us were disturbed survivors, so our learning was not great. Getting us to act like normal people was the priority. Slowly, I began to enter the real world, but I now know how disturbed I was. I was destructive and secretive, I had difficulty sleeping, waking nightly to nightmares, and bed-wetting was a nightly event.

In 1948, my parents had to flee Poland — apparently my father's brand of socialism was not what the new Polish Communist Party wanted. We left on false passports, all on the same day, but using different routes. My brother Jim, who was two by this time, left with Mum, on a train going through Czechoslovakia. I left with Dad, on a train going through Germany. Such was the haste and secrecy that the only 'person' I could communicate my thoughts and fears to was my dog, Rex. We took him to the station; there, Dad explained to me that we had to leave him. I was so used to knowing that I could lose someone I loved, but that I had to survive, that, whilst I knew I would miss him, I left him on the platform without even questioning my reasons.

Just before we left, my parents took me to see Auschwitz. And one of the things I remember from that visit is that I did not really want to identify with the inmates who'd been there not so long ago. I think you could still smell them; Auschwitz then was certainly different from the Auschwitz that I saw recently. I identified with the guards, the Germans. The pictures from that visit show me pretending to be a guard. So I was quite a screwed-up kid.

We went to Paris, where I proved too much for the local school to handle. So I was put into a boarding school where there were only child survivors, and the effort was to try and make us 'normal'. There was no formal teaching. I recall that, after six months, I still had not made a close friend or been able to communicate in any deep manner with anybody — but the bed-wetting did eventually stop there.

My parents, meanwhile, had decided to leave Europe. They looked at a cheap map of the world and chose Melbourne as the spot to come to live. Had the map been better, I am sure we would have ended up in New Zealand or, at best, Tasmania.

Our ship to Australia took many weeks to reach Perth, and the journey was full of incidents, as there were two decks of Jewish refugees and also two decks of members of a Baltic States SS Division and their families. Early on, I remember a major commotion, as one of the people recognised a man who had been his guard in a concentration camp.

After a brief period in Melbourne, my mother found an aunt in Sydney, so we moved to Sydney and settled there. In Sydney, for the first time, I began to recover.

In Australia, because I was allowed to, I was able to quickly become Australian — and I will never be anything else. When I came to Australia, I was nine, so my first real schooling was in Australia. Within three months, I'd forgotten how to speak Polish, and I spoke only 'Australian'. I think I'm a very good Australian. I mean, if we lose at cricket, I don't sleep at nights — that is how I am Australian. This is the country that gave me dignity; it gave me the privilege of belonging. I was an almost-nothing when I arrived here, because I had no country, and I had no people I could talk to. Here, from my first school — Bondi Beach Primary — children came to talk to me, and I sensed and felt it was safe to start responding to their warmth.

We moved to Maroubra and, soon after that, I finally began to come alive, to interact with peers at Maroubra Bay Primary School through sport — particularly rugby. It was a wonderful place to bond with my fellow students, and I began the long journey to enter the world as a 'normal' human being.

But the term 'normal' carries a wide range of meanings. For many years, I still woke up with nightmares once or twice a week; even today, since I started writing this, they have come back. I could not read books about the Holocaust, maybe because I spent many years of my life listening to the stories — and no book will ever tell you what a survivor will tell you, when he thinks you're a fellow survivor, in a quiet room.

So, after that, not only did I become Australian, I did not even want to be particularly Jewish. And I did not identify myself as a Holocaust survivor till well into my forties. I knew I had been there, but I convinced myself (despite the nightmares) that I really had no memory of the period. I did not particularly identify myself as Jewish. I was Jewish because my parents were Jewish and I was a good son, but I did not particularly want to be Jewish until 1967.

In 1967, I was a surgical registrar at the Camperdown Children's Hospital. It was about two weeks before the Six-Day War, and I'd just come off a very rough day. It was about 2 a.m. I sat down in front of the news on the ABC, and they said, 'The straits at Tiran are closed.'

I was so uninvolved that I wasn't quite sure what was going on there. I was too busy at work. I was concerned, but it was 'over there'. And then, the TV said that an Iraqi general had come to Jordan with his troops and had said, 'We're going to kill all the Jews in Israel, and then we're going to kill the Jews in the rest of the world.'

And, really, it was like a veil had lifted off my face. All of a sudden, I got so angry. I was furious, fuming. I mean, this guy was telling me that he was going to come and kill *me*. I got so angry that by the end of that week, I was in Israel. I volunteered, and went to Israel as part of a team of doctors. In fact, we got stuck in Italy, because the war broke out while we were travelling, and I came to Israel two days before the end of the war. I wanted to go and fight. I consider myself the world's greatest coward but, at that stage, I was crazy.

I ended up working for three months in a neurosurgical hospital. In Sydney, I had been working as a surgical registrar in children's neurosurgery, and I was just what was needed in Israel: a junior doctor. Israel, at that stage, was full of overseas volunteer doctors, but no junior ones. So I did work, and I had a wonderful time. In fact, I met my wife there, so I actually got a bonus for being such a 'brave' fellow — though it was really done out of sheer anger. I've acknowledged my Jewishness far more since then — but it really was the threat by a third party that caused me to do this.

Even then, though, I did not acknowledge that I was a Holocaust survivor. I thought I was a child who'd lived during the Holocaust. And, you know, you can be as clever as you like: I used to wake up night after night with these nightmares, and yet I could never bring myself to believe that they had anything to do with my survival.

They were nightmares that I have woken up with thousands of times in my life; and yet, until the very end, I did not acknowledge myself as a survivor. As an adult, I have a problem, because I'm still learning about my childhood. In reality, I just put a heavy gate in front of it; it was just a horrible event, and every time I opened the gate, a little bit more of the horror escaped. It didn't please me, so I closed it again. Only now am I beginning to open the gate a bit more, because I realise that closing it does not make it go away.

When the Australian Association of Holocaust Survivors was formed, my late mother went and joined the committee. Sadly, before the committee met, she passed away. But when she went on the committee, she decided to put it on my conscience, and she said, 'Look, I'm going to go on the committee, but one day you will take my place.'

I said, 'Oh, go away, Mum. Leave me alone.' Afterwards, when she died, it was on my conscience for several years. She wanted me to be on the committee, and I should have been on it. It took about three years, but I finally went on the committee.

Doing this was a stroke of luck. We had an international meeting of Holocaust survivors in Sydney, and I only went to the meeting for one day. There, I was pounced upon by a wonderful lady, Sarah Moskovitz. Suddenly, I was being interviewed and put at ease by this understanding scholar who had, as I subsequently found out, devoted her life to helping child survivors understand their lives.

Somehow, she convinced me to come to her hotel room for a chat the next morning. It had to be then, as she was leaving to go back to the United States that night.

I arrived, she started talking and, suddenly, things came pouring out of me. The memories became real; for the first time, I realised who I was and what I had experienced. After three hours, I walked out of the room a different person.

I began to acknowledge the fact that, not only was I a survivor, and not only did I have a store of memories, I had actually experienced a lot of things. I recall them now, and I acknowledge the fact that, in a way, I have a knowledge which is almost unique.

You see, the adults knew what they were getting into and what was happening. I was a child. I did not know that this was not normal life. As far as I knew, everybody hid in cellars and did not talk in public, and it was usual for a boy to walk around dressed as a girl. (Why I did not become a transvestite is beyond my comprehension, but I managed to contain myself, obviously!) I just thought, as a child, that this was normal; that it always was normal to be hiding, to be scared. It took me many years to realise that I could talk in public. At the age of five, I believe I was about as street-wise as a 40-year-old, and as social-wise as a newborn.

At first, I had great difficulty with any form of social intercourse. I had great difficulty in presenting myself so that I'd be noticed, because in my youth I was told, 'If you're noticed, you're dead.' I like to think that I overcame these difficulties, as I now lecture extensively, and I love it. I have made a number of TV appearances, and I no longer feel terrified that people will recognise me for what I am.

Eventually, I began to realise that some of my responses were not normal, but were instead conditional. However, even today, I have to consciously control them: it is hard for me to get up from a table and leave something on a plate. It is almost impossible. If I am served a plate of food, I have to eat every bit of it, and I cannot leave anything. And that goes back to the war, because I was always told, 'Finish everything on your plate. You do not know when your next meal is coming.' I feel guilty leaving food. It probably took me 40 years to realise why I felt guilty when I left the table. It was because I was too full.

Many child survivors had a double problem: they also had parents who were survivors. So, because survivors brought us up, we already had a different upbringing.

Another thing I did not realise for many years is a habit of mine: whenever I enter a strange room, the first thing I look for is another way to get out. This is an unconscious action. I was well into my fifties before I even realised I was doing it. I recall that I was a keynote speaker at an international conference and, as I walked in to give my talk, the delegates were clapping, and I realised I was not anxious about checking all the doors and windows of the hall in case the Germans burst in. That night, I finally realised that I had been doing this all my life and had not been conscious of it.

One of the things that the war did to me is to make it so difficult for me to think about those times: I have such difficulty in talking about it at times. I can talk about it, but I do not want to think about it. I spent five years of my life sitting in dark rooms, underground, in garbage dumps, and in wardrobes, thinking about what would happen to me. I am not keen to think about it any more. Crying is something I have difficulty with. I was conditioned in childhood that if I cried, I could die.

I graduated in medicine and went on to become a surgeon in Sydney, where I worked until the age of 50. Somehow, whilst loving my work and life, I felt I was unfulfilled. As I became more aware of myself, I began to want more; but I was not sure what.

I have had a very lucky life, but one of the luckiest moments was on that trip to Israel in 1967, when I went to a wedding of a distant cousin, and was introduced to my future wife, Rachel. It is not a cliché: I fell in love at first sight, and now, 40 years later, I am pleased to say that nothing has changed. Rachel, herself the daughter of Holocaust survivors, somehow understood me and my problems, and she has been my main support in my journey to this point. We formed a relationship based on love, and we also became best friends. We have no secrets, and anything we do is done as a team.

We have three great sons — Ron, Guy, and Ariel — all of whom have a sense of responsibility, compassion, and understanding that makes us proud. We feel we have achieved some great things through them. This chapter is not long enough for me to tell you about my five wonderful grandchildren.

In 1990, our eldest son, Ron, was in the UK studying to become a musician. I decided, with urging from Rachel (she understood my sense of something lacking even better than I) to take a year off work so that we could go and live in London to be with Ron. Ariel, the youngest, was then 11 years old, and we felt he could afford to miss school in Australia for a year. Meanwhile, I was going to enrol in an undergraduate course in my great love — archaeology.

By the end of the first year, I had fallen in love with the subject. Being a mature student, I had time to start a research project into the diseases of the ancients, and my knowledge of medicine allowed me to use the newest technology. My first paper, published that year, is said to have opened up a whole field of research into ancient diseases. I went on to finish my degree, and have embarked on a whole new career. I was able to identify the DNA of ancient bacteria, and this area is now the main focus of my work, although I have continued to practise medicine at a less intense level.

Within a few years, I was invited to come to the Hebrew University Medical School, where I became a Visiting Professor. I also became a Visiting Professor at the Centre of International Health at the Royal Free Medical School and the University College London Medical School in the UK. Thus, my life now alternates between laboratories at those two institutions, as well as between the many international contacts I have made.

Sadly, I only come to Australia now for family visits. In 2007, I was fortunate to win a Sir Zelman Cowen Fellowship at Sydney University, and was able to spend a month in Australia, lecturing, working, and seeing the Rabbitohs play.

On Holocaust Memorial Day a few years ago, we went to a ceremony at the memorial for the fallen from Zagwlembie (Bedzin, Czeladz, Dabrowa Gornicza, Kromolow, Modrzejow, Slawkow, Sosnowiec, Strzemieszyce, Zagorze, and Zawiercie), our district in Poland. The memorial is located in the foothills of Jerusalem. One of my beloved granddaughters was sitting on my lap, listening to the speeches, when she turned to me and asked, '*Saba* [grandpa], were you in the war?'

'Yes,' I replied.

'Who won the war?'

'I did!'

'How did you win the war?'

'Because,' I said, 'you are sitting on my lap asking a question on this day.'

I guess it was with this conversation that the significance of my survival finally hit me.

In September 2008, I went back to the area with a group of survivors, saw my home town, the house I was born in, and the areas where most of my family lived and perished. I will not describe my emotions — it would take another chapter.

The trip was to inaugurate a memorial (in the square from which they once almost transported me and my mother to Auschwitz) to the Jewish resistance fighters of the area, one of whom was my uncle, who died in the resistance. The ceremony was quite moving: there was a large attendance of dignitaries from Poland and Israel, such as ambassadors, and there were Israeli flags all around. We had sat down in a VIP tent when, suddenly, a brass band sounded, and in marched 200 fully armed Polish soldiers, followed by 200 members of the Israeli army, in full uniform. This was quite a moving moment for me. At the end of the ceremony, after the Polish national anthem, when the band struck up 'Hatikvah' (the Israeli national anthem), it became too much — I had never, until that moment, cried in public (I had been told never to do so as a child), but that day, even that lesson was lost.

My final thought, as I write this, is to realise how my family has grown, and how the teaching we were given by our parents — to help others, never to allow hatred to govern our lives, to make sure we gave back and did not just take — has shaped all our lives. My two brothers both work in fields relating to helping people: Jim is Chief Justice of NSW, and Alan is Professor of Surgery and Dean of the Clinical School at St Vincent's Hospital in Sydney. They each have three kids who are growing up like mine, as fine human beings, willing to give to society and not only to take; each of them has benefited from the wisdom inculcated into their father by our wonderful, fearless, and dedicated parents. The success of each member of our family represents a victory for our late parents against intolerance and racism. Thus, my final thought is: in what way would the world really be a better place if the two so-called 'sub-humans' Majloch and Gustava Szpigelman had been killed by the fascists? This is something that anybody with racist views about any ethnic group should consider.

Last Days in Poland (anti-clockwise from top): Mark Spigelman's 1946–47 class at the Warsaw Ghetto Fighters' School, Katowice; Mark posing as a guard (rather than an inmate) by the infamous gallows at Auschwitz, 1948; a Jewish tradition continues in 1947 with the school Purim play, in which Mark wanted to be a Persian warrior rather than a Hebrew slave; Mark posing as a guard again, during the same visit to Auschwitz.

PAUL KORNMEHL

With a bit of *Mazel*...

I remember it clearly, as if it was yesterday, the day Germany invaded Holland. It was 10 May 1940. I was still in college, in my hometown of Scheveningen; shortly after the invasion, Jewish students were no longer permitted to attend.

Since I could no longer attend college, I started working in my father's hosiery factory during the day. As news of raids on Jewish homes emerged, I started spending my nights at the railway stationmaster's house. I did this for the next 17 months. My elder brother, Itscho, also took to spending his nights away from our family home.

On 17 November 1941, my girlfriend Melitta and I left Scheveningen for a place called Bergem Op Zoom, near the Belgian border. Another Jewish couple, the Eismans, came with us.

While in Bergem Op Zoom, we rented bicycles, and stocked up with food for two to three days. Then we started cycling towards the Belgian border. Just before we approached the border, we were stopped by Dutch *Marechause* — special police in blue uniforms — who asked us where we were heading. I told them that we were going to visit a nearby Jewish cemetery. One of the *Marechause* sensed our real intentions and told me not to go straight ahead, because the Germans were there. Instead, he said, we should take the first street to the right, leave our bicycles at the end of that street, and set off on foot. He also said we would meet a farmer there who would let us go across his property into Belgium. We did as we were told and, sure enough, there was a Dutch farmer who took us over the border.

Once in Belgium, we took a tram to Antwerp, and there I contacted a school friend who helped me to send a letter back to my parents, David and Rachel Kornmehl, via Switzerland. I needed to let my parents know that we had made it safely to Antwerp, and also that the way was clear for them to follow us. But it wasn't safe for us to stay in Antwerp. We spent only one night there, then journeyed on to Brussels.

In Brussels, we stayed with a woman who owned three brothels, all of them next to each other. This woman was kind enough to protect us from some of her clients: her establishments were frequented by German soldiers, and every evening we had to be inside by 6 p.m. to keep them from seeing us. Most nights, we hid in the laundry.

We waited for nine days for some friends, the Jaegers, to join us. However, they never showed up. We found out later that they had lost all their money in card games, and hence could not finance their trip.

In December, on the advice of the underground movement in Brussels, we took the train from Brussels into Occupied France. When the train had crossed the border and stopped in Nancy, we got out, crossed the platform, and went into the waiting room for the night. It was very crowded — there must have been about 500 people in that waiting room. In the middle of the night, the police came and shone their torches at us. Because it was a very cold winter, we had blankets to try to keep warm, so we quickly hid our

Before the journey: Paul Kornmehl and Melitta Heuschober off Scheveningen, 1941, and (inset) Paul in 1940.

faces in our blankets. By a stroke of luck, the police did not lift the blankets to look at our faces.

We waited in the waiting room for six or seven hours, and then took another train to Liesle. In this train, there were about 70 French POWs who had escaped from the Germans and were making their way into unoccupied France. They instructed us to get off at the seventh stop and on the left-hand side of the train to escape detection by German soldiers, who were getting onto the trains from the right-hand side.

After getting off the train, we walked for about ten hours in thick snow and ice into unoccupied France. We were following a canal, and we often had to crouch and hide in the snow and ice to avoid German soldiers, who were only a few metres away, on the other side.

Even in this time of terror, we found a little humour. There was a female prisoner of war in front of us whose dress was quite ridiculous. She wasn't wearing warm, comfortable winter clothes like the rest of us, but a fur coat, patent-leather high heels, and a red hat with a long feather! Melitta and I couldn't stop laughing and, in some ways, it must have helped us get through that terrifying ordeal.

When we finally reached Liesle, we were ordered to report to a detention centre. I asked for 24 hours' grace, and checked into a hotel. Whilst there, I managed to ring my sister Anna, who was already in Marseilles with her husband, Isaac, and their young daughter, Paulette. Anna managed to send a Frenchwoman, who accompanied me to the police, and she bribed one of them with 25,000 francs. From him, we managed to secure a permit to leave for Lyons.

In Lyons, I went to see the Dutch consul, Mr Jacquet, who was known to be a very kind and helpful man. He gave us our passports.

Within days, we also managed to secure our *sauf-conduits* (travel permits) from the police, after bribing them with cigarettes. With the permits, we were able to leave for Marseilles.

I made several trips between Marseilles, Lyons, and Nice; but, instead of getting a travel permit each time, we started forging the papers. On one of my trips to Marseilles, I was caught with the forged exit papers. I was interrogated and tortured for up to 18 hours without a break. I was held in the cellar of an old castle, about 60 feet below ground level, and wasn't allowed out for many days. How many days I can't tell, as I was in total darkness the whole time. It felt like eternity.

All through my ordeal, I remained polite, and swore in my best

French that the papers I held were genuine. I was then brought before a judge. During the hearing, the judge summoned me to approach the bench. He whispered to me that I would be followed upon my release.

After my release, I noticed that I was indeed followed by two men. I quickly checked into a different hotel from the one I was staying before my arrest, then escaped through the back door.

While Melitta and I were in Nice, the rest of my family joined us, including my brother, Itscho, and his wife, Rita; my older sister, Berta, her husband, Max, and their two sons, Siegfried and Manfred; and my younger sister, Anna, her husband, Isaac, and their daughter, Paulette. The day before we split up to go our separate ways, most of us had our photo taken by a street photographer.

From Marseilles, we journeyed on to Monte Carlo. The Prince of Monaco, from his exile in America, had assured Jews that they

Reunion in Nice: (Back row, left to right) Anna and Isaac Rose, Rita and Itscho Kornmehl, Berta and Max Wolf, Melitta and Paul Kornmehl. Manfred and Siegfried Wolf stand in front.

would not be harmed in his principality. My parents and Berta and her family were already there. But, suddenly, Berta and her family were rounded up and put on a train that was headed ultimately for Poland. Having received word that the train would first stop in Marseilles to pick up more Jews, we returned to Marseilles, and there I managed to bribe the police. For 100,000 francs, I managed to get Berta and her family off the train.

All of the family except for Melitta and myself now set out to cross the Pyrenees into Spain. Melitta and I remained in Marseilles. We ended up spending seven months in unoccupied France, and it was there that we got married. The date was 16 March 1942.

It was getting increasingly dangerous for us to stay on in unoccupied France. More and more Jews were being rounded up and transported to concentration camps. We were getting more and more fearful for our lives. At the same time, we were waiting for word from our contact in Switzerland as to whether my family had made it to safety in Spain. But word never came.

Finally, Melitta and I decided to travel to Perpignan, a town close to the Spanish border. Melitta was allowed to enter Spain, but I had to go to the Spanish consul in Pau, a town about 60 kilometres from the Spanish border, to get him to certify that I was not fit for the French army. This was because I was of military age. Although the consul could see that my papers were forged, he took pity on me, and signed the certification that authorised my entry permit. With that, I was allowed into Spain, where I was reunited with Melitta.

We then set out for the port of Barcelona. We were lucky to leave France when we did, because the very next day — 11 November 1942 — the Germans moved into the unoccupied part of the country as well. After that, crossing into Spain would have been extremely difficult, if not impossible.

By now, Rita, together with Berta and her family, were already in Madrid. I learnt, however, that my mother, Anna, and Paulette were being held in a camp on an old convent site at Figueras, while the men — my father, Itscho, and a family friend,

Jacob Markuszower — were in an internment camp at Miranda de Ebro. This camp held about 60,000 men, both Spanish political prisoners and foreign refugees, including a number of escaped French POWs, who were housed in a separate barrack. My father and his companions were at least not going hungry there, as food was donated by a number of American Jewish charitable organisations, among them the American Jewish Joint Distribution Committee, commonly known as 'the Joint'.

Melitta and I could find no help in Barcelona, so we travelled on to Madrid. There I went to a large speciality store, and asked if anyone could speak French. I wasn't used to the Spanish food and was feeling very ill and weak, and I urgently needed some medicine. A very kind lady appeared from the back of the store and started to engage me in conversation. I was so overcome with emotion and exhaustion that I started to cry. I poured out my family's story to her, and she very kindly offered the help of her brother. Her brother owned the store and had been Spain's ambassador to France at the start of the Spanish Civil War in 1936. I was then introduced to her brother, Pecastain, who in turn introduced me to a Spanish count by the name of Salgado, who was also a general in the army. Salgado happened to be in the store in order to try on some suits.

Salgado was very genuine and was keen to help me. He somehow managed to track down just where my female relatives were, and obtained their release. The wonderful thing was, not only did he secure the release of my female relatives, but he also managed to free the other women in that camp. When he told me to expect no fewer than 86 women the very next day, I had my doubts. But, with the help of a fellow Jew, I went ahead with obtaining food and writing materials for that number. I prepared it all in blind faith, reasoning that whatever the consequences, they would be far worse if I made no preparations and the promised 86 arrived with nothing done.

Indeed, 86 female prisoners arrived in handcuffs by train the next day, with my mother, Anna, and Paulette amongst them.

They were then taken to a prison in Madrid. But Salgado was very friendly with the governor of Madrid, and he managed to convince the governor to liberate the women the next day. It was a very happy moment for me; but, of course, I couldn't stop there. I still had my father, Itscho, and Jacob to rescue. With Salgado's help once again, I managed to secure their release from the camp at Miranda de Ebro four weeks later.

At about the same time, my other relatives — Rita, Berta, Max, Siegfried, and Manfred — also arrived. So all 14 of us made it!

Salgado kindly arranged for our exit permits to leave Spain. We were so anxious to leave that we took whichever ships arrived first, in either Spain or Portugal. My father, Melitta, and I took a ship to Jamaica; my mother, Berta, Max, Siegfried, and Manfred took a ship to Surinam; Anna, Isaac, and Paulette went to Canada, and Itscho, Rita, and Jacob Markuszower to British-Mandate Palestine.

While in Jamaica, I volunteered for the Dutch army. I joined the

Jamaica bound: Paul Kornmehl and Melitta Kornmehl on deck with Paul's father, David.

In training: Paul Kornmehl (left) during commando training in Guelph, Canada.

Royal Dutch Brigade 'Princess Irene', and received commando training in Guelph, Canada, and Wolverhampton, England. I joined the observers for the brigade's 25-pounder artillery.

By May 1944, I was training at Dovercourt, on the Essex coast in southern England. Thirty of us were told that we were going on a secret mission to North Africa — but, in reality, we were going across the Channel to fight in Normandy. D-Day, the Allied invasion of France, was imminent.

The Royal Dutch Brigade landed on Juno Beach that August, and took part in the Allied advance to the Seine. I was in charge of the Observation Post. That meant I had to climb up high on a hill or tree with binoculars, so that I could see which way the Germans were coming. I would then alert the soldiers, via walkie-talkies, as to the Germans' whereabouts and what direction they were coming from.

We set up a Bailey bridge, a transportable bridge that an expert could set up in a few hours, and 15 of us went across the bridge to the other side of a river. Unfortunately, the Germans destroyed the bridge; we could not swim back, as the river was mined, and we had three trucks with us on our side of the bridge. I and the 14 others dug ourselves into the sand during the day, and would come out at night to try to find the enemy. The bridge expert was building another Bailey bridge, but we were cut off for about eight days. We couldn't cross the enemy lines, and we were stuck there.

Out of the 15 men we started off with, six were killed and six were wounded. It was sheer luck that I and two other men were unharmed.

In recognition of my services, I was awarded 14 medals from France, Belgium, and the Netherlands, including the Wilhelmina Cross.

After the war, Melitta and I decided to immigrate to Australia to begin a new life. By then, we had two young children, Jim and Yvonne. In October 1952, we set sail for Sydney, and arrived the following month. Our third child, Anita, was born in Sydney.

I went on to establish the Kolotex brand of hosiery and, a few years later, the Glomesh range of ladies' fashion products. For many years, I have been involved in the business and Jewish communities in Australia, Israel, and in Europe.

I often think about those war years. I think about my family, and about the other Jews we knew in Holland before the war. I then think about how lucky we were. Despite having to walk across several countries, despite being captured several times and interrogated and jailed, our whole extended family made it to safety. Unfortunately, most of the other Jewish families that we had known so well were not so lucky. Most did not survive.

In deciding which country we would settle in after the war, we were incredibly lucky. Our decision was based simply on which country would be first to accept us, and which ship had the space.

Paul Kornmehl's Wilhelmina Cross: Awarded with 'Normandy 1944' bar.

In ending up in Australia, we found a warm and loving country, and people who were kind and welcoming. We found people who cared about families — just like we did — and we found that our ways were accepted without discrimination.

Despite making a new home in Australia for myself and my family, I never forgot where I came from. I brought up my three children and five grandchildren to know and understand Jewish traditions — not just the religious side, but also the care of others in the family. I stressed the importance of education to them all.

During the last ten years, I became involved in the development and growth of the Kornmehl Centre — a Jewish preschool that is now part of the Emanuel School in the Sydney suburb of Randwick. More recently, I also helped set up the Kornmehl Family Hebrew School, weekly classes run by Rabbi Yanky and Leah Berger of the Chabad, Double Bay.

I am still grateful that my family had a second chance to survive, and I am proud to feel that I have given Australia at least as much as this country has given to me and my family.

At the preschool: Paul Kornmehl at the Kornmehl Centre in Sydney's Emanuel School, 2000.

RUTH LEISER

The Holocaust survival of the Katz family, 1941–44

The Katz family arrived in Sydney on 31 March 1951. There were four of us: my parents, Nachum and Berthe, my brother, Jack, and me. I was 16, Jack was 14. We had been on the run, or in transit, for the past ten years. From 1941 to 1944, we had been under Hitler, in what is now Lithuania. In 1945, we had fled to Poland. We fled Poland too, crossing the border illegally into Czechoslovakia. From there, we made our way to Austria and, finally, to Bavaria, in the American zone of postwar Germany. There, we spent over four years in a total of three Displaced Persons camps.

Our new life in Australia started with many difficulties. While still in temporary lodgings, where we had only one room, my mother fell and broke her hip. Her recovery took a long time, with months in hospital, and years on crutches. It fell to me to help my father by cooking, washing, and tending to my mother's needs. I also worked in a little cake shop that my father opened in King Street, Newtown. There was a tiny so-called 'residence' upstairs, to which my mother was brought on a stretcher from hospital.

In Australia: Berthe and Nachum Katz in Sydney's Rose Bay, about 1964.

Jack was going to school, but he also helped when he could — for example, by delivering pies from the shop.

We spent three years in Newtown, working very hard — especially my father. We became members of the Newtown Shul, and slowly started making some friends.

In 1954, my father sold the shop. Soon after, he bought a much larger cake business, Jasper's cake shop, on the Corso in Manly. I, of course, went with him, though reluctantly. My father bought his first Holden, and we moved to a flat in Bondi. Jack finished school and, as time went on, I did all kinds of courses, time permitting. The Manly business proved very successful, but the hours were extremely long — seven days a week.

In 1960, my father finally decided to sell it and retire. He had made some modest investments that secured him and my mother an income for the remainder of their lives. They enjoyed 18 years of peaceful companionship with their growing family, until my father's death in 1978. By coincidence — a providential one, perhaps — my parents and I bought units in the same building, so I was able to help care for my father during his final illness. I was also able to look after my mother until she died in 2001.

Jack became a lawyer, and now has four children and seven grandchildren. He is still in practice.

As for me, since 1988, I have worked as a broadcaster/journalist on SBS Radio's Yiddish program. In 1998, I was appointed head of group for Yiddish, a post I occupy to this day. I have one son, who is married with a five-year-old daughter, Hannah, and a three-year-old, Sophie. He and his family live in America. Both Jack and I have been members of the Child Survivors Group since its inception. I have acted as the group's treasurer for most of that time.

My father, Nachum Katz, was born in Bendzin, Poland, in 1899. As a young man, he served in the Polish army towards the end of the First World War, and also in Poland's War of Independence in 1920. He earned many decorations and medals, the most important being the *Virtuti Militari*, second class. He was one of only a small number of Jewish soldiers to win the *Virtuti Militari*, Poland's highest decoration for bravery, and he always wore a miniature of it in his lapel. In later years, it opened many official doors that were otherwise closed to Jews.

While stationed in Vilno,* my father and a number of other Jewish soldiers were welcomed into the home of the Orzechowski family. The Orzechowskis lived on their family farm, known as Kotlovka, seven kilometres from town. They had seven children, five girls and two boys, and for many years they kept a flat in Vilno to allow the children to attend school. They went two and three at a time, depending on their ages.

My father's chance meeting with the Orzechowskis led, ultimately, to his marriage, 12 years later, to Berthe, the fourth of the five Orzechowski daughters. Berthe was considerably younger

---

* Now Vilnius, the capital of Lithuania.

Before the war: Ruth Leiser's mother, Berthe Katz, née Orzechowski.

than my father; she was born in Vilno in 1910. After their marriage, she moved to Bendzin, where my father was already established with a home and business. But she found it difficult to settle down there. Somehow she did not fit in, and she was homesick for her family. My father, on the other hand, very much liked her parents' way of life on the land. So, after some deliberation, he decided to try his hand at farming, only on a larger scale than my grandfather's farm.

Through a land agent, my father found a suitable estate on the main highway between Vilno and Kovno, which was then the Lithuanian capital.† Godulin, as the estate was called, lay about 28 kilometres from Vilno, and belonged to a Polish gentry family who lived in Warsaw. They relied on a manager, but the

---

† Now Kaunas.

estate was badly managed and, consequently, run down. My father began negotiations to obtain it. This was no easy matter, as Jews were not allowed to own land. The feat was accomplished partly due to my father's war record, and partly thanks to intervention and string-pulling by a great friend of my grandfather, a Pole and very large landowner who was then the president of the Farming Association.

In 1933, a little over a year after their marriage, my parents made the move from Bendzin to Godulin. The nearest town, Mejszagola, was four kilometres away. As a provincial town and the seat of the local municipality, Mejszagola had a town hall, a mayor, a local farming association, a police station, a post office, a school, a bus station, and so on. It also had a good-sized Jewish community of perhaps 200 people, who all lived fairly well. The community was served by the usual Jewish institutions, as well as shopkeepers and tradesmen.

The year 1933 was also notable for another, more ominous, event: it was the year that Adolf Hiter became chancellor of Germany.

Godulin had a great deal of land, including orchards, cultivated fields, and its own forest. It had livestock of every description and a number of buildings, including a large residence. It also had 11 peasant families who lived and worked on the estate permanently and, at planting and harvest time, it attracted many seasonal workers from around the district.

Farming in that part of Poland was still very backward. My father was a very capable man and, with the help and expert advice of my grandfather, he soon brought in many changes: mechanised equipment, more modern farming methods, better conditions for the workers, and much more. In a few short years, Godulin became quite prosperous, and a showplace for the whole district. It became famous for its marvellous horses, which my father bred and was very proud of. For as long as I can remember, my father used to tell us stories about his favourite horses, some that he alone could handle. Godulin also had champion bulls and herds of milk cows, not to mention the produce of the land, which was sold either through agents or directly to mills, breweries, the army, and so on. The fruit orchards were usually sub-contracted seasonally.

My father gained great respect, admiration, and even devotion, not only from his own workers, but also from the neighbouring farmers, large and small, all around the municipality. He became known far and wide as 'Pan' Katz: 'Mr' Katz. He was also generous to the many poor small farmers in the district who could not produce enough from their own land to feed themselves and their animals over the long winter months. Because my father always helped them with whatever they needed without taking any payment, some of them would come at harvest time and do a few days' work in order to show their gratitude.

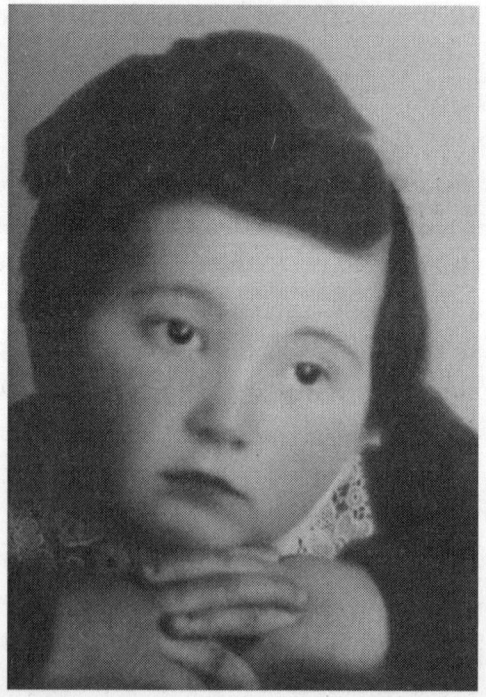

Ruth Leiser as a child of four: A portrait from 1939.

My father had a shortwave radio, and the few broadcasts my parents heard from Moscow (and, after 1938, from German-occupied Prague) left no doubt that bad times were ahead for the Jews. Some of Hitler's speeches chilled them to the bone.

In September 1939, Hitler attacked Poland. Right away, the Polish army commandeered all my father's horses. I vaguely remember the whole herd being led away — not that it did the army any good, for Poland was overrun in three weeks. The Germans advanced from the west and the Soviets from the east, and they partitioned Poland between them. Godulin was in the Soviet half. But, somehow, my parents, Jack, and I were able to go on living there very happily and in harmony with everyone — both man and nature.

Communications with the German-occupied half of Poland were cut off, but terrible rumours reached us about what was happening to Jews there — rumours so terrible they were hard to believe.

Then, on 22 June 1941, Hitler launched his invasion of the Soviet Union. Eastern Poland lay directly in his path, but when Hitler's army marched into Vilno, it encountered no resistance. In fact, certain sections of the local population welcomed the German troops with flowers and applause.

The local Jewish population, by contrast, had watched Hitler's advance with alarm and a foreboding of disaster. Our worst fears were soon borne. In Vilno and all the surrounding areas, the Germans fell upon the Jewish population almost at once. They began mass killings, frenzied killings, in order to liquidate as many Jews as possible, as quickly as possible. In June 1941, Vilno had a community of 80,000 Jews; by December, thousands had been killed.

Our own ordeal began when a detachment of German troops turned off the highway into the avenue of trees that led to the estate. They were looking for fresh provisions. At this early stage, we owed our lives to two ordinary German soldiers. The two came into our house and asked, by sign language, for butter and eggs.

Taking a risk, my father answered them in German. This aroused their curiosity as to who he was and how came he to speak German, as the locals spoke only Polish. They must have realised our identity immediately, and they asked my father certain questions. When he answered, 'Yes, we are Jewish,' the two soldiers looked at each other and went outside. A few minutes later, they came back and told my parents to quickly disappear, as their commandant was a *Judenfeind* (enemy of Jews) and would finish us off straight away. One of them illustrated by drawing his finger across his neck, as if cutting his throat from ear to ear.

Terrified, my parents grabbed us children, and left through the back door. We fled through the orchards, across the fields, and through woods to a neighbouring farmer.

A few days later, when the Germans had gone, we returned to Godulin for a short time, my parents trying to decide what to do, all the time in a state of grave anxiety. A few days later, or perhaps a week, a nearby farmer and friend came, riding his horse at full gallop, and informed my parents that he was just returning from a meeting outside the council in Mejszagola, where the liquidation of the Jews was being discussed. It was to take place on the very following Saturday. He told my parents how a voice in the crowd was heard to ask, 'And what about Katz?' The reply was, 'Katz will be the last one.'

My parents heeded their friend's warning. Hastily, they packed a few belongings and some valuables — only what they could carry — and, as soon as it was dark, we all crept silently out of Godulin and into the woods, leaving our beloved home forever. I was six years old, and Jack was four.

We fled as far from Godulin as possible, through the fields, pastures, and woods, my parents and us, two small children. It was the beginning of our titanic struggle to stay alive, to survive this horrific period, which lasted three long years.

We went as far as our legs would carry us. My father knew the area well, and chose to ask for help from the most isolated farmers,

Nachum Katz, Ruth Leiser's father: A holder of the *Virtuti Militari*, Poland's highest decoration for bravery, pictured in Bavaria after the Second World War.

especially those whom he had helped in their time of need. The first few months, we hid in a variety of barns, stables, attics, cellars, and all manner of hiding places; but more often it was out in the open. We had to move very often. Nobody, even with the best intentions, wanted to keep us for long, as sheltering us endangered their own families. Autumn was approaching, and it was getting colder and colder every day.

We hid in the barn of an old and very primitive peasant who used to get drunk daily, quite often in the company of one or more of his cronies. Their subject of discussion was always 'the Jews'. As time went on, our protector became more and more abusive, jeering insults and wild accusations at Jews — 'except you, Panie Katz,' he would always add. My parents saw the danger he posed, and were very apprehensive. They feared that, while drunk, he might kill us all.

So, one night, when he was very drunk, we crept quietly out of the barn and into the forest. But where were we to go? It was already extremely cold. The ground was iced over everywhere. After wandering in the forest for half the night, we came upon a stream. It was one of those times when my parents' situation was so desperate, so hopeless, that they considered suicide rather than to face falling into the hands of the murderers. But these thoughts only lasted a moment. 'What about the poor children?' they thought. 'We would have to drown them first.'

My father suddenly remembered that there had once been a forester's hut somewhere in the area. It had been abandoned years before. We resumed our wanderings, and looked for it for hours. Finally, near despair, we found it. Only part of it was still standing, but it gave us some shelter from the cold, even if being there put us at the mercy of anyone who might discover us. That was our home for the next week or so.

Once again, my father started setting out at night, leaving us in the hut, while he went and approached various farmers for help. Fearing for their lives, they all refused. Harbouring Jews was punishable by death. Even the most isolated farmers knew about the seven gallows in the centre of Vilno, where seven Christians had been hanged for helping Jews. The bodies, bearing large placards, were left hanging for a long time as a warning.

Night after night, my father left us and went to try to find a more secure hiding place. Some of the farmers would have weakened out of friendship if it had been only my parents, but they were reluctant to hide a whole family. A few said, 'If it were only you … but children!'

Eventually, a former worker from Godulin, who now had a tiny farm of his own, agreed to hide us on his land, in a hole in the ground where potatoes were stored for the winter. It was an open hole where we could half stand, half crouch, with the top covered by tree branches. The farmer brought us some bread and potato soup every few days, and we managed to survive this way for a short time, in spite of the cold. But, after a few weeks, he too told us we had to leave. He was afraid to have us on his land because, he said, someone might see footsteps in the new snow, and that would lead them to our 'bunker'. This was a time when Jews were being intensively hunted. Any Jew who was found was killed on the spot, with any available weapon, preferably an axe.

It was becoming bitterly cold. My father continued to go out, night after night, to yet other farmers, begging them to take us in. Every time he left us, we were terribly afraid. He was our rock; somehow, we felt more secure when he was with us and we were together. It became a pattern: a farmer friend would finally take pity on us and, for a while, give us shelter and food. If we were lucky, our hiding place would be in a barn, or a stable, or a cellar, or even in a shed in the pigsty. Mostly, though, it was out in the open, in one hole or another dug in the ground and camouflaged.

So we went from one hiding place to another, staying in each sometimes for days, sometimes for weeks, sometimes for months. We were always starving, dirty, and terrified of every noise and shadow — but we were alive, and we were together. We survived this way until sometime in 1942. Then, my parents felt that they could no longer go on. They were completely drained, physically, emotionally, and spiritually. The only thing that kept them going, one day after another, was their desperate wish, almost an obsession, to save their children, whatever the sacrifice, deprivation, or humiliation.

By that time, the most dreadful horrors had befallen the Jews of Vilno and its outlying townships and rural areas. Thousands of Jews had lived on farms and in small communities in the district. Almost immediately after Hitler's forces occupied Vilno, tens of thousands of these Jews were murdered in the most gruesome and cruel way. They were buried in mass graves in the Ponary Forest, some miles from the city. The rest were herded together and locked up in the Vilno Ghetto.

Among the first to be killed was my mother's entire family. All of them, except for us, had gathered on my grandfather's farm to be together in a time of danger. On Yom Kippur in 1941, the father, mother, sisters, brother, cousins, aunts, uncles, nieces, nephews, all the children, in-laws, the young and the old, together with all the Jews in a ten-kilometre radius, were herded together at certain points and, from there, they were led to their deaths. At gunpoint, they were forced to go to a smaller forest, the Wieliciany Forest, dig a huge ditch, and strip naked. Then, they were brutally and mercilessly murdered. Beatings and acts of extreme brutality were also committed during the march to the place of execution. Local peasants, some of whom witnessed part of the death march, told us, after the war, that my poor grandfather Zelig, who was a *tzadik*‡ among men, who lived a pure life full of love and charity for others, died horrifically on the way to Wieliciany. He was beaten to death, and left to die where he fell. Such was the end of a most wonderful and saintly human being, a Talmud *chochem*§ who studied as a young man under the famous Chafetz Chaim in his equally famous yeshiva in Radin. May they all rest in peace.

We continued our life in hiding for well over a year, always in fear, always hungry, dirty, and listening for every sound that might betray us. Jack and I seemed to feel and understand the gravity of the situation, not questioning anything, not asking for anything. We were silent and obedient, needing only our parents to cling to.

Even this form of existence ran out in the end. Those few farmers who were shielding us, each without knowing about the others, could no longer do it, for fear of getting caught. Hostile peasants were very clever at sniffing out Jews hidden anywhere

---

‡ Righteous person.
§ Scholar.

in the area. Another disaster for my parents was that my mother realised she was pregnant, and probably in an advanced stage.

One of my parents' farmer friends told them that there were still a few work camps outside the Vilno Ghetto. He knew where one such camp was. My mother decided to investigate. Dressed as a local peasant woman, she went there with the farmer in his horse and cart, and drove past the camp to determine its position and the possibilities of joining it. It turned out to be, as he had said, a work camp drawing on the ghetto for slave labour. But, because it was 14 kilometres away from the ghetto, a single barrack had been built to house the labourers. There were approximately 400 of them.

The camp had barbed wire all around it and, apart from the barrack, it had two sheds: one serving as a so-called kitchen, and the other as a latrine. There was a gate with a watch-house manned by armed Lithuanian guards. The work consisted of digging up *torf* (peat), a kind of mud that was then shaped into bricks and used as fuel when it had dried. The camp was only casually guarded, and it looked as if it would be possible to slip into it with the prisoners.

Our situation was desperate. To remain in the open forest would mean certain death, and there was no one left at that time who would take us in. So my parents decided to try and smuggle the family into the camp with a work party, there to share the fate of the others.

The camp, known officially as Rzesza but nicknamed 'the *Torfowisco*' (Polish for 'the place where you dig *torf*'), was about 30 kilometres from us. We set out to walk, travelling through the forests at night, avoiding roads and inhabited places, and hiding in bushes or fields by day. At last, we reached the camp safely and, somehow, joined its inmates. Children were a rarity in the camp, but there were a few, so we were lucky, for the guards seemed to tolerate our presence.

The barrack had double bunks so overcrowded that some people huddled in corners on the floor. There was no bedding of any kind, and we had to live in the rags on our backs. A daily portion of watery soup and a bit of bread was the only food. My parents worked at digging *torf* with the others, up to their knees in mud. We children kept quiet and out of sight of the guards, who were known to enjoy a little cruel sport.

We spent about four months in the camp, but soon after we reached it, my mother's time drew near. My parents were told that in the ghetto there were doctors, and some kind of hospital still existed. My mother decided that she had no choice but to try to join a returning work party and smuggle herself into the ghetto.

With a heavy heart, my mother left us in the barrack, in the full knowledge that she might never see us again. She might soon be dead, and so might we be. We all knew that any of us could be killed at any time. But she managed to slip into the ghetto and there she had the baby, a beautiful boy. He was disposed of immediately, and she never saw him again. She said later that, at the time, being numb with despair, she did not care. It was a foregone conclusion that the baby could not be saved. Her only concern, her desperate worry, was for us and our safety.

After the birth, she became very ill. Later, it was thought that the afterbirth had not come away, possibly owing to the many months of immobility she had spent in our cramped 'bunkers'. There was a doctor, but he could do nothing for her, not even give her hope. Her condition was critical. Even in normal times, before the war, such cases were usually fatal. In the ghetto, it was a virtual certainty. My mother knew she was dying. She recalled that she managed to scribble a note to my father, which someone managed to smuggle to him in the labour camp. It said: 'I am dying, we will not see each other again, do whatever is possible to save the children.'

As her condition worsened, she became delirious with extreme high temperature. She was taken out of the so-called ward, so as not to die in front of the others, their own misery and despair being bad enough. Nobody was bothered with her any more, as death was an accepted daily occurrence in the ghetto. There was one nurse, however. My mother recognised her as an old school friend. She checked on my mother now and then, in the dark corner of a corridor where she had been put to die, all alone.

It is not known how long she was in that state of delirium, but one day the nurse came near her and was amazed to find her conscious. Her temperature dropped, and the crisis appeared over. The nurse ran to fetch the doctor, who, after looking my mother over, stood back in disbelief, exclaiming, 'If you survived this, then maybe there is still hope for all of us! Maybe a miracle will happen and the whole ghetto will be saved.' My mother willed herself to live. My brother and I like to think she recovered so as to come back to find us still alive in the barrack.

Though I was only seven years old at the time, I clearly remember the utter desolation I felt when my mother left, and my happiness when she returned. I also remember, as if it were yesterday, being inwardly excited about the baby that I expected my mother to bring. A wondrous thing, a baby! But when my mother returned without a baby, even at that age, I knew how to suppress my inner disappointment, and to not ask any questions.

One of my most haunting memories from that period is the way that my mother looked at me, and at Jack, when she returned from the ghetto. It was a look of such love and gratitude for having found us still alive and waiting for her. Only as an adult, many years later, did I fully realise how she must have felt then. Our little family always felt, even after liberation, that the hand of G-d was shielding us, and that we were meant to survive as a family. In the end, we were one of the very few Jewish families who did survive the Nazi occupation of Vilno.

Yet, the worst was still to come. During our time in the *Torfowisco* camp, my father became involved in the Polish underground. My father knew many Polish resistance members who had collected stores of arms after the collapse of the Polish army in the face of Hitler's blitzkrieg in 1939. He also knew where a

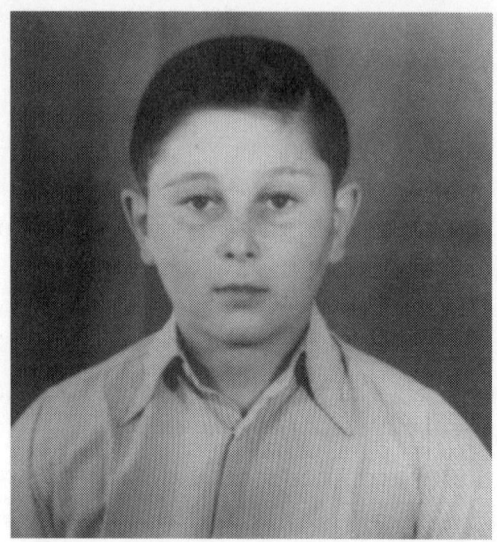

Jakob Katz: Ruth Leiser's brother, later known as Jack.

cache of small-arms had been buried on the Godulin estate, when the Soviets occupied the eastern half of Poland. He used to sneak out at night, underneath the barbed wire, and go through fields and forests to various Polish contacts, buy whatever arms he could get — revolvers, hand grenades, ammunition, and so on — and bring them back to the camp, where they were hidden under the floorboards.

This whole operation was done in the utmost secrecy. Only a few selected people were involved. They included those who had their own contacts in order to smuggle the arms into the ghetto, where there were groups planning a resistance movement. This movement never really eventuated, but many would-be members managed to escape from the ghetto, join the partisans, and fight gallantly against the enemy.

By this time, conditions in the ghetto were desperate. Most of the old and sick, as well as the children, had already been liquidated. There was starvation, and only the fittest survived from day to day. Even they had no hope left. A feeling of doom lay over them.

Towards the end of our period in the camp, one of my father's

Polish contacts in the underground betrayed him to the Gestapo. One day, the ghetto police, the scum of the Jewish people, arrived in the camp, talked to the camp guards, and came to where the people were digging *torf*. They asked which one of them was Katz, and when my father was pointed out, they arrested him before he had time to run. He had not realised in time that it was him they were after. He and my mother pleaded with them to let him go, to return to the ghetto and say that there was no such man in the camp, but to no avail.

At a signal from my father, my mother crept away from the *torf* pit, and set out through the woods to a neighbouring farm, where my father had a couple of revolvers hidden. The idea was that, with a gun, he might be able to escape from his guards en route to the ghetto. But the police sensed that something was in the air and, without delay, they bundled my father into their horse-drawn cart and sped away.

In the ghetto, my father was brought before the *Judenrat* chief, Jacob Gens, and the chief of the ghetto criminal police, Salk Dessler. With them, too, he pleaded not to turn him over to the Gestapo. But that is exactly what they did.

When my mother returned to the camp with a revolver under her breast, faint from running, trembling, and out of her mind with worry, it was too late. Her despair and distress were extreme. To be arrested by the Gestapo for any reason, even a minor one, almost always meant death. When the charge was smuggling guns into the ghetto, it could only be death.

In spite of it all, her first instinct was to think of us children. She had the presence of mind to smuggle us out of the camp, and she found a kind farmer in the area who hid us in his barn until she could return. The farmer brought us some food, and we stayed there, without moving around, for days or weeks. I don't know how long it was, but we stayed there all alone and, most importantly, we kept very quiet and did exactly as my mother had instructed us. We just stayed there and waited, my little brother and I.

While we were waiting, my mother smuggled herself into the ghetto by joining a working party that was being marched into it. She did this with a young rabbi, Israel Gustman, the only rabbi from Vilno to survive under the German occupation. He remained a lifelong friend of my parents. There was no question of saving my father, but together they tried, at least, to smuggle some food to him. With the greatest difficulty, my mother managed to obtain a few potatoes and onions for him, even though she herself was at the point of starvation.

My mother and the rabbi approached the *Judenrat* and begged them to intervene. There were even individuals who offered to collect funds with which to obtain my father's release, for if he were found guilty of the charge, the repercussions for the remaining Jews in the ghetto would be horrendous.

My father was held in the Gestapo prison for ten days. He was interrogated night and day, tortured, beaten, hung with his arms tied behind his back, and beaten again and again, but he did not confess, nor did he betray any of his comrades or their locations. He denied everything and did not weaken once during his ordeal. He knew that he would die, but he wanted to protect the ghetto. He knew that if he confessed to smuggling guns into the ghetto, the Gestapo would wipe it out, along with everyone inside it.

We can only speculate as to what really happened and how it was achieved, but my father was quietly released from the Gestapo and returned to the ghetto. It was a miracle without equal in the ghetto's annals. My parents found each other, and together returned to the *Torfowisco* camp with yet another work party.

My mother recalled with great sadness how, on their way out of the ghetto, near the gates, they were forced to witness the flogging of a woman who was caught bringing in a few beans in her hair-bun. The woman, a famous Jewish singer before the war, was stripped naked, put on some sort of bench, and flogged mercilessly. Ever afterwards, her inhuman screams haunted my mother's memory.

While the Gestapo officers were interrogating my father, he overheard a conversation to the effect that orders had come in to liquidate all the work camps outside the ghetto. When my parents returned to the camp, he passed this information on to a few people, and everyone agreed that our days there were numbered. This information spread very quickly and, that afternoon, a mass escape was attempted. By cutting the barbed wire in a spot behind the latrine — the least visible spot from the guardhouse — a number of people escaped. We were among them; but, lacking a plan and driven by panic, we ran aimlessly into the woods. To make matters worse, for the only time in the whole three years of our lives under the Nazis, I had developed a fever and couldn't walk. My parents had to drag me by both arms.

Before long, we were all surrounded by the Lithuanian guards. They fired a few shots and, in a few minutes, rounded us all up, hitting people at random with their rifle butts, and herding us all back into the camp compound. Everyone felt a helpless and hopeless resignation. Most people who had no knowledge of the countryside were resigned to staying in the barrack and facing whatever would come. Even if they managed to get away from the camp, they wondered, where would they go? In any case, they were physically and spiritually broken and helpless, with no strength left.

For their part, my parents decided not to wait even until the next day, for then there could be twice as many guards, and it would be too late to do anything. So, once again, they took all our lives in their hands. That very night, when things had quietened down, we managed to crawl under the barbed wire again. My father, in a state of extreme anxiety and tension, held it up for us. Escaping with us were our friend Rabbi Gustman, his wife, and his daughter, Pesia, who was the same age as me.

Under my father's guidance and through his strength, we all crawled under the barbed wire and away, first into the high grass and then, as quickly as our legs would carry us, into the forest and through the fields, as far away from the camp as possible, before we all dropped from exhaustion. Once again, my parents had to drag me. Remarkably, after being dragged most of the night and finally dropping on the damp ground, I found my fever had gone.

No doubt it would have been easier without children, especially one with a temperature, and my weak little brother, who had to be carried some of the time. But my parents had decided long before then that, if it were humanly possible, we would all survive or die together. We were told after the war that a few others, mostly single men, made an escape similar to ours. As for the rest, some of the inmates were sent back to the ghetto. The rest were shot, and the barrack was set on fire.

Meanwhile, we hid in the forest, or in fields, or in high grasses during the day, and went on at night back to the area my father knew, and to the farmers who had helped us before we entered the camp. We did this day after day, covering a fair distance, until we felt that we were not being followed.

After a few days, we came across a very isolated farm, deep in the forest. My father approached the farmer and begged him to give at least some of us shelter, at least for a while. Very reluctantly and with much hesitation, the farmer agreed. It was decided to let Rabbi Gustman and his family stay there. The rabbi had never had any contact with non-Jews, and if he and his family had had to fend for themselves in the forest, they would most certainly have perished. Happily, the rabbi, his wife, and daughter were lucky enough to survive there until the liberation.

We were not so lucky. We wandered around in the forest for days, without food or water, and with my parents near despair. One of my most vivid flashbacks from that period is of how, one night, we had to cross a small river or creek with very high banks. The bridge was a thick cut-down tree with some sort of railing — either a rope tied to each end, or it may have been a strip of timber, but it was certainly very flimsy. First, my father led my mother across; then he came back, picked up my brother, and carried him across. Then he came back for me. With me, he had a problem, for I refused to move. I was too afraid to step onto the tree, and I was too big for him to carry across. He was very weak himself by then. I do not remember how my father managed to get me across. I suppose that I had no choice but to 'walk that plank', but to this day, I can see the black water far below and remember how scared I was to cross it.

At the end of the forest, we came to a farmhouse. My father knocked meekly on the windowpane, and when the farmer appeared, my father begged him to let us stay in his barn for at least a day, as we were too exhausted and starved to go any further.

The peasant took pity on us, gave us food, and allowed us to stay for a few days. Then one night, he harnessed his horse to the cart and drove us, by back roads, a further 15 kilometres into our former territory, where we could seek shelter again.

Again, we spent days in the forest, while my father went to different farmers he felt he could trust, and asked for help once more. Some gave him bread and other food, which he brought to share with us, but all refused to take us in, for fear of their own lives.

According to my mother's calculations, it was spring or early summer of 1943 when my father approached a peasant named Sylvester and his wife Zuzanna, who had two children of similar ages to Jack and me. They lived on a tiny farm on the outskirts of a village called Osinówka, deep in forest country. Both Sylvester and Zuzanna had been in service on our estate before the war, leaving only when they inherited this farm. They were so poor that they could barely feed themselves, their few chickens, or their single cow and pig. They also had a horse that they had struggled to buy and could not afford to keep.

My father begged Sylvester and Zuzanna to hide us once more, as they had done for a short time in 1942. He argued that, as we had been through so much already, and had come so far and were still alive and together, maybe we were meant to live, for the war could not last much longer, and so on. Sylvester deliberated for a while, and then said, 'Another Jew I would not let over my threshold, but with you I will share my last bit of bread.' With that, they agreed to hide us again.

Their hut was small and primitive, even for that region. It was one room with an earth floor, with the pigsty and a small barn all under the same straw roof. Inside the hut there was a brick oven (the bricks were homemade of clay) with a flat top used for sleeping on. The oven served as a sort of room divider; one side was for cooking and heating, while a bed stood at the back of it, hidden from view by a tattered curtain. A coarse wooden table and benches, some very primitive cooking utensils, and some wooden plates and spoons were all their worldly possessions.

Underneath the oven, Sylvester dug a hole for us, with an entry hole large enough for a body to slide in. The opening was then covered by a board, and over this was thrown household rubbish, old clothing, rags, whatever they had. An old bed was moved on top, as a final camouflage.

This hiding place was smaller than the space you would find under a small table. The four of us would slide in — first my father, then my mother, then my brother, and then myself. Many years later, I worked out why we used to slide into that hole in that order: it was easier for children to climb into a hole in the ground if the parents were already there. So the four of us would slide in, with my parents at the back and us children facing them with legs intertwined, unable to move and in total darkness. It was impossible to dig any deeper, as water was coming through. We sat like that in the damp and dark, and only came out at night, when we slept on top of the oven, if it was considered safe.

Sylvester and his family were really very poor. Even the bit of watery potato soup that they shared with us was a burden for them. My father tried to help by going out at night, preferably on dark nights, to more distant farmers, in order to safeguard our location, and to beg for whatever food these farmers could spare. He would bring this back, together with whatever news he could find about what was happening in the outside world. A few times, he was given luxuries — a few lumps of sugar, a few apples. As famished and weak from starvation as he was, he denied it to himself, and brought it all back for the children. My mother kept a lump of sugar like a treasure, and gave us a lick every now and then as a treat.

Several months passed, and we got used to our rat-like existence. With every day that passed, our hope grew that 'maybe a miracle will happen and we will survive'. This kept my parents going, one day at a time. During these optimistic moments, my parents used to discuss things, and talk about a possible future, although the chances seemed very slim. Even if we survived, they would wonder, could the children ever grow up to be normal adults, leading normal lives?

One night, around September or October 1943, during one of my father's nighttime wanderings, one of his farmer friends warned him to be very careful. This friend had overheard a certain person boast in Mejszagola that he knew where Katz was hiding.

'This time,' the person had said, 'I will get him.' My parents found out after the war that the same Pole who had betrayed my father to the Gestapo while we were in the camp had found out that he was still alive, and so, for his own protection, had tried to find him and eliminate him. This person was in the Polish Underground, and was in contact with some of the partisan groups whose members included a few men who had also escaped from the *Torfowisco* camp. My father was friendly with them, and had told them the story of how he had survived before the camp, and where we had been. Under the guise of trying to 'help Katz', the informer had discovered the approximate district where we had hidden and were likely to be again.

The informer denounced my father to the Gestapo for the second time. As a result, several plainclothes Gestapo men were dispatched to the area, with pinpointed villages, to 'find Katz'. My parents were devastated by this information, but could do nothing.

There was nobody left within a night's walk to turn to for help. Saying nothing to Sylvester and Zuzanna, lest they tell us to go, they hoped against hope that their fears would not come to pass. Their anxiety and desperation were so extreme that even Sylvester noticed their deterioration for, by then, both my parents had lost more than half their bodyweight, and were unrecognisable from their former selves. My father's normal weight was 105 kilos, all of muscle. Physically he was exceptional. In his youth, he used to show off by bending steel bars over his knee, tearing apart metal chains, lifting tremendous weights, and so on. After the liberation, he weighed just 46 kilos.

We existed with this danger hanging over us until February 1944. One day, Sylvester noticed that there were strangers in the village. After a while, they began heading in our direction. At that moment, my parents were totally numb with fear and despair, paralysed by helplessness. There was no chance of escaping this time.

The Gestapo men came in and demanded to know where Katz was hidden. At first, Sylvester denied any knowledge of Katz. He knew of him, he said, but he had heard that he was dead. The Gestapo did not play around with him for very long. They took Sylvester to a corner, put a revolver to his head, and promised to spare his family if he told them where Katz was. And, out of sheer terror, Sylvester told them.

Inside the bunker, we could hear everything that was happening. In despair, my parents knew that for us it was all over, but for the final agony. The terror my parents felt at that moment I am unable to put into words. We children may not have quite realised the full gravity of the situation, but we knew that it was very bad, and we were terribly afraid.

The Gestapo men rushed toward the bed, moved it aside with their feet, pushed away the rubbish that we had as camouflage, and exposed the opening to our hiding place. With revolvers pointing down at us, they shouted '*Heraus!*' (Come out!) Since I was nearest to the opening, I crawled out first. Jack came next, as we had been sitting side by side, then my mother and, finally, my father. Although the Gestapo immediately began to search us, particularly us children (people were known to hide valuables on children), the sight of a whole family momentarily took them aback. The way we looked must have betrayed even to them what we had been through already.

They demanded gold, jewellery, guns … My mother recalled that as I was being body-searched, I was white as a sheet and terrified, wringing my hands like an old woman in distress, with tears running down my cheeks.

When the leader demanded to know where our 'jewellery and guns' were, my father suddenly fell on his knees like a man possessed. He started to beg them not to kill us, to let us go, to have pity, to spare us, and so on, with such dramatic eloquence and emotion that the Gestapo men must have been stunned, even fascinated, by the audacity of this Jew. He said to them, '*Panie* [sirs], you must have families of your own, children, wives … All we want is to live! Please spare us; all I want is to save my children, the war is nearly over!' Of course, there was much more. My mother recalled that she really thought he had lost his mind. Seeing him begging the Gestapo to let us go, he seemed possessed by some extraordinary power, or madness, especially since they had orders to find and kill him. The rest of us were an unexpected bonus.

The miracle was that the Gestapo men allowed themselves to listen. My father, emaciated though he was, must have possessed some kind of power whereby the Gestapo, especially their leader, hesitated to pull the trigger. The scene went on for several hours. At one stage, one of them became impatient and kept repeating, 'Let's get on with it and finish them off!' But still, the leader hesitated.

Something extraordinary happened that afternoon. The Almighty saw fit to touch the hearts of murderers who had killed countless Jews, and most likely would go on to kill others. They let us go.

The Gestapo men ignored Sylvester and his family completely and, as soon as it was dark, they led us out into the forest. Even then, my parents were not sure what they were going to do with us. There was still the possibility that they were going to shoot us. But, instead, they told us to leave the area. We had to leave, because they would have to report to headquarters either that they had shot us or that they hadn't found us.

For us, it was an unbelievable miracle. After the Gestapo men disappeared into the night, we stood there under a tree in the snow, our parents trying to collect their thoughts and decide what to do, not knowing which way to turn, still in shock, and hardly able to believe that we were still alive and together.

From this point on, however, our plight became even more desperate. Even for us, the conditions were almost unendurable. It was deep winter and, apart from the bitter cold, the trees were bare. It would be impossible to hide in the forest out in the open, and there was absolutely no one in the vicinity to whom my father could turn for help.

After everything that Sylvester and Zuzanna had done for us and endured because of their friendship for us, they still continued to help us. It was too dangerous for all of us to go on staying with them, even though they were willing to take us back in.

Zuzanna especially was fearless. But my parents' nerves were shattered by the traumatic experience, coming on top of the constant fear and terror, and they knew it could not be. They also had us children to think of — how could they return us to a hiding place known to the Gestapo?

After standing in the forest for a while, my parents decided that my father should go back to Sylvester's to let them know that we were alive, to talk things over with him and Zuzanna, and to collect the few bits of clothing we still had there that were necessary for our survival.

The whole situation seemed unreal. That whole afternoon when the Gestapo came, Zuzanna had crouched outside with her ear to the window. She had heard everything. Now, she kept crossing herself and repeating that my father was the greatest *advokat* in the world, and surely must have been possessed by a special power to make the Gestapo do what they did.

Sylvester remembered an old, abandoned hut somewhere at the other end of the forest and, during the night, he led us there. The hut had once been used as a bathhouse or country sauna for all the local peasants. It contained a few suspended planks of timber to sit on, and a pile of stones and rocks that were heated and used to make steam when water was poured over them. There was ice and icy water everywhere, with no way for us to warm up. My parents sat us children on those planks, and my mother remembers how she took off her only petticoat — it had been on her back so long that it was quite stiff — and wrapped it around my brother's frozen legs. There was nowhere for my parents to sit other than on the icy surface of the floor, so my mother had to crouch. We almost froze to death there, but it was still better than being entirely out in the open forest. Sylvester brought us whatever food they could spare and, in this way, we stayed there for some time — days or weeks.

One night, we heard a lot of shooting that appeared to be quite near. After that, my parents were too afraid to stay there, not knowing who was lurking around outside.

My parents used to counsel each other on what to do and where to turn. Finally, feeling insecure in the hut, they followed their instinct and decided to leave. One night, they took us each by the hand, and started walking in a new direction into the forest. By morning, we had reached a clearing with a farm in the distance. My father recognised it, and thereby found his bearings.

Daylight was our enemy. As dawn was approaching, we made our way into the farm, and crept into the barn. The dogs barked so loudly that they roused the farmer. He came out into the barn, shouting, 'Who's there?' My father knew the farmer from before the war, and answered, 'It is I, Katz.' The farmer recognised my father's voice, but when he saw him, he was shocked by his terribly emaciated appearance. He shook his head in disbelief.

The sight of us all must have evoked some pity in him, because he allowed us to stay in the barn for a few days, and even brought us cooked food from the house. At night, my father went out again to try to find us a place to hide. Our present farmer was a kind man, but we had to leave, as he was expecting a visit from his daughter and son-in-law. The son-in-law was no lover of Jews, and the farmer said it would be suicide for us to remain.

My father approached yet another farmer, one who had subsidised his meagre holding by working part-time in Godulin before the war. My father had helped him many a time between harvests, but up till now, he had avoided him. For one thing, his little farm was situated right on the highway between Vilno and Kovno. More importantly, my parents did not trust him at all. He was very primitive, and if he felt that we had anything of value, he would very likely have killed us himself. But this was nearly the end. Even we knew that the Germans were retreating, and that it was only a matter of time. And my parents had no alternative. There was no one else they could turn to. So my father went to this farmer in the middle of the night, and knocked lightly on the window to get his attention.

After much pleading, and a promise of a reward after the war, the farmer agreed to take us in, on condition that our hiding place should not be inside a building. He dug a hole — slightly bigger than a grave — outside the barn wall, with a small hole beneath the barn wall as an entry from inside the barn. The entry to the hole was covered with a pile of straw, and the outside hole was camouflaged with logs, tree branches, and general bits and pieces from around the farm. In this hole, we sat in all weathers, day and night. When it rained, we still sat in it, until the water had drained away into the earth. Every few days, the farmer brought us some food — just enough to keep alive. But he took pleasure in telling my parents that the Germans were once again advancing.

There we stayed until the summer of 1944. By then, the German army really was retreating from the Soviets, and we found ourselves in the added danger of being on the frontline between the two armies. Farm buildings were on fire all over the district, as far as the eye could see, and nearly all the farmers fled with their families to safer ground, away from the frontline. Our current benefactors decided to leave as well.

The farmer came quickly to tell us that they were leaving. He plunged a parting gift into the hole: a loaf of bread and a jug of milk, which got half filled with soil as he pushed it down. 'You're as good as dead here,' he added, shrugging his shoulders as he left.

So we were left there alone. We had no choice but to stay, as there were German soldiers everywhere. The fields were full of German tanks, and on the highway there were endless columns of all manner of German military vehicles, all retreating from the Russian advance. We knew that if we could last just a little longer, our deliverance was near, maybe as near as a few days.

During those last days, we experienced yet another miracle that saved our lives. Again, it was due to my father's presence of mind. A German tank broke down on the highway and pulled into the farmyard, possibly looking for water to carry out repairs. Some of the crew got out to look around. As they were passing the pile of timber that concealed our bunker, one of them started to poke around, saying that the pile of wood and the assortment of branches looked suspicious. 'I wager there are Jews or partisans under there. Bring me some hand grenades and we'll find out,' he said, and he dispatched one of the soldiers back to the tank for grenades.

Hearing this, my parents were stricken with terror and despair. To have come so far and suffered so much and, in the end, to die within sight of liberation! But my father, keeping his head even at a time like this, came up with a plan. He could not show himself, as his appearance would certainly have betrayed our identity. So he urged my mother to take us children, crawl out of the bunker through the pile of straw, go out of the barn and walk up to the Germans as if we were the owners and had been hiding from the artillery.

My mother was terrified. She was trembling, her mouth was dry, and she clenched her teeth for fear of visibly chattering. Yet, she composed herself sufficiently not to arouse their suspicion. Almost in a trance, she did what my father had urged. With Jack and myself clinging to her, she crawled out of the bunker, and walked out of the barn and into the daylight. We children were conditioned that in daylight we had to hide, so we were doubly terrified; but, with my mother, we approached the Germans.

She started to speak in Polish to the one who looked like the leader. She repeated exactly what my father had instructed her to say, that we were hiding from the bombs, and that she was just on her way to the well to give the children water, and so on.

Luckily, the German seemed to understand Polish, and did not doubt her story.

One of the Germans kept insisting, in German, 'Where is her husband? Let him come out.' Fortunately, the leader did not respond. As this talking was going on, a soldier came up with an armful of hand grenades, but the leader waved him away, as if to say they were no longer needed. And, soon afterwards, they left.

Unable to believe our luck in having cheated death again, my parents decided to leave that bunker and take their chances out in the open, in the fields and marshes, which would give us the most cover.

For days and days, we wandered around on the frontline, with artillery fire, bombs, and *katyusha* rockets falling everywhere, all around us. The Germans did not retreat easily, and the Russians had to fight for every bit of territory. My father kept moving us from spot to spot, in order to avoid being hit by the shells. He told us to listen for the whistling: 'When you hear the whistle, it has passed you.' Everything around us was on fire: the whole horizon, farm buildings, knocked-out tanks ...

The best shelter seemed to be in the woods, but this particular area was swampy, and we kept sinking into the soft ground. My father went ahead, testing the ground, and we followed him in single file, back and forth for many hours, until we came out into a clearing.

We saw a farmhouse in the distance, and headed in that direction, totally exhausted. This farm was a bit more removed from the highway, and we hoped it might still be intact.

The farmer was still there. He had not left, he said, because his children were very sick and could not be moved. He told my father that we could go into the barn; but, for some reason, my father hesitated and led us instead inside a clump of bushes at the side of the barn, where we crouched in the furthest corner.

Some hours later, a group of German soldiers showed up, looking slightly disorientated. Searching for partisans, they dashed into the barn, into the stable, here and there, shooting at random everywhere. They fired a few shots into the bushes where we were hiding. My father held a hand firmly on both of us and signalled with a glance for total silence, for we could see them, and that made it all the more frightening. Thank G-d, the bullets missed us. One bullet went through Jack's cap, yet he didn't make a sound.

We hid in that bush for a few more hours, but everything went still. There were no more sounds of bombs or gunfire; a silence fell that was almost eerie. All we could hear was the buzzing of insects, so we slowly ventured out of the bushes and into the daylight. It felt very strange and new. We were no longer used to moving around in it freely and without fear.

A while later, we saw two men, soldiers, who popped out of the forest and headed towards us. My parents' first impulse was to run, to hide ... but somehow they did not move. The soldiers came closer and, even from a good distance, we could see that they were not Germans. They were Russians, tired and slightly bedraggled, who had become separated from their unit. Each carried a rifle on his shoulder.

My parents' relief was overwhelming. To be face to face with our liberators, at last! These two ordinary Russian soldiers were a sight that we had longed for, not believing that we would ever live to see it, for three long years.

One of the soldiers asked my parents if they had seen any Germans. When they replied, 'Not for a few hours,' the soldier pointed to his ear and said, 'Do you see your left ear? So you will see Germans here again!' After asking, 'Which way to Berlin?' they left.

We knew then that the day of our liberation really had come. We were free again after three years of unbelievable suffering and hardship. Thanks to the Almighty and to my parents' endless courage, endurance, and will to save us, we had survived against seemingly hopeless odds.

My mother began to cry, and we children clung to her and cried as well. My father too — we all cried. Overcome by the release of emotions and tensions held back for so long, my parents clutched us and held us close. They were unable to grasp the fact that it really was all over, and that we were alive and together.

To this day, and for the rest of my days, I will remember with gratitude and warmth those two ordinary Russian soldiers who were our liberators, our deliverers, our long-awaited saviours.

Immediately after our liberation, we made our way to Vilno. There, we joined the small community of survivors who were coming in from the provinces, together with the partisans. Our friend Rabbi Gustman became the community's spiritual leader. At that early stage of our new life, every survivor needed help and consolation. For six months, we lived in close contact and friendship with him, until we left, in an effort to reach the West.

Rabbi Gustman, his wife, Sonia, and their daughter managed to reach the American zone of Germany as early as 1946. From there, the Jewish Refugee Organisation immediately whisked them off to the United States, all red tape having been specially waived.

In New York, Rabbi Gustman gave speeches and became quite a celebrity, for Vilno had been famous throughout the Jewish world as a city of great learning and culture. It is said that it was Napoleon who called it the *Jerushalayim D'Lita*, the 'Jerusalem of Lithuania'. And from this second Jerusalem, Rabbi Gustman was the last surviving rabbi. He obtained a post in an American congregation and, in time, became a great Judaic scholar, famous throughout the religious Jewish world. From 1960 to 1970, he was a dean of yeshivas for the USA and Canada. In his older years, he moved to Jerusalem, where he was head of a yeshiva until his retirement.

My parents corresponded regularly with the Gustmans until the *rebbetzin* passed away in 1978, the same year as my father.

Their daughter, Pesia, also lives in Jerusalem. She is married to a rabbi, and has six children. In 1989, while on a visit to Israel, I made a point of visiting them.

After the war: Berthe and Nachum Katz in Traunstein, Bavaria, 1949; Ruth in Traunstein, 1949, and with a Zionist youth group (middle row, second from left); the Katzes visiting the memorial to the victims of the Dachau concentration camp.

LEXIE KESTON

For exchange to Palestine

I was born in Krakow on 20 November 1938. I wasn't quite one year old when Poland was overrun by Nazi Germany.

My very first memories are of my mother, father, and maternal grandmother living together. I believe this was in the Krakow Ghetto. I remember that my grandmother was hidden almost continuously from the Germans. The method was simple: she lay on a bed completely covered in doonas, to make it appear as if the bed was empty. At this time, my grandmother was not only quite elderly, but also frail and blind. I don't know how long she was with us. I do not remember her being taken away — I only know that from one day to the next, she was no longer with us. The Nazis found her, took her away, and eliminated her. I never saw her again.

The other memory I have of the ghetto is of my habit of sitting outside on the front steps of the building where we were living. I did this even though my mother had told me not to.

One day, someone passed me, and I fell off the steps onto broken glass, and severely cut my top lip. I went inside, bleeding

Before the ghetto: Lexie Keston on her grandparents' farm in Czechow, Poland, about May 1940.

profusely, with my top lip cut into two. I remember my mother being absolutely shocked and devastated. She took me to a very fine doctor who happened to be in our vicinity. This doctor sewed up my lip with a long needle, without anaesthetic. My mother was crying, and I was the one who consoled her, keeping myself from crying, and telling her that it didn't hurt. This incident left me with the smallest of scars, thanks to the fine surgeon who did the operation. Had he not been such a fine surgeon, I could have been left with an ugly, disfiguring scar. That is what I think my mother was fearful of. However, it worked out fine: unless I point out this little blemish, no one notices it to this day.

What year was this? I can only say that it was prior to 1943, because that's when we were transported to Bergen-Belsen. I don't remember the trip from Krakow to Germany. It was probably by train.

The Bergen-Belsen camp was located near Hanover, in northwestern Germany, on the site of a former army camp. In 1943, a section of it was designated as an internment camp for European Jews who were to be exchanged for German citizens held by the Allies. It was transformed from a prisoner-exchange camp into a 'regular' concentration camp in March 1944. The *Bergen-Belsen Book of Remembrance** records that poor sanitary conditions, epidemics, and starvation led to the deaths of thousands of inmates. One of them was Anne Frank, who died in March 1945, just a few weeks before the camp was liberated. By the end of the war, hundreds of similar concentration camps had been erected across German-occupied Europe.

My memories of Bergen-Belsen are of a time when I was constantly sick. My mother was always worrying about me, as she had no medications with which to alleviate my sickness or pain.

I remember one occasion when my mother went to the fence separating the barracks. There was always some sort of illegal barter going on at these places. I do not know what my mother was trying to obtain — maybe it was an aspirin for me. She got caught. As bad luck would have it, some high-ranking Nazi was visiting the camp that day, and we feared that my mother would be made an example of, maybe even put to death. However, it didn't happen. What punishment she received I do not know, but she came back, and I continued to be with her.

I have no memory of ever being hungry. The only food I remember receiving was a watery soup with a few vegetable pieces in it. There was a certain woman who was in charge of distributing the food. I remember that if too many vegetable bits were in the ladle, she would drop most of them back into the big pot. I remember this woman as being fatter than the rest of the people there. I know we were given bread, but I only remember the soup.

The latrines were an awful, scary experience for a little child. They were as illustrated in the Steven Spielberg film *Schindler's List*: a long plank that we sat on, over a cesspit. I always feared that I might fall off the plank, though I never did.

I remember transports arriving more and more frequently. We

---

* Foundation for Memorials in Lower Saxony, Bergen-Belsen Memorial, Bergen-Belsen, 2005.

could hear terrible happenings in the barracks next to us. People were beaten, and we could hear dreadful screams through the night. The next day, the dead and injured were taken out of the barracks. I don't know whether we could see anything, whether the reports we had were facts or just rumours. I remember that it happened more and more often, and I remember the discussions about this.

The section of the Bergen-Belsen camp that my parents and I were in was Section 3, the *Sonderlager* or 'special camp'. In this camp were Jews who held special documents, such as foreign passports or entry papers. My father, for example, had a passport for Palestine, for he had gone to Palestine in the early 1930s. He had returned to Poland after a few years, and then married my mother.

According to the *Bergen-Belsen Book of Remembrance*, the special camp held more than 9000 Jews. Amongst these were two transports of Jews that arrived in late 1943 and 1944 from Poland (including some 2400 from Warsaw, Lwow, and Krakow), France, Holland, and other parts of Europe. Despite their documents, which their holders had considered a ticket to life, these Polish Jews were deported to their deaths at Auschwitz by mid 1944.

During the final months of the war, however, several groups of these 'exchange Jews' were transported out of Axis-occupied Europe. German authorities transferred several hundred to neutral Switzerland, and at least one group of 222 Jewish detainees was transferred from Bergen-Belsen, by way of neutral Turkey, to British-controlled Palestine.

By April 1945, Allied armies had pushed deep into Germany from both east and west, and British troops were approaching Bergen-Belsen. So, in order to keep them in their hands, the Germans decided to transfer the remaining 'exchange Jews' to the Theresienstadt camp, in Czechoslovakia.

To implement this scheme, three trains crammed with prisoners left Bergen-Belsen in early April. My parents and I were on the first of these trains. We were marched out of the camp on a very cold Friday morning, 6 April, to walk the six kilometres to the station. I have no personal memory of this. It is, however, well documented.

On the way to the train, the inmates saw a neighbouring village for the first time in two years. In it, Germans were living normal lives, in houses with curtains and bicycles leaning against the gate. The villagers seemed untouched and unmoved by the horrors going on in the nearby camp.

My train left on 7 April with some 2500 people — 400 from the special camp, and 2100 others. Among them were many different nationalities, including Dutch, Slovaks, Hungarians, Poles, and others. We spent seven days aboard that train and, in those seven days, it covered only 80 kilometres. There were constant stops and starts as the officer in charge awaited orders about what to do with us. His final order had been to take us across the Elbe, but he didn't follow it. Perhaps he realised that the Americans were very close, and that by letting us live, he had a chance of securing his own survival. However, many of his prisoners did not live to see the imminent downfall of the Nazis, or the day of their own liberation.

Again, I must say that I have no personal recollection of this horrendous journey, in unhygienic conditions, with many of the prisoners on the brink of starvation. I do, however, vividly remember getting off the train when the Nazis who were guarding us fled from the approaching Americans. I remember very clearly picking up a gun dropped by the fleeing guards. I also remember that this gun was promptly grabbed from me — that I have never forgotten, and I remember it as if it happened yesterday. It was Friday, 13 April 1945, at Farsleben, 16 kilometres from Magdeburg.

I now know that our classification in Bergen-Belsen was not 'Jew', which was the usual classification for Jewish prisoners. Rather, we were classified as 'For Exchange to Palestine'. Altogether, we were in Bergen-Belsen from 15 July 1943 to 6 April 1945 — nearly two years. All of this is recorded on the identity documents that were issued to us by the United States army after our liberation.

Shortly after liberation, we were taken to the town of Hillersleben. There we were lodged in houses belonging to

Germans. I don't know whether the occupants had fled when the Americans arrived, or whether they were evicted so that we could stay in their houses. I remember the house where we stayed had a beautiful bed with sheets and doonas. There were lots and lots of toys, more than I had ever seen in my life. In one of the rooms, there was a large table completely covered in toy soldiers.

I don't know whether it was in Hillersleben, but we were still in Germany when a number of Zionists came, with the aim of organising transportation for people who wanted to go to Palestine. Being now six years old, I immediately decided that this was where I wanted to go. My mother found me in the queue and asked me what I was doing there, to which I replied, 'I want to go to Palestine.' As she took me away, she told me that this was only for the 'orphans', and not for me. Why I wanted to go I don't know.

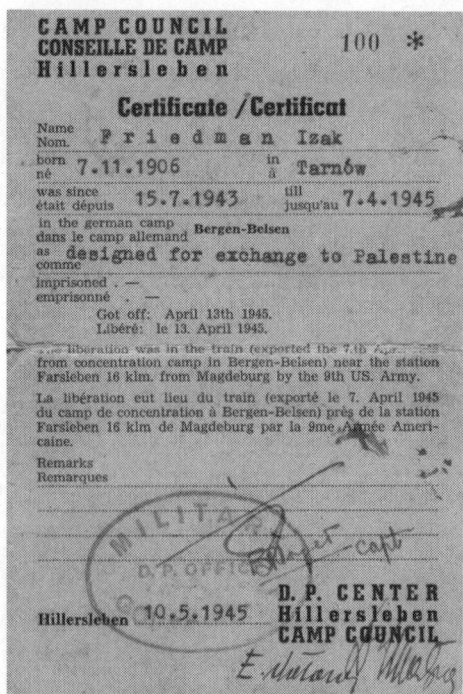

For Exchange to Palestine: The certificate issued by Hillersleben Displaced Persons camp to Izak Friedman, Lexie Keston's father.

Maybe I thought that where I was had been so horrible that any other place on earth would be much better.

After a short time, many of the Jews who were now 'stateless' in Germany were dispersed to different European countries. We were sent to Belgium. During the five years that we stayed in Belgium, we remained 'stateless' citizens.

Shortly after our arrival, I was sent to the sanatorium Preventorium Leon Poriniot at Biez, where I spent almost a whole year. I was hospitalised to cure me of TB and of my inability to keep any food in my stomach. I used to vomit every day, and I also suffered from some other health problems. After the years of deprivation and starvation, I needed medical help, which I did receive in that wonderful place. It probably saved my life. Had the war dragged on for much longer, I don't think I would have survived.

While I was in the sanatorium, my parents were living in Brussels, trying to re-build their lives. I remember when I came back from the sanatorium that I had forgotten how to speak Polish and could only speak French. For a little while, I could not communicate with my own parents, and I think that was a devastating experience for them. However, it was not too long before I was able to speak Polish again, so it was a very short-lived trauma.

I think that my health was still poor. My parents found a kind woman, in a village called Ruisbroek in the countryside outside Antwerp, who wanted me to come and stay with her. I did this on a number of occasions. She, her husband, and her son were all very good to me. The family were Flemish Catholics by the name of Van Roy. Mrs Van Roy looked after me well, and fed me lots of good food at a time when food rationing was still in force. The Van Roys owned a butcher shop, and the servings of meat at dinnertime were gigantic. When I was with this family I suffered from too much food, rather than from too little — so much so that I used to be sick from over-eating.

Mrs Van Roy developed a special bond with me, and was very keen to adopt me, although she had three children from her first

Mrs Van Roy

marriage, and a son, Flor, from her current marriage. This, of course, did not and could not happen. She asked me while I stayed with her to call her *Moe*, the Flemish word for mother, and of course I did. I spent some of the happiest times of my life there. I used to play with one of her granddaughters, whose name was Florence. She was a couple of years older than me. We played every day, going on bicycle rides and picnics, and skating on the frozen river.

To me, that place was paradise. The Van Roy family home had a beautiful big garden, with many fruit trees. The one I liked best was the cherry tree. The cherries were a two-coloured variety, white and red. She also had a little foxy terrier dog. He was not that fond of children, and once he actually bit me. But I wasn't frightened of him, and I liked to play with him and give him pieces of meat.

Every Sunday morning we used to go to the local Catholic Church. It was so large that it could have been a cathedral. I enjoyed going to church with Mrs Van Roy. But I remember many times in Brussels, when I was in the street outside the apartment block where we lived, children would yell abuse at me. '*Sale Juif!*' they would shout: 'Dirty Jew!' Why did those children do that? After all the suffering of the Holocaust, there still was so much anti-Semitism in European countries. And today, it is on the increase once again.

We spent five years in Belgium. By the end of 1949, there were grave fears amongst the Jewish people living in Europe that there would be another world war, and many decided that it would be safer for them to leave Europe for places as far away as possible. No one could contemplate a repetition of what had happened only a few years earlier. My parents also thought this way, and they applied to immigrate to the United States, Canada, and Australia. The Australian visa arrived first; so, to Australia we went.

We sailed from Genoa aboard a ship called the *Surriento*, with six to eight people to a cabin. We arrived in Sydney many weeks later, in January 1950.

On our arrival at the Woolloomooloo Docks, we were met by

After the war: Lexie Keston and her parents in Brussels, 3 August 1945.

people from the Jewish Welfare Association who took us to a beautiful place, a boarding house that the association had in the harbour-side suburb of Greenwich. I remember being in our room on the first floor, and seeing for the first time a hibiscus bush with its beautiful, large, colourful flowers. I often used to look out and admire those blooms. Sydney, Australia, looked beautiful from my window.

I went to school, and life became fairly normal for me. I picked up English quite quickly and easily; but, throughout my school years, I had a problem admitting to anyone that I was Jewish. The conscious memories and fears of the war were still very much with me.

I did not like to hear any discussion of the war. Whenever my parents discussed the Holocaust with their survivor friends, I would just walk away. I did not want to hear any of it, or think of it. I wanted it totally out of my life.

I did find that I was most comfortable with Jewish friends. I was always worried with non-Jews — worried that they might be anti-Semitic, and thus dislike me once they knew that I was Jewish. However, I will say that since I came to Australia, I have never, ever personally been the target of any anti-Semitic insult or slur. To me, Australia is the most wonderful country that I could possibly live in. I am most grateful that fate destined me to come to this beautiful country with the most amazing people of goodwill and big hearts.

Recently, I had the incredible good fortune to learn more of the liberation of our train at Farsleben. Because of a chance meeting with two people who work at the Bergen-Belsen Memorial in Germany, I discovered the names of two US tank commanders who were the first to arrive at our train after the guards abandoned it on Friday, 13 April 1945. They were sergeants George C. Gross and Carrol 'Red' Walsh.

I also came upon some 11 photos taken on that day by Sgt Gross and his commanding officer. The photos were of the train and some of the survivors from it. When I looked at those pictures of the desolate region and the physical appearance of the survivors, it just made me cry.

The moment of liberation: Survivors from Lexie Keston's train greet US tanks near Farsleben, 13 April 1945. (Picture by Major Clarence L. Benjamin, courtesy George Gross and Matt Rozell.)

I must confess that the photos did not trigger any memory in me, though I found them a stark record of the events of that day. As much as I tried and wanted to remember, I did not. The only memory I have of the day of my liberation is picking up the gun.

Finding and seeing these photos was a most emotional discovery for me. That it happened some 60 years after the actual event is almost impossible to believe.

The following passage is an extract from 'A Train Near Magdeburg', George C. Gross's memoir of that day:

> On Friday, April 13, 1945, I was commanding a light tank in a column of the 743rd Tank Battalion and the 30th Infantry Division, moving south near the Elbe River toward Magdeburg, Germany ... [A]lthough we knew the fighting was at last almost

Above: As survivors spread out looking for food of any kind, on the hill to the left people are resting — some of them forever. Sixteen people died of starvation before food could reach the transport.

Below: Smiles for the liberators. The girl on the left was so weak from hunger that she could hardly stand.

Above: English-speaking Gina Rappoport, a survivor of the Warsaw Ghetto, told how the transport, after leaving Bergen-Belsen, had crisscrossed central Germany in an attempt to avoid Allied troops.

Below: Men, women, and children from the transport. (All pictures on these pages by George C. Gross.)

over, a pall had been cast upon our victories by the news of the death of President Franklin D. Roosevelt. I had no inkling of the further grim news that morning would bring. Suddenly, I was pulled out of the column, along with my buddy Sergeant Carrol Walsh in his light tank, to accompany Major Clarence L. Benjamin of the 743rd in a scouting foray to the east of our route. Major Benjamin had come upon some emaciated Finnish soldiers who had escaped from a train full of starving prisoners a short distance away. The major led our two tanks ... down a narrow road until we came to a valley with a small train station at its head and a motley assemblage of passenger compartment cars and boxcars pulled onto a siding. There was a mass of people sitting or lying listlessly about, unaware as yet of our presence. There must have been guards, but they evidently ran away before or as we arrived, for I remember no firefight. Our taking of the train, therefore, was no great heroic action but a small police operation. The heroism that day was all with the prisoners on the train.

Major Benjamin took a powerful picture just as a few of the people became aware that they had been rescued. It shows people in the background still lying about, trying to soak up a bit of energy from the sun, while in the foreground a woman has her arms flung wide and a great look of surprise and joy on her face as she rushes toward us ...

I pulled my tank up beside the small station house at the head of the train and kept it there as a sign that the train was under American protection now. Carrol Walsh's tank was soon sent back to the battalion, and I do not remember how long the infantrymen stayed with us, though it was a comfort to have them for a while. My recollection is that my tank was alone for the afternoon and night of the 13th. A number of things happened fairly quickly. We were told that the commander of the 823rd Tank Destroyer battalion had ordered all the burgermeisters of nearby towns to prepare food and get it to the train promptly, and were assured that Military Government would take care of the refugees the following day ...

We stood in front of the tank as a long line of men, women, and little children formed itself spontaneously, with great dignity and no confusion, to greet us. It is a time I cannot forget, for it was terribly moving to see the courtesy with which they treated each other, and the importance they seemed to place on reasserting their individuality in some seemingly official way. Each would stand at a position of rigid attention, held with some difficulty, and introduce himself or herself by what grew to be a sort of formula: the full name, followed by ... the origin and the home from which the person had been seized. Then each would shake hands in a solemn and dignified assertion of individual worth. Battle-hardened veterans learn to contain their emotions, but it was difficult then, and I cry now to think about it. What stamina and regenerative spirit those brave people showed!

Also tremendously moving were their smiles. I have one picture of several girls, specter-thin, hollow-cheeked, with enormous eyes that had seen much evil and terror, and yet with smiles to break one's heart.

Little children came around with shy smiles, and mothers with proud smiles happily pushed them forward to get their pictures taken. I walked up and down the train seeing some lying in pain or lack of energy, and some sitting and making hopeful plans for a future that suddenly seemed possible again. Others followed everywhere I went, not intruding but just wanting to be close to a representative of the forces that had freed them. How sad it was that we had no food to give immediately, and no medical help, for during my short stay with the train sixteen or more bodies were carried up the hillside to await burial, brave hearts having lost the fight against starvation before we could help them.[†]

[†] Reproduced with permission from Matthew Rozell's 'World War II Living History Project' at Hudson Falls High School, New York State, www.hfcsd.org/ww2/Interviews/GEORGE%20GROSS/george%20gross.htm.

I have developed a warm relationship with these two wonderful men. George is now 83, and a retired professor of English, living in San Diego, California, while Carrol is 85, and a retired judge of the Supreme Court of New York State. We have exchanged many emails, and I cherish very much the experience of having found these two men. In my heart and soul, I honour them for being part of my liberation, and for enabling me to regain a normal life. I think that I also mean something to them — for they also never thought that someone from that day, 61 years ago, would find them and have the opportunity to say 'thank you'.

I have also obtained many articles from Germany that have helped me gain a broader understanding of my years in Bergen-Belsen. I am grateful for the help extended to me by the people from the Bergen-Belsen Memorial.

This part of my story would never have come to light if not for the wonderful work of Matthew Rozell, a history teacher at Hudson Falls High School in New York State. It was his website that provided the opportunity for the photographs and the story written by George Gross to be exposed to the world. So, in fact, the website was the catalyst for my discovery of the information on my liberation.

George Gross's account is also an unbiased witness testimony of the events of the day of my liberation, Friday, 13 April 1945. George is not Jewish. His account is an impartial illustration of Hitler's other war — the 'War Against the Jews' — and it carries all the more weight for that. It is a valuable counterbalance to the distortions of revisionists, who are still trying to play down the sufferings of the Jews during the Holocaust.

I admire the survivors who speak of their experiences, who teach the younger generations, and who serve as guides in the permanent Holocaust exhibition at the Sydney Jewish Museum. I still don't think I have come to terms with my Holocaust past. I think it still controls and affects my daily life. But I think that having discovered so much more information such a long time after the war, I

US tank commanders George C. Gross and Carrol 'Red' Walsh.

may be on my way to finding closure and some inner peace.

My life now consists of spending quality time with my two granddaughters, nine-year-old Jessica and her sister Rebecca, aged seven. They are indeed a core part of my life. My little family consists of Jessie and Becky's parents, Helen and Anthony Epstein, together with my younger daughter, Anne.

Every day, with great interest, I read newspapers on the internet, and try to keep informed as to what is happening in the world. I retain a very special interest in Israel. To me, a peaceful Israel is of the greatest importance to world Jewry. I believe the need for a Jewish sanctuary in Israel is of paramount importance to Jewish people everywhere. Had we had the independent state of Israel in the 1930s and 1940s, there would not have been a Holocaust of six million Jews.

Hitler did not win.

EVA GRANT
Eva's story

I was born in the city of Martin (then called Turčiansky Svätý Martin), Slovakia, in December 1940. At that time, my family lived in the city of Trenčín, 60 kilometres to the south-west. My father, Bartolomej Steiner, known to all as 'Berci', was a successful dentist there.

My father was born in 1906 as the fifth of eight children, and grew up in the village of Bolešov, where he attended the local Jewish school from 1911 to 1915.

There he learnt three alphabets: Latin letters, the old German *Kurrentschrift*, and Hebrew, which the pupils had to practise with their heads covered. A gregarious boy, and good at languages, he learned to play the violin gypsy-style. He also had a good singing voice, and, at the age of ten, he mastered the ancient Hebrew chants known as *niggun*. He grew up steeped in Jewish custom, ritual, and liturgy. He was deeply religious, but he was also tolerant. He never argued about religion, and he always got along with people, whatever their nationality or faith.

In 1915, my father enrolled in the Trenčín Gymnasium, a Hungarian Catholic secondary school. It was not unusual in the mixed society of those days for Catholic schools to have a high Jewish enrolment. About half the boys at the Gymnasium were Jews — his brother Arpád was already a pupil there — and in the convent school attended by their sister Aranka, a majority of the girls were Jewish.

The First World War was now raging, and Arpád, Aranka, and my father all had to board in Trenčín to go to school. In peacetime, they might have commuted from Bolešov, as it was just 20 kilometres from Trenčín, but the wartime rail service was too unreliable. In addition, the Austro-Hungarian army had taken over half of the school buildings, which meant that teaching hours had to be extended from 7.30 a.m. to 8.30 p.m. That made it very difficult to commute, even if the trains were running.

The war cast its shadow in other ways. The family's eldest son, Karl, had been called up, and was serving on the Romanian front. In 1916, the father of the family — my grandfather, Eduard Steiner — was also called up. As a result, the family soon ran short of money.

That June, Aranka had to leave school altogether, while Arpád had to move back home and take his chances getting to Trenčín by train. Fortunately, under the new timetable, his classes did not commence until 2 p.m. But he too was eventually called up. All this left my father boarding on his own in Trenčín at the age of ten.

By mid 1918, after four years of war, the Austro-Hungarian Empire was tottering. In October, it collapsed, and the war on the Eastern Front was over. At the end of the month, my grandfather came home from Serbia, where he had been serving; and, a few days later, Arpád returned from Italy. Karl had last been heard from on the Western Front, where he was listed as missing, but he too finally returned — in his case, from a French POW camp.

The reunited family now found themselves citizens of the new nation of Czechoslovakia. For my father, this meant a change in the staff of the Gymnasium, and a change in the language of instruction. It had been Hungarian, which he spoke well, but the curriculum was now taught in literary Slovakian.

This he soon picked up, but my grandfather was doubtful about the prospects for Slovakian as a professional language. The times were still turbulent, and he wanted my father to learn a skill that was independent of a particular language. So in June 1919, my father left school, and, in December 1920, he began training as a dental mechanic in the spa town of Trenčíanske Teplice.

From this time on, my father's ambition was to graduate as a dentist. His path to this goal was far from smooth, but he always kept his eyes firmly on it. From 1925 to 1929, he sold dental equipment, and in 1930 he got practical experience with a non-Jewish Sudeten-German dentist by the name of Morgenstern. Dr Morgenstern then appointed him to operate a branch surgery, and in 1931, he took the dentistry exam — in Slovakian, even though his studies had been in German.

In 1931, with equipment borrowed from Dr Morgenstern, he finally opened his own surgery in Komjatice, in the south of the country, near the Hungarian border. Ironically, he wasn't fully accepted by the highly Orthodox Jewish community in Komjatice until 1936. In that year, he married Magda, a 'southern' girl who came from that community. Four years later, she became my mother.

My father and his new bride did well in Komjatice. They were a respected couple with a six-bedroom house with a two-room surgery.

In 1938, however, the shadow of Hitler fell across them, and across all of Czechoslovakia. Following the Munich Agreement, Germany seized the Sudetenland — Hitler's 'last territorial demand in Europe' — and much of the rest of Czechoslovakia was carved up. Hungary annexed territory in southern Slovakia, and my father was expelled from Komjatice — not as a Jew, but as a Slovakian. He and my mother had to leave their home and move north to Trenčín.

Father and daughter: Berci Steiner in about 1935, and (inset) Eva Grant.

Worse was to come. In March 1939, Germany took over all the rest of the Czech lands. Slovakia became nominally independent, under the regime of Monsignor Jozef Tiso. In 1940, with the Second World War well under way, Tiso passed a series of Nazi-style Aryanisation laws, depriving Jews of the right to own businesses. In November 1940, Slovakia became a formal ally of Nazi Germany. I was born in the following month.

Despite the Aryanisation laws, my father was still able to practise as a dentist, as some exemptions were made in Slovakia for Jewish businesses that were deemed vital to the economy. He retained this exemption even after the introduction in September 1941 of Tiso's so-called Jewish Code, modelled on the Nazi Nuremberg Laws, and the start of the deportations of Slovakian Jews to Auschwitz in March 1942. But things became more and more difficult.

In 1943, we were forced to leave Trenčín for my father's home village, Bolešov; there, stone-throwers forced us to move on to Bánovce. I remember feeling excluded from the playground in Bánovce, without knowing why. I know now that because I was Jewish, it was against the law for me to go into it.

In autumn 1944, Germany crushed a national uprising in Slovakia and occupied the whole country. All of Slovakia's remaining Jews, without exception, now faced deportation. My family's situation was becoming increasingly desperate; we could have been arrested at any time. My parents decided to leave Bánovce and take refuge in the attic of a local farmer. With my father, my mother, and me, there was my grandmother, Matilda Steiner, as well as a colleague of my father's. My grandmother couldn't help pacing up and down on its creaky wooden floorboards, and this was very dangerous, as it could give away our hiding-place. It would only take one stranger to notice the sound, and we could be betrayed. So, the next night, the farmer took us in his horse-drawn wagon to the forest near Bánovce, where many other Jewish families were hiding.

In the forest, we joined some other Jewish families who were hiding in a tunnel they had dug for themselves. However, it was very

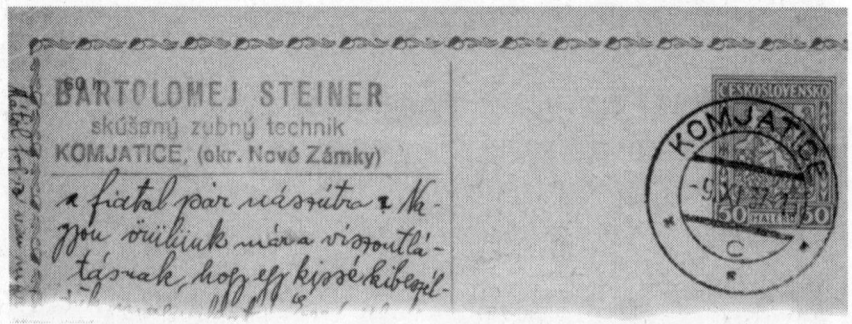

Postcard from Komjatice: A section of a postcard Berci Steiner sent from Komjatice in 1937, the year before his expulsion from the town.

cramped inside, so you could only crawl on all fours. My mother felt claustrophobic, so we had to go to another part of the forest.

There, a hole was dug that we called 'the bunker'. It was covered by tree branches, and we had a fire burning in the centre to keep warm. I know this because my little coat caught fire at the back, and I had it like that to the end of the war. We survived with the help of a man from Bánovce who brought a basketful of food once a week. We paid this man well, but he was risking his life; today, he would be called a Righteous Gentile.

Once, during our months of hiding, my mother begged the man from Bánovce to take her and me back to his home, so that we could have a bath. Late that afternoon, as we were on our way back through the forest, the two of us were caught in crossfire between partisans and the Germans. A bullet flew past my mother's ear. From there on, she carried me, and we both fell into a ditch.

Our time in hiding ended when, one day, we heard marching soldiers go by. When their noise subsided, my father went out to

Long-lost photo: Eva Grant with her parents, Magda and Berci, in Bánovce, in about 1942, before the family was forced into hiding.

see who they were. Two stragglers caught sight of him, and called back their whole unit — some 70 men. As a result, the soldiers tied the four adults to separate tall trees, ready to be shot.

At this point, I woke up crying, and came out of the bunker. I instantly understood the scene I came upon. I had been warned constantly not to make any noise because 'they' would find us; and now they had come!

Once the captain of the unit saw me, however, he started to scratch his head. He asked my mother how old I was. 'Three and a half,' my mother replied. He replied that he had a dark little daughter just like me and he didn't know where she was, whereupon he had a change of heart and ordered everyone untied. Then they marched us out of the forest with them.

I remember how small I was; I remember feeling the weight of the many layers of clothing, topped by my light greyish coat; and I remember walking through forest pathways, holding my parents' hands. Once we were out of the forest, the soldiers sent us to the concentration camp at Sered.

The Sered camp was situated at a rail junction. The Germans used it to sort out the thousands of victims and send them all to different concentration camps.

We waited for three days to be processed, and in all that time, we were given no food. A few of us were locked in a large schoolroom with soldiers who were bandaged from head to foot. They were lying on the floor in two straight lines. I stared at them, because many of them were smoking, and the puffs of smoke were emanating from their bandaged heads.

When we were called out to be sent on, there was great desperation. Families were torn asunder by brutal separations. No one knew where they and their loved ones were being taken. We were all clinging to each other. Some 20 years ago, I wrote a poem likening this to a storm tearing a tree out by its roots and scattering the leaves and branches, while each leaf tries desperately to cling on.

Before my mother died, in 1990, she told me that when the

men were separated from us at the railway in Sered, my father broke away from his line, and came over to kiss her goodbye. The German guards beat him up for doing that. All her life, she kept this, and other very painful scenes, inside her aching heart. Each time she released something, she broke down badly, so I could never ask very much.

While awaiting his fate in Sered, my father met his uncle, Julius Kučera. Sharing the one scrap of paper, each of them managed to write a last message to Julius's son, Karel, known as Karcsi. This is what it said:

Dearest Son

It is half past seven and still no decision. But there is still hope of God's help.

I take this opportunity to say a last goodbye.

This last message of mine could be a keepsake for future generations.

Remain God-fearing!

I wish you the life any father would wish to a good child.

God protect you!!

Your loving father,
Julius

My father wrote:

Dearest Karcsi!

Should your father travel with us, I will do my best to make life easier for him.

I hope that you survive all this in good health.

Please do what you can for my mother, wife and child.

When all this is over, see to it that my dear father gets a headstone on his grave.

> Greetings to your brother, sisters and to my brother Feri.
> The Almighty shelter you all.

Love, Berci

The note was smuggled out by a sympathetic railway guard. By the time it reached Karel, he himself was awaiting deportation in Sered. But he survived the war, and the note has indeed been a keepsake for future generations. My uncle Feri shared it with us when we visited him in Bratislava in 2005. By then, he was 92.

From the Sered camp, my father was sent to Sachsenhausen, then to Buchenwald, and finally to Bergen-Belsen, where he perished. He was one of those for whom liberation came too late; he died on 8 May 1945, the very day of Germany's surrender.

My grandmother, my mother, and I were put on a cattle train bound for Theresienstadt concentration camp. Recently, as I was looking at some German documents, I realised that my fourth birthday passed unnoticed, as we spent it crammed into that awful train.

We arrived at Theresienstadt in December 1944. The journey had taken weeks, and we were starving. The hunger and cold tormented everyone. I came down with pneumonia. I was also suffering from impetigo, and the skin all over my body was infected where I had scratched it. I mention this because in 2003 my dearest friend asked me, 'How did they die?' I could only blurt out, 'They were sick.' The topic never came up again.

In the camp, I was put into a cot, where I cried for hours on end. I have an ever-present memory of the other little children being minded in a noisy, crowded room. I was standing in the cot, crying, when the other children ran to the windows to see the new transports arrive. This was a major event. We all identified with it and understood, because we had all arrived in the same way.

This scene was powerful, and afterwards, I always longed to meet those children. I suppose I wanted a reunion. I yearned to be with those children again, because it was just not possible for other people to be in that same emotional space.

In Theresienstadt, my mother did shift work, splitting mica for use in fireproofing German aircraft. She kept a small piece for years afterwards. She often had to go to her factory in the middle of the night, terrified, with the guard-dogs barking in the pitch darkness. She had to leave me behind in the barracks, and these countless separations have never left my memory. The danger was real and constant. Because of my age, I developed separation anxiety, which I now understand, but still find hard to overcome. We spent seven long months in Theresienstadt, and for much of that time I cried bitterly for my mother.

In 2003, I received a photo from Tel Aviv. It showed a family group: my mother, my father, and me. I'd never known that such a photo existed. For a long time after I received it, I stared at the way my father was holding my arm so tightly, securely. That was the security I lost.

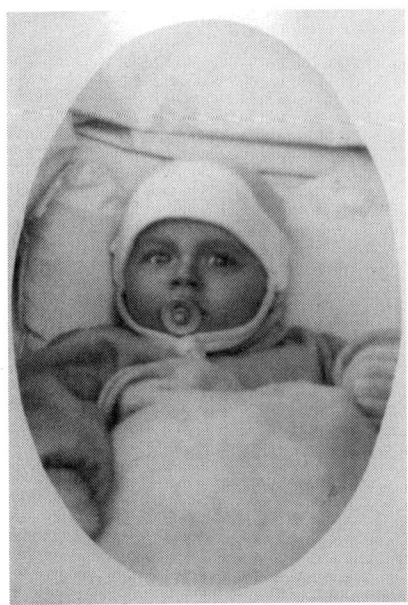 

Young victims of Auschwitz: Eva Grant's cousins, Miklós and István Finyes.

On 3 May 1945, two days before Germany surrendered, the Nazis handed our camp over to the Red Cross. In June, the Soviets arrived and formally liberated us. We were put on passenger trains, and we returned to Slovakia. But we were full of bitter sadness, as 99.9 per cent of our family members had not returned.

In 1949, together with a handful of surviving close relations, we immigrated to Israel. There we lived in Jerusalem for seven years, a good and enriching experience.

In 1956, we began a second immigration saga by moving to Australia. I went to high school in Sydney, and when I left school, I became a pre-school teacher, specialising in deaf children. As a result of all this, I now speak English, German, Hebrew, and Hungarian, and I have some understanding of Slovak and Yiddish.

In 1960, I married my dear husband Fred Grant (formerly Grossman). He was also from Slovakia, and he too had lost almost all of his family in the Holocaust. His mother and brother died in Auschwitz. This helped make us very compatible. Sadly, he died of mesothelioma in 1987.

Our only child, John, was born in 1961; he brought us great pride and joy. I love to sing his praises, and do not ask for more.

Fred was interested in forming a child survivors' group; but it didn't happen until 1987.

One day, I met another child survivor, Eva Engel. Shortly afterwards, she phoned me and asked if I thought it would be a good idea to form a group of people who had survived the Holocaust as children. I said yes, especially so that there would be someone to remember all those little children who had perished and had no one else to remember them, because their parents had also perished. I was thinking particularly of some photos I had received from Canada that very week. They were of two boys, first cousins of mine, who had died in Auschwitz with their parents. I had never seen their picture before, and their faces haunted me.

Several weeks later, a few of us coined the title 'Child Survivors', and the Sydney Child Survivors Group was born.

In October 2005, together with John, I returned to Slovakia for the first time in 56 years. We managed to find the grave of my grandfather, Eduard, in Bánovce. We had it repaired, and we re-gilded the names of the six adult children who perished in the Holocaust — Alžbeta; Karol; Arpád; Aranka; my father, Bartolomej; and his younger sister, Renata. It was a poignant task for us; we had in our minds my father's plea, as he faced deportation at Sered, that his own father should be commemorated with a headstone which he could not supply.

In Memoriam: The grave of Eduard Steiner in Bánovce, Slovakia, with the names of all but two of his adult children.

ELIZABETH LEVY
My childhood

I was born on 17 April 1938 in Krakow, south-western Poland, to Henek and Lusia Reiss. I was named Elzbieta Anita Reiss, although everyone called me by the affectionate diminutive 'Elzunia'. However, the first family name I knew was not Reiss, but Daraz. That was the name on the false papers that saved us. Similarly, my first religion was Roman Catholic. I learnt to pray for my loved ones every night. I had to kneel beside my bed, cross myself, and say: 'In the name of the Father, the Son, and the Holy Ghost, please look after ...' I still remember it: '*W imię Ojca, i Syna i Ducha Swiętego ...*'

My father's family, the Reisses, were mostly owner-farmers, with estates near Belz in the wider Lwow district of south-eastern Poland. My mother's family, the Hermans, lived in the city of Lwow. Until 1919, this part of Poland had belonged to Austria. During the First World War, the Reisses and the Hermans had taken refuge in Vienna itself, where both of my parents went to school. Consequently, they grew up speaking fluent German.

At home, my parents spoke Polish. Yet, in inter-war Poland,

they suffered discrimination: as Jews, they were prohibited from Polish government employment, restricted in study opportunities, and treated unequally in academic examinations. Occasionally, there were pogroms, to which the authorities turned a blind eye. Nevertheless, their families lived full and happy lives. Each of my parents graduated in civil engineering at the Lwow Polytechnika.

Early in August 1939, concerned at rumblings of an imminent attack by Nazi Germany, my parents sent me, together with my Catholic nanny, Zosia Janowska, to my grandparents' farm at Oserdow, in Poland's east. There we were received by my father's mother, Rudolfina, and by his brother, Ludwig.

On the first of September, Germany launched its blitzkrieg. Krakow was bombed, and my parents fled, joining me in Oserdow. It was a long way from the frontline, and seemed, at first, like a haven of peace; but on 17 September, the Soviet Union invaded Poland from the east. Oserdow came under Soviet rule, and so did we. My parents, as land-owning capitalists, feared that the communist authorities would arrest them, so they fled to Lwow, taking me with them. In Lwow, they hoped to find employment and so make themselves part of the 'approved' working class.

At first, life under the Soviets was reasonable. We lived with my maternal grandparents, Simon and Regina Herman. My mother found work as a design engineer with the Government Railway Department. My father found a job in the Government Mills Trust, which was nationalising all the flourmills. However, Communism soon wreaked havoc with the economy. Banks and other major institutions were nationalised; private buildings and businesses were expropriated; farmers were evicted from their properties. Many people had to follow in our footsteps and move to the big cities. Among these people were my grandmother, Rudolfina, and my uncle, Ludwig, who now joined us in the Hermans' small apartment.

Lwow was soon bursting at the seams. Unemployment rose and food became scarce: essential food was rationed, and there were long queues to get it.

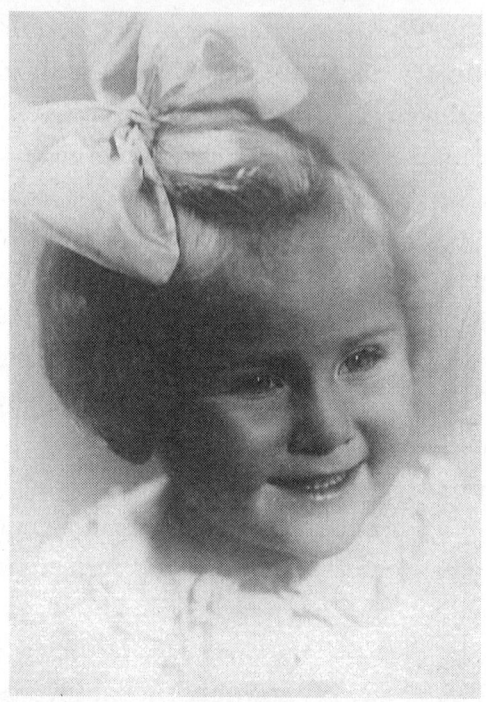

'**Elzunia**': Elizabeth Levy as a child in Krakow, Poland.

Among my father's first cousins, the closest to my father was Josef Reiss. Their mothers were sisters, their fathers were brothers, they were similar in age, and they had virtually grown up together. When Josef, who was an officer in the Polish army, answered the military call-up by the Russians, he expected to be recruited to fight Germany. Instead, the Russians assembled the Polish officers and deported them to Russia. Years later, the German army discovered mass graves in the forests of Katyn. The graves contained the bodies of thousands of Polish officers, in uniform, their documents in their pockets, their arms tied behind their backs, each with a bullet-hole in the back of the head. Josef's name appeared in the published record of the massacre.

The Russians deported hundreds of thousands of Poles to a fate everyone feared: labour settlements in Siberia. 'Capitalists' were the main targets but, at one stage, single young males also appeared to be in their sights. Josef's parents received one postcard from him, and soon afterwards, they were deported, as if their relationship with him had brought them under suspicion.

Meanwhile, Germany had annexed the western territories of Poland and set up a so-called 'General Government' to rule German-occupied central Poland, including Krakow. At that stage, conditions under the General Government appeared relatively tolerable. When a joint German–Soviet commission was set up to facilitate the return of refugees from the Soviet zone of occupation to the German General Government, many thousands of people registered to return. But, instead of sending those who registered back to their homes, the Soviets deported them to the USSR.

I was lucky to acquire a playmate when my three-year-old cousin, Felus, arrived from Kharkov to stay with us. His parents — my mother's brother, Edziu, and his wife, Rozia — were idealists who had believed so strongly in communism that they had moved to the Soviet Union, where Felus was born. Unfortunately, Edziu was now imprisoned in Moscow, a victim of Stalin's purge of the communists of Western Ukraine. Rozia had sent Felus to us so that she could follow Edziu to Moscow, in the vain hope that she might succeed in obtaining his release.

In June 1941, Nazi Germany broke its non-aggression pact with the Soviet Union, which had opened the way to their joint carving-up of Poland. The German army overran Eastern Poland and pushed on deep into the Soviet Union. As the Soviets hurriedly withdrew from Lwow, the jobs of both my parents folded; yet they declined an offer to leave with the departing Soviets. Instead, they chose to remain in Lwow, even at the risk of coming under Nazi control — which, they believed, had been relatively benign in Western Poland.

Under the Nazis, however, life in Lwow became progressively worse. Laws designed to persecute and humiliate Jews were implemented. Jews were ordered to wear the blue-on-white Star of David, which made them prey to attack by any anti-Semitic Pole,

Ukrainian, or German. My parents told me it was 'a decoration'.

Jews were also subjected to countless rules. They were excluded from public transport and public parks and, if not employed, could be picked up on the street and forced into heavy manual work. Non-Jews (termed 'Aryans') were prohibited from associating with or trading with Jews, or from helping them in any way, on pain of death. Despite this, my nanny, Zosia, stayed with us, caring for Felus and me as if we were her own children. Then, in May 1942, her cousin unexpectedly arrived to take her home to her family in Krakow.

Intermittently, there were large-scale, and often violent, round-ups of Jews for deportation. The euphemistic German term for such a round-up was an *Aktion*. As rumours spread concerning the fate of those who had been deported, it became apparent that the Jews were facing annihilation by one means or another. Yet, amazingly, many people refused to believe this, and they continued to hope.

For a time, my father worked at moving furniture for the Gestapo. Most of it had belonged to Jews who had been evicted from their properties. He also managed to find work for a company, rebuilding the war-damaged Lwow railway station, and thus indirectly working for the Deutsche Ostbahn, the German rail network in the east. This, my parents hoped, made us essential to the German war effort, and so might save us.

But in August 1942, there was a major *Aktion* that lasted several days. By that time, 11 of us were crammed into the Hermans' flat. Then the flat was requisitioned, and we were told to vacate it within six days. This shattered our lives. We could no longer stay together as a family; we had to disperse. Each group had to work out what to do, where to go.

In November 1941, the Germans had designated an area of Lwow as a ghetto, and decreed that all the Jews in the district must live there. It was poor, overcrowded, and ominous. My Herman grandparents now had no choice but to move to the ghetto. They moved in with relatives, taking little Felus with them. That decision sealed their fate as, within days, they were forcibly taken elsewhere, to perish no one knows when, where, or how. My grandmother, Rudolfina, was at that stage employed at the *Städtische Werkstatt* (city workshop) for Jewish women. Before we had time to plan where she should go, the Gestapo arrived at her workplace, and she and her workmates were taken to Majdanek concentration camp.

For my parents, the time had arrived to take a desperate step — one that would ultimately save us. They took off our identifying Stars of David and incinerated them, together with all the 'Reiss' documents. Then they took on the identity of an authentic Catholic couple, Stasia and Piotr Daraz, whose birth certificates my father had purchased from a dealer. The certificates had addendums about their marriage. No child was mentioned, but delayed registration of the birth of a child was not unusual at the time.

We spent one critical night with Stanislaw Wilczek, a Polish childhood friend of my father's, who took us in, even though helping Jews was punishable by death. As the Gestapo was offering a reward for informers who identified Jews, we fled to Warsaw, where my parents were not widely known. There, they felt, they would be less likely to be recognised and denounced.

'Daraz' is the first family name I remember having, and Roman Catholic was my first religion. Having me live the part of a Polish Catholic ensured that I would not give the family secret away, and also spared me the immense burden and responsibility of lying. My parents had to live the lie every minute of every day. They had to act their parts, know all the relevant family details, including those of our notional extended family; they had to be able to expand on places and events, and had to be prepared to corroborate each other's stories if they were challenged.

By 1943, we were living in Legionowo, a town outside Warsaw. Mrs Bielicka, the mother of one of my father's workmates, had let us a room in her cottage. The men were working for a Warsaw building company, Stolzman, which had contracted to rebuild the

Skierniewice station, near Warsaw, for the Ostbahn.

They lived all week in Skierniewice, and came home on weekends. My father had got this job thanks to Wenceslav Poniz, who had been one of his old tutors at the Polytechnika and had since been appointed a professor at Warsaw University. He had taken a great risk when he recommended my father, for he knew him to be not Piotr Daraz, as purported, but Henek Reiss, a Jew.

I remember begging my mother to send me to kindergarten, and my frustration at her refusal. But the most vivid experience of that time for me relates to Mrs Bielicka's brood of hens, which I remember herding into their pens every night. I was especially thrilled to be given two newborn chickens as my very own pets. I named one Pieszczoszka ('Snuggle-pie') and the other Strzepczycka ('Speckledy'). As they grew, they learnt to recognise me, and each would respond when I called her, running to me and jumping into my outstretched arms.

Unfortunately, an epidemic struck the birds and decimated the flock. Worse still, the few remaining healthy chickens had to be killed before they too became ill. With a heavy heart, I delivered Pieszczoszka into my mother's arms, and watched while she put her between her knees and cut her head off. Headless and bleeding, the poor thing ran around the house before finally dropping. That evening, there was a delicious meal of baked chicken. I remember trying not to eat it, but the smell was irresistible.

One day in January 1944, my mother took me on a very important excursion on the train. I remember asking why I was wearing my best white coat with its fur collar. At our final destination, I remember being in a room with a lot of men in uniform. They were very friendly, smiling at me, making kind, approving sounds, stroking my hair. I now know that this was Gestapo headquarters in Warsaw. The previous day, they had arrested my mother on the street. They had held her there all day, accusing her of being Jewish, which she vehemently denied. They had subjected her to intensive questioning, measuring her face and examining the roots of her hair. As the day wore on, she began to insist that she needed to go home to feed her little girl, who was alone. Finally they released her, but withheld her documents. If she returned with me the next day, and if they were convinced that I was not Jewish, they would return them.

The documents included Stasia Daraz's birth certificate, and a travel pass to Muszyna, near the Slovakian border. My parents had arranged to escape Poland across the Carpathian Mountains, and travel via Slovakia to Hungary. The documents were essential to the plan, and to forego the plan and stay in Poland was akin to suicide. That is why, against all advice, my mother took a gamble on my blonde hair and small nose, and returned with me to the Gestapo. Her confidence was boosted by her fluent German, which enabled her to forge a rapport with her interrogators.

That day, she did indeed recover her documents. Encouraged, she requested a certificate stating that her documents had been examined and found to be correct, 'since my features must look somehow suspicious, and I would not like to go through the same unpleasant experience again'. The Gestapo officer told her that in such an event she could refer to his office.

We left Legionowo on 19 January 1943 and travelled by train to Krakow. There I spent the night with Zosia, while my parents stayed with friends, Irka and Henek Haber, who were to accompany us on our trek.

In the morning, we met our guide and took the train to Piwniczna, a village on the Slovakian border, near Muszyna.

That night, we set out along a snow-covered road. Suddenly, our guide gave the prearranged signal, 'Z', to show he had spotted German border police. Instantly, we moved to the side of the road, where I sank up to my neck in snow and became stuck, unable to move. I started to scream but, immediately, a firm hand was clapped over my mouth, and I began to suffocate. 'Do not dare make a sound,' my father threatened, as he eased the pressure.

I didn't walk much after that — the guide carried me on his

back. We climbed over the mountain peak that formed the border, and clambered down into Mníšek, our first Slovakian village. That night, we continued into the next village.

We rested the next day, then walked on, the following night, into a small town. There we waited for two days, while our Polish guides returned for the Habers. Our two families would undertake the crossing into Hungary together.

Next we took a two-hour train trip to the large town of Prešov, where we were received by hospitable Slovakian Jews. But, for all their care, we did not feel safe, especially as the two fathers were accommodated in the synagogue, sleeping on two tables. Slovakia was, after all, a German ally, and by 1942, three-quarters of Slovakia's Jews had been deported, mostly to Auschwitz.

We spent three weeks in Prešov, waiting while contacts were established with new German guards on the Slovak-Hungarian border. Two young Slovakian Jews escorted us. I crossed that border once again on the guide's back. I remember being frightened, especially seeing my mother repeatedly slip and fall in the snow. I also remember 11-year-old Rysio Haber running forward and back again, driven by fear, excitement, and the excess energy of youth.

We spent our first night in Hungary in Kassa, sleeping on two single beds, one for each family, sharing our warmth with masses of bedbugs.*

The next day, still led by the two young men, we boarded a train for Budapest, where the Polish government-in-exile in London had established a committee.

The committee provided us with documents, and we moved into a refugee camp in Kadarkut — one of a number of camps that the government-in-exile had set up for Polish citizens in Hungary.

We were amazed to see that the Jews of Hungary — another German ally — were still free. But, in March 1944, two months after our arrival, the Germans occupied Hungary, and soon the

---

* Today, Kassa is Košice, in Slovakia.

round-ups and deportations of Jews began there, as well. My parents watched with horror as the Jews of Kadarkut, refusing to believe the horrible fate that awaited them, gave their keys to the local mayor and boarded the trucks that would take them on the first leg of their journey to Auschwitz.

Motivated by the very real danger of being denounced as Jews, my father managed to find work in nearby Taszar, a tiny village where the Germans had begun to build a large military airfield. Building had stopped, but the construction company employed my father as an engineer to measure and draw the work done to date, for the purpose of invoicing the German military. We moved into a one-room worker's hut at the airfield, and lived there for nine months. We were still there when the Soviets liberated Hungary in December 1944.

It was in Taszar's tiny school that I started my formal education, in Hungarian. My mother had taught me to read and write Polish, but this was my first actual school, and the lessons were in a new language of which I could not understand one word.

After the liberation, we moved to Budapest, and there, I attended a large school, also Hungarian. We were still using our Daraz papers, and I attended Catholic scripture classes there. I remember being able to recite the Ten Commandments in Hungarian by rote, mouthing the words without any idea as to their meaning. The school also participated in a ceremony in a Catholic church. I remember the class queuing up in front of the priest's cubicle to confess our sins. I was worried because I could not think of any sins I had committed. Finally, I decided on the episode of the apple. It was part of my lunch but, after just one bite, I had thrown it away, and to make things worse, I had not told my mother. I said my two Hail Marys, which took no time at all. This made me feel quite inadequate, as all the other children had a lot more to tell the priest, and they stayed much longer in the church. I wondered what they could possibly have done. Anyhow, I received a sort of confirmation certificate.

At some stage, I must have been influenced into anti-Semitic thinking. I remember walking in the street with my mother, when I spotted a baby in a pram. I remember saying to her, 'Look, there is a Jewish baby!'

'How do you know the baby is Jewish?' my mother asked.

'Because the baby is so ugly. Jewish people are particularly ugly, aren't they?'

'I don't know,' was her reply.

I remember thinking that she did not seem to agree, and wondering if, therefore, perhaps my statement was not correct.

On 25 May 1946, my little sister Krystyna was born in Budapest. Our parents thought Krystyna, like Elzbieta, was an international name, translatable into whatever language we would adopt. I have always known that she was born for my sake, so that I would never be totally alone in the world.

At this time, many refugees were being welcomed home as they returned to their countries and their families, who, although hurt by the war, remained as cohesive, loving entities. For us Jews, however, Poland no longer felt like home. It now held all our loved ones in mass graves, unidentified, anonymous. Moreover, the people of Poland were the same ones who had condoned anti-Semitism in the past and, in some cases, had even denounced Jews to the Nazis. We wanted to go to the West.

At 6 a.m. on 23 June 1946, amid great secrecy, we left Budapest in a truck. Our departure had to be secret, because it was illegal; it was organised by the Palestinian Zionist organisation Brycha. We then travelled by train to Vienna.

Two weeks later, we were transferred to a DP camp, a camp for Displaced Persons, in Ulm, Germany. We lived there for six months. I remember the large group of Jewish orphans there, marching and singing Hebrew songs, and planning to migrate to Palestine. I also remember having a scooter and a boyfriend.

In Ulm, I found out that I was in fact not Catholic but Jewish. I never asked anyone what the words meant. I simply decided it was a label; referring to some invisible thing inside one, something one was born with, like a heart. I also learned that we had pretended not to be Jewish in order to avoid being killed by the Germans. I was shocked to hear that people had wanted to kill us, even though we had done nothing wrong, and that so many equally innocent people had been purposely killed by others. Up till then, I had not known about the war at all. I realised then that one was not in control of one's own life, and resolved to try to enjoy each day, in case something should happen to me the next day. I was eight years old.

From Ulm, we travelled to Paris, a major transit point for refugees heading for the West. We lived there for a year, all four of us sharing one room in the Hotel Mirabeau, which had been rented for Jewish refugees by the 'Joint' — the American Jewish Joint Distribution Committee. We ate in the large dining room, and the food was atrocious, but I was tiny for my age, and my parents forced me to eat every morsel.

I travelled to school on the Metro, and tried to learn French. I suffered recurrent tonsillitis, and had my tonsils removed under local anaesthetic as a day patient. I sat, tied to a chair, with my mouth clamped open, and watched each bloody tonsil on its way into the kidney dish. Subsequently, the tonsils grew back.

At long last, Michael Eisner, a Jewish civil-engineer friend from Poland who had settled in Australia before the war and had a large steel-construction firm in Sydney, sent us a visa to Australia. To obtain this visa, he had guaranteed to provide us with accommodation and work, so that we would not be a burden on the country.

On 17 January 1948, we embarked from Marseilles for a six-week voyage aboard the Egyptian ship *El Sudan*. At first, we slept on three-tiered bunks in the cargo hold, which was divided into gigantic separate-sex dormitories. Later, we joined some other families, and slept on deck to avoid the heat of the equator, hanging blankets to make separate 'suites'.

We arrived in Melbourne, and then flew to Sydney, in February 1948.

We lived in a rented apartment in Milsons Point. The other three apartments in the block also had Jewish immigrant tenants, and we formed a very friendly community. The Habers arrived shortly after us, and lived directly below us.

At nine years of age, I was a very responsible and serious child, and could be trusted to look after my baby sister, Krysia, who was then less than two years old. I used to take her to the park and, on one occasion, had to protect her from stones thrown at us 'foreigners' by local children. But it was wonderful to be living opposite a park, next to Sydney Harbour, close to the Olympic swimming pool and to Luna Park.

When I turned ten, I had my first birthday party. It was a success, although my mother could not fathom why the children passed over the cocoa and other continental fare, preferring the lime fizzy drink and white bread covered in 'hundreds and thousands'.

I was enrolled in 5th Class at Milsons Point Primary School. I remember my early struggles with English, my fifth language after

The Reisses at Balmoral in Sydney, 1948: Elzbieta, Lusia, Krystyna, and Henek (Elizabeth, Lucy, Christine, and Henry).

Polish, Hungarian, German, and French. When a child asked for my 'address', I refused. How could she expect me to give her my one and only 'dress'? I thought indignantly. English would be the language in which I would receive most of my education, and I learned to appreciate it, but Polish is the language that resonates with my childhood. Its use of special soft sounds added at the end of any noun or name to make it diminutive and affectionate remains in my heart.

I was a diligent pupil at Cremorne Girls' High but, being foreign and non-Christian, I remained an outsider among the children, and only had one friend, a Czechoslovakian girl, who, when her father found out I was Jewish, was forbidden to see me after school.

I was happy when I attended a few meetings of the Zionist youth movement Habonim, where we learnt about Israel and danced Israeli folk dances. There the Jewish young people welcomed me as one of their own and, for the first time, I felt that warm feeling of belonging, thus positively forging my identity as one of the Jewish people. This was cemented at university, where the Jewish students socialised together, forming friendships and often marrying each other.

Thinking back over the events of the war, I reflect that I was born into a very large family of about 150 souls, of whom only a handful survived, mostly those who had left Poland before the war. Only one survived in Poland, and he was hidden by his non-Jewish wife. Despite our good life in Australia, my parents' happiness was always marred by that loss.

The credit for the initiative, ideas, and tactical plans for our survival, and the attention to detail in executing them, belongs to my father. And he never lost his optimism and sense of humour. This sustained my mother who, in turn, was brave and encouraging in her support of him.

Several Poles helped us, some of who are acknowledged at Yad Vashem, the major memorial to the Holocaust in Jerusalem. There they are recorded as Righteous Gentiles who risked their own lives to help Jews. Their sincere friendships were possible because my parents spoke Polish and shared the Polish culture with them.

Being able to speak German was also very helpful to my parents. This was facilitated by their exposure to it during the First World War when, as children, they lived in Vienna. Ironically, in that war, my father's father, Filip, fought for Austria against the Russians.

The only organised help we received as Jews during the war was from the Slovakian Jewish community, supported by the Joint. In Hungary, the Polish government-in-exile supported us as supposedly Catholic Poles. Brycha, the illegal Palestinian Zionist organisation, arranged our escape to the West from Soviet-occupied Hungary. Further organised help sustained us after the war: the United Nations supported the DP camp in Ulm, and the Joint supported us in Paris. Finally, Australian Jewish Welfare paid our fares to Australia.

I was most fortunate to have always been with my parents, who provided me with love and protection. I was sheltered from any conscious knowledge of the danger we were in, and I remember only a few moments of fear. I was never hungry. Although I never saw a toy, a chocolate, or a cake, I did not miss those things, and I remember my childhood as happy. My parents — not any home, neighbourhood, or country — were my base. My parents consciously tried to minimise the impact of the Holocaust upon me, teaching me to love and trust, and not to hate or be vindictive. However, I believe the Holocaust shattered any faith they may have had, and I had no religious education or participation whatsoever.

The Holocaust has shown me that a highly civilised, educated, and religious society can organise and commit acts of extreme immorality, depravity, and cruelty. My hope for the future depends, on the one hand, on increasing the bonds of friendship, understanding, and mutual tolerance between peoples; and, on the other, on Jewish autonomy as represented by the state of Israel.

I thank the wonderful people of Australia for giving me the opportunity to live and work in freedom and equality. I have now lived here happily for nearly 60 years. I have tried to repay this gift by treating everyone with kindness, sincerity, and respect, and by working ethically and diligently in my profession as a pathologist. I have made many friends, and believe this to be the best country in the world. I love Australia with all my heart.

CESHA GLAZER

Like a sack of potatoes

I was born on 15 March 1923 in Serock, approximately 30 kilometres north of Warsaw, to Josef and Miriam ('Etka') Oryl. As it was Purim when I was born, my parents called me Ester. I changed my name to Cesha during the war, and since my marriage in 1947, I've been known as Cesha Glazer.

When the Second World War broke out, I was living with relatives — my great-uncle Josef Goldfein, and his wife, Miania — in Warsaw, where I was attending high school. My war began on the very first day, 1 September 1939, when air-raid sirens announced the beginning of the German invasion of Poland and the first bombs fell on Warsaw.

The blitzkrieg fell on us with full force. Within a month, Warsaw was occupied by the Germans, and Poland was carved up between Nazi Germany and Soviet Russia.

In 1940, the Germans decreed that by the first of October, all of Warsaw's Jews must move into a ghetto that they had created in the centre of the city. The ghetto was already very crowded when we arrived. We couldn't find anywhere for the whole family to live together, so we had to split up. My mother and father went to the flat of my cousin Lea, just one room and a kitchen at 4 Elektoralna Street. It was so small that my parents had to sleep in the kitchen. My sister, Szajndla ('Saba'), then 11 years old, found a place at our great-aunt and great-uncle's in Pawia Street. They had rented a room in a large apartment, but the whole apartment was crammed with people. In every room, there was at least one family, often of four or five people, with just the one kitchen and the one bathroom between them all. As for me, I went to live with cousins of my mother, Josef and Frania Wielkabroda, at 74 Dzielna Street. Their daughter Roza and I were in the same class at high school.

Before we went into the ghetto, I had been helping Uncle Josef, as I called him, in his business. He bought industrial fats from abattoirs, and supplied them to be used in producing soap. But, even by December 1939, it was dangerous for him to venture out to see clients and collect money. It was easier for me to move around, because I did not look Jewish, so I did that work for him.

Once confined to the ghetto, Uncle Josef had no way of carrying on his business. I felt uncomfortable that he and his family were supporting me, a 17-year-old, so I offered to sneak out of the ghetto whenever possible and pick up some of his business.

In the beginning, I went out and returned mostly through the law courts, as they straddled the ghetto boundary. I would go into the courts from Leszno Street and go out on the 'Aryan' side, in Ogrodowa Street. This was dangerous, as the Ogrodowa Street entrance was guarded by Polish policemen, and I did not have the proper documents. But, for a number of months, I got away with leaving and re-entering the ghetto, using different points of exit and return. I kept it secret from my parents, as they would have been horrified if they knew.

As time went by, it got harder to find ways of getting out of the ghetto, and even harder to get back in. I remember one day very vividly: I was running late, the curfew was approaching, and

Class VIc in Serock, 1936: Cesha Glazer (at that time, Ester Oryl) is second from the right in the second row.

I could not find a point of entry back into the ghetto. It was too late to reach a place to spend the night on the Aryan side, even if I could find one. Soon, the German patrols would be on the street … this would not end well. I was getting desperate. I knew of a few places at which it was sometimes possible to cross, but they were also too far away to reach before the curfew.

Suddenly, I remembered hearing of some smugglers who used a building in Freta Street. This building, on the Aryan side, adjoined another building inside the ghetto, and the smugglers used this as a route to send goods in from the Aryan side.

In terror, I ran there and was told, yes, they could help me — for a fee, of course. I paid the fee. Then I was asked to follow a man up a flight of stairs. A rope was put around me and, without a word of warning, I was lowered — rapidly, like a sack of potatoes — to the ground on the ghetto side. There, someone put me back on my feet. The complete surprise and abruptness of that drop, without a word of warning, was a terrible shock to me, and for many years, it tormented my dreams — or rather, my nightmares.

It was very difficult for my family to find any employment inside the ghetto. Our modest reserves ran down very quickly. Ultimately, we had to rely on the communal kitchen for a bowl of soup and a slice of bread a day. In desperation, I proposed to my parents that I should leave the ghetto and find a way to earn money for our livelihood. Without telling them that I had already been going in and out for some time, I argued that I could get away with it, as I did not look Jewish and could blend well with typical Poles.

There was a demand for couriers between the ghetto and the Aryan side, but it was highly dangerous work. Only desperate people would take the risk, but I was desperate. My parents at first opposed my plan; but, when they saw that this was the only way of surviving, they finally consented.

With the help of some Christian friends and some people in the ghetto who were eager to use me as a courier, I was able to obtain a Christian birth certificate and rent a room in Targowa Street, outside the ghetto. At this time, the Germans issued a new ID — in German, a *Kennkarte* — for all Poles. I received one in the name of my new identity. I was now officially a Polish Catholic, Czeslawa Kaska — 'Cesia' or 'Cesha' for short.

It will not be all right

In the next few years, I had many harrowing experiences. I remember the day, in April 1943, when I went back to the Plac Krasinskich, or Krasinski Square. My school had stood there until it was destroyed in the German bombing in 1939. I came back now because Krasinski Square overlooked the ghetto and was the best point for observing what was going on inside it.

From this vantage point, I saw with my own eyes the smouldering remnants of the ghetto. The Warsaw Ghetto Uprising was in progress down below; the remaining Jews of Warsaw were perishing in a hopeless and desperate fight for their dignity. Meanwhile, in Krasinski Square, a merry-go-round was still operating to the sound of gay tunes. I stood there with a fake smile on my face and despair in my heart, listening to a woman proclaim, 'At least the Germans had done one thing right — getting rid of the Jews!'

I vividly remember the visit of two blackmailers (*szmalcowniki*) to my apartment. These opportunists were in search of easy money, and they suspected me of having dealings with Jews. At that time, I was in fact hiding six fellow Jews in a partly bricked-up alcove in an apartment at 45 Sienna Street. I can still recall how my heart was racing as they nosed around. But I had to look calm and innocent; the slightest noise or any hesitation could have given us away and ended in disaster.

Another vivid memory is my encounter with a mixed group of Jewish men, drawn from most of occupied Europe, who were brought to Warsaw from Auschwitz to clear up the rubble where the ghetto had stood. They came to Winter's Laundry, where I was working, and I remember my desperate efforts to help them.

But nothing was more harrowing than the time when I learned what had happened to my family. It was in July 1942, when I returned from a trip to Podhajce (near Lwow, and presently in Ukraine). I was told that deportations from the ghetto had begun. At the time, it was still possible to make contact with the ghetto by phone, and a friend from there rang me to tell that my parents were all right. Only my great-aunt Miania had been taken, and my parents were looking after my great-uncle Josef.

I took the news with mixed feelings. A few days later, I was again called to the phone, which was situated in the dining room. On my way to the phone, my landlady's brother stopped me. He said that he had an excellent new joke and would share it with me after I took the call.

The caller informed me that, unfortunately, my whole family

Cesha Glazer working in Winter's Laundry, Warsaw, 1944: The laundry, which cleaned German uniforms, was visited by prisoners (below) who had been sent from Auschwitz to a camp in Warsaw itself.

Escape attempt: At the laundry, Cesha Glazer helped a Jewish prisoner from Greece, Saul Senor (left, and wearing sunglasses, above) attempt to escape. The attempt failed; Saul was later hanged in front of the other Warsaw prisoners.

had been taken to the *Umschlagplatz* — German for 'transit point'. I knew what that meant ... it was where the deportation transports left from. Regardless of the turmoil in my heart, I had to stay calm. On my return, after that phone call, I had to listen to the joke and even laugh heartily, notwithstanding that I did not comprehend it and hardly heard it. I went to my room and closed the door. I was on the verge of exploding with emotion, but I still could not allow myself the luxury of releasing my feelings. I had an appointment, and had to leave shortly for the meeting; under no circumstances could I leave looking distressed or with red eyes, because that would invite questions.

The person I was to meet was a Polish policeman, Leon Rybacki. He was a real friend, and very helpful to us during those difficult years. When we met, he already knew what had happened to my family and expressed his sympathy. It was too late to save my own family but, ironically, the purpose of this meeting was to work out the logistics of smuggling a family of four out of the ghetto. Ultimately, that rescue was successful. But my own family, I was sure, had gone to their deaths. I know now that they were sent in cattle-trucks directly to the Treblinka death camp, south of Warsaw.

At some point in my conversation with Leon Rybacki, I used an optimistic phrase that was popular during the German occupation: *Jakos to będzie*. It was a similar expression to the Australian saying 'She'll be right.' But, instantly, I realised how fake and fallacious it sounded. 'No,' I said to myself, 'it will not be all right. Never, ever!' And I've never used that expression again.

The rings

Early in the twenty-first century, I received the forms and instructions concerning Holocaust Victim Assets Litigation. I had to try to decide whether I had any claims against Swiss entities relative to assets looted by the Nazi regime.

At first, it seemed to me that I had no claims. I am a Holocaust survivor, but I came from a poor family. We had no bank accounts or safe deposits to be looted. But, on reflection, I came to the conclusion that, yes, I had a very strong claim.

Serock, our hometown, was in a part of Poland that the Nazi regime incorporated into Germany as the so-called 'Warthegau'. In December 1939, all the Jews in this area were woken up in the middle of the night and marched many kilometres to the nearest train station with only what they could carry. There, they were told to undress; then, they were searched, and any valuables were taken away.

My mother had only her wedding ring, and that was taken from her. Later, when I was living outside the Warsaw Ghetto under the identity of Cesha Kaska, I bought my mother another wedding ring, because I knew the loss of the first one had meant so much to her. This second ring was taken away from her when she went to her death in Treblinka.

So I think that in the tons of gold bars that the Swiss banks laundered for the Nazis, there were two wedding rings that belonged to my mother — and, through her, to me and to my daughters.

I am sure that in the gold bars there were also wedding rings and other jewellery belonging to other members of my family — my grandmother, aunts, uncles, cousins, and others. There would also have been gold fillings.

But my main claim was for those two wedding rings, which were of great emotional significance to me.

CHARLES FELDMAN
A fortunate childhood

I was born in the Rothschild Hospital in Paris on 4 December 1937. My sister Jacqueline was then nearly seven. She too had been born in Paris, on 18 January 1931.

Our parents were from Poland. My mother, Paulette, was born Pessa Hudessa Flambaum, in Rawa, in 1910. My father, Icek Feldman, was born in Lodz in 1903. They married in Lodz in 1929, and migrated to France in the same year. At first, they stayed in a small hotel, but then they moved into an apartment in the 11th Arrondissement, a district known for its small shops, bars, and dance halls. Both my parents worked hard in tailoring and were happy in their new life.

We lived at 3 rue Froment. Jacqueline went to a public school on the corner of rue Froment and rue Bréguet, and later, I did too. A few minutes' walk away was the Place de la Bastille, where the July Column marked the site of the storming of the Bastille prison in 1789. It was crowned by the famous sculpture the Spirit of Liberty.

In 1939, Germany invaded Poland and my father volunteered for the French army; but, instead of being sent to fight the Germans, he was sent to French North Africa. He was still there in May 1940, when German tanks poured into France. The French army collapsed as quickly as the Polish one had done. On 14 June 1940, the Germans marched, unopposed, into Paris. Eight days later, France surrendered.

Charles in about 1940.

In July 1940, Marshal Pétain founded his collaborationist government in the southern city of Vichy. His government was anti-Semitic, and we soon discovered that this was no mere lip-service to German racial policy. Only three months later, the Vichy government introduced the so-called *Statut des Juifs* (Law of the Jews), the first of a series of laws that aimed to exclude all Jews from public life in Vichy France.

Paris was under German occupation. In spite of this, my father returned there around January 1941. For several months, he was able to resume his work as a tailor, even though he was limited to working from home. But in May 1941, he received the *billet vert*, a special letter requiring Jews to report to the authorities. When he presented himself, he was arrested and sent, together with many other 'foreigners of Jewish race', to an internment camp at Pithiviers, south of Paris. There he remained for over a year.

From June 1942, my mother, Jacqueline, and I — and all the other Jews in France — had to wear the yellow Star of David that marked us publicly as Jews. Then, on 15 July, Jacqueline heard something terrible from Jeanine, her best friend at school. Jeanine's father, a policeman, had told her that the Paris police were planning a secret operation for the very next day. They intended to round up all the Jewish women and children.

Jacqueline ran straight home to tell our mother. Her story seemed unbelievable, and Mum decided to wait until morning to see what would happen. But she took one precaution. She went to our concierge, Mme Joly, and asked her to say, if anyone came looking for us, that no one was at home.

Early the next morning, the gendarmes did come, just as Jeanine had said. Courageously, Mme Joly told them that we were not at home. They came upstairs anyway, and banged on our apartment door. Inside, my mother had a handkerchief to my mouth, and we all kept very silent. They tried to push the door open, but eventually left, assuming we were not home. We were amazed that they hadn't heard us. Later, Mme Joly came up and told us that we had to leave, as the police were coming back to seal our apartment door.

All this happened on 16 July 1942. We later learned that the very next day, the 17th, my father was deported from Pithiviers to Auschwitz. We never saw him again.

The Yellow Star: A Star of David bearing the word *Juif,* French for 'Jew'. (Photo courtesy of Sydney Jewish Museum.)

Father was very close to a cousin by the name of Goldwasser. He too had been sent to Pithiviers, but his wife Rachel and their two children, Bernard and Jeanine, still lived nearby. Mum wanted to warn them that the police would now be looking for them as well. She ran to their apartment, but it was too late. They had already been taken. We never saw them again either.

When she came back, Mum hurriedly packed a small suitcase. Then she showed Jacqueline how she had sewn fabric and gold coins onto her dress to make them look like buttons. She told Jacqueline that if anything happened to her, she should tear the coins off and use them to survive.

We made our way to the train station. Non-Jews were not affected too much by the German occupation and, as it was holiday time, lots of people were travelling to the countryside. This was fortunate, as it allowed us to meld into the crowd.

We caught a train going south to try to get to the so-called 'Free Zone'. Being ruled by Vichy, it was hardly free, but at least it wasn't occupied by the Germans, and so it remained until the end of 1942.

During one stop on this journey, French police with dogs boarded the train. Mum quickly gave the ticket to Jacqueline, and went to hide in the toilet. With her, she took our identity papers, which were stamped with a large J. Then came another piece of luck: to save money, she had only bought a single combined adult-and-child ticket. When the police inspected it, it looked correct. All the same, they asked Jacqueline what she was doing on her own with a young boy. 'I'm visiting friends in the countryside,' she replied, with such conviction that they didn't ask her anything more. The other passengers — who were all women — looked straight ahead through all this, and didn't say a word.

Meanwhile, in the toilet, Mum had collapsed, and it took her a while to recover. She kept looking through a crack in the window to see if we had been taken. If we had been, she would have run out after us.

At last, we left the train. I don't know how Mum knew what to do next but, somehow, we joined up with other families who were running away. We met a man who was supposed to lead us across the patrolled boundary to the 'Free Zone'. After we had all paid him, he left to check out the route. He took the money with him — and he never came back.

Eventually, we set out anyway, with someone else leading the way. In pitch darkness, we walked across fields, sometimes diving to the ground to avoid searchlights sweeping across it. Both the Vichy authorities and the Germans were on the lookout for infiltrators. But we made it across the line, with Jacqueline carrying the suitcase and Mum carrying me. Soon we arrived in the little town of Limoges.

In Limoges, we booked a room in a private house. With papers identifying us as Jews, we couldn't go near a normal hotel. But our money quickly ran out, and soon we were reduced to sleeping in doorways and eating out of rubbish bins. Jacqueline remembers Mum staying awake and holding me all night. I don't know how she did it.

We couldn't go on like that. At her wits' end, Mum decided to give herself up. We were actually on our way to the police station when a young woman suddenly tapped her on the shoulder and inquired if we were Jewish. Mum, believing we had been found out, said yes. Incredibly, it turned out that the woman was a member of the French Resistance. She led us to a safe house.

Almost immediately, we were separated and sent to hideouts organised in conjunction with a Jewish organisation called OSE — *Oeuvre de Secours aux Enfants*, or Children's Aid Society — and a network of religious and resistance groups. As I was not yet even five years old, I was put in a nursery in Limoges itself. Jacqueline was sent to a children's home called Le Couret, a magnificent property with huge grounds in the area of Haute Vienne. Jacqueline remembers going to the station with Mum, who had dressed her in two dresses and two pairs of pants. 'Take care of them,' she said, 'they're all you have.'

My mother was first sent to a tiny place called Argy, where she worked briefly as a maid at a gentleman's residence called (I believe) Lante de la Fleur. Then she was placed with the family of Pierre and Simone Moreau, on their farm 'La Bieterie', about 40 kilometres from Châteauroux. She stayed in hiding there, working as a farmhand, until the liberation.

Jacqueline and I were eventually moved to a place not far out of Limoges. It was a large old house in a very small village called Poulouzat. For a while, it was a fine hiding place — but only for a while: the hiding places of Jews were often betrayed for the sake of the reward offered by the authorities. Many Jewish children were caught and sent to death camps in that way.

Our hiding place in Poulouzat was betrayed, but we were warned at the same time. The very young left hurriedly in trucks. I left amongst the first, and my sister, who should have waited with the older children, managed to leave with me. We were saved, but the older children were caught. Later, we were sent further south to a town called Castera-Verduzan, in a remote area not far from the Spanish border. We were placed in a Catholic convent, where nuns looked after us. We stayed in hiding there until the end of the war.

At the end of the war, OSE came to pick us up, and sent us to another home, the Chateau de Corbeville, a beautiful chateau in Orsay, very close to Paris.

Eventually, with the help of OSE, we were reunited with my mother, whom we had not seen since being separated from her two-and-a-half years earlier.

My mother acted strangely, and not in the way we had expected. She was suffering from trauma. The Moreau family kindly allowed my mother to stay on the farm for a short while after the war, giving her the opportunity to travel to Paris to arrange to move back into our apartment. She found that, after we'd fled in July 1942, Mme Joly, the concierge, had had her daughter move into it to look after our belongings. For this we were very thankful.

My mother at first did not want us to return to live with her. She felt inadequate, incapable, and scared. Everyone else in our family was lost and gone. But Jacqueline was now almost 15, and she was made to return home. There, she learned right away how to sew and earn some money. I was left in the orphanage and, subsequently, moved to another home called Les Glycines, in the Draveil area of Essonne. I remained there until 1948.

Meanwhile, some distant cousins from Australia were making enquiries about surviving relatives. These cousins, the Pakulas, first contacted us, and then obtained permits for us to immigrate to Australia. My sister was the first to go, in March 1949. She stayed with the Pakulas and, not long afterward, she married Louis Pakula.

My mother decided to send me to Australia, too, to join my sister. It felt quite normal at the time, but I wasn't even 13 years old. She got the tickets for a train to Italy, and I sailed from Genoa, on my own, in December 1950.

My mother was to join us later, but, in the meantime, she had met a man called Henry Landowitz. He too had lost his loved ones in the war, and they decided to live together. Henry did not want to go to Australia. In 1956, they were married, and they chose to remain in France, while I stayed with Jacqueline in Sydney. It was only much later, in 1977, that my mother finally came to Sydney to live with Jacqueline.

Jacqueline had two children: Rina, in November 1950; and Irwin, in January 1953. Her marriage ended in divorce a few years later. She later married a man named Tony Dale.

I went to school for three years, and after Jacqueline's divorce, I went to work. I joined a Zionist organisation, and had already decided to settle in Israel when I met my wife, Anna Asz, in 1959. In 1961, we left for Israel to settle on Kibbutz 'Yisrael'.

Our first son, Etienne, was born in Israel in 1961. We returned to Australia in 1962. Our second son, Bart, was born in Melbourne in 1963. Our daughter Romy was born in Sydney in 1966.

I have no qualifications, and I have worked at many jobs, the main ones being taxi-driving, selling insurance and, most successfully, in retailing ladies' clothing at the markets and in shops.

Today, I have seven grandchildren. Our two sons went to Israel and married Israeli girls, but their work has taken them out of Israel. Our daughter lives in Sydney, close to us.

I am now 70 and retired. As I look back, I marvel at the series of chances that allowed Jacqueline and me to survive those years of hiding in wartime France. They were dark years, and we only came through them because of our mother's courage, the kindness of strangers, and extraordinary good luck. For us, in spite of everything, it was a fortunate childhood.

NAOMI GOLDREI

Mummy will be back soon

In 1942, I was three years old and living with my mother and grandmother in Sosnowiec, in German-occupied Poland. None of us had heard from my father since he set off to join his Polish army unit in August 1939.

At that time, my mother was working as a waitress. In the evenings, after she came home from work, we ate our supper and she would bathe me. Then she helped Grandma with her bath. If I was still awake, she would sing me a lullaby or read me a story.

One evening, I was not asleep, and was waiting for my story, when I heard heavy footsteps on the timber staircase. Grandma must have heard them, too, because she asked to get out of the bath much earlier than usual.

I heard sharp knocking on the door. My mother was busy helping Grandma and did not go to the door. The knocking grew louder. When my mother finally opened the door, there were two men there who spoke German. Everyone knew German in my family. Grandma had come to Poland from Austria and spoke fluent

German. Sometimes she even told us anecdotes in German.

I do not remember anyone translating the conversation with the two men, so I must have understood it all by myself. One of them asked my mother for her name. After she had identified herself, they asked her to accompany them to the police station. When my mother asked why, they said that it would be clarified when she arrived there. She asked if she could say goodnight to me and take her coat. Mummy came to me, gently stroked my head, and said a few words in her soft voice. '*Dobranoc Zosienko, mamusia zaraz wruci.*' 'Good night, my dearest Zosia, Mummy will be back soon.'

I must have been very frightened, for I couldn't say a thing. After I regained my voice, I called Grandma, and asked her why the men had taken Mummy to the police station.

'It's probably some misunderstanding. Mummy will be back soon,' said Grandma. She may have believed it but,

Naomi Goldrei with her grandmother
in Sosnowiec, Poland, in autumn 1943.

somehow, the change in her voice made me doubt her, and a sad and fearful feeling overcame me.

In the morning, my *niania*, or nanny, arrived very early. Hastily, she spoke to Grandma, whom she knew well, as she had also been my mother's *niania* years ago. Then she came to me, hugged me passionately, and said, 'Don't worry, my dearest. I will do everything possible to get your mummy back to you.'

To this day, I cannot explain what possessed my mother to do what she had done. I do know that without her mentor and older brother Lutek at her side, she was at a loss, incapable of rational decisions, and relied solely on emotion. Any other explanations that come to mind defy all reason. Therefore, I suspend judgement, and keep to the facts as my mother presented them to me years afterward:

A friend of my father's by the name of Stefania had approached my mother and asked her to be a witness in an adoption case. Without asking any questions, my mother agreed. It was put to her that it was for the good of the child. The mother of this child could not support her daughter without the father, who was in jail. My mother was unaware that the papers were pre-dated, and therefore false. Nor was she aware of the real purpose of the scheme. When the father unexpectedly got out of jail, the scheme backfired.

All her life, my mother firmly believed that she was set up by my father's friend, who had wanted her job. In her eyes, this disgusting affair was another in the considerable list of black marks my father already had against him. My mother was incarcerated for three days in the police station, before a hearing in the magistrates' court. None of the other people involved in the plot was arrested.

Niania came on the second day and again said she would do everything possible to get my mummy out. When she came on the third day, she was almost running. I was outside, playing in the yard, when I saw Niania cracking her knuckles as she rushed up the staircase. I followed her. She opened the door and fell on her knees.

'*Jezus Maryja*, they are sending my mistress to prison! I was in the magistrates' court this morning. I told them, and I tell you, she is innocent, she is too trusting …'

While she was talking, tears rolled down her cheeks, and she was gasping for air. Grandma was speechless. As she helped Niania to her feet, tears rolled down her sombre face. On 19 November 1942, my mother was sent to the same prison as Lutek.

I was left at home with Grandma. Apart from Niania, no one came to visit us anymore. I do not remember seeing any of my cousins or my uncles or aunties for a very long time. I vaguely remember visiting my aunt Cela with Grandma, and staying at her place for some days.

Many years later, my cousin Janka sent me translations of German letters that she had received from her parents. On 29 April 1943, Janka, who was in a labour camp, received a letter from her father. It said, in part:

> Both grandmas send you their love. Grandma and Zosia are staying with us. Little Zosia always consoles your mum, saying that you will soon return home. She does not allow anyone to touch your things. She keeps 'writing' letters to you.

I learned from Janka's letters that we were with her parents for four weeks. There must have been bad news in every letter, for every time Grandma received one she cried. One morning, we received a letter with a red swastika at the top. I was beside Grandma when she opened it.

'Oh my God!' she exclaimed. 'We have an eviction order.' With the letter in her hand, she ran to the fishmonger's apartment, where she stayed for a while. When she came out, she said to me, 'Come my dearest, we have a lot of work to do. We're moving to a new home, in Srodula.'

Srodula … I knew that name. Niania lived not far from Srodula, and she often mentioned the latest goings-on there.

Little did I know, the part we were going to was behind

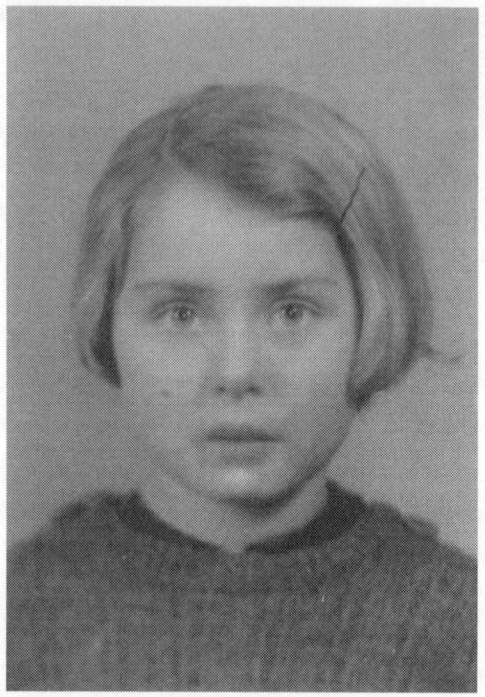

Naomi Goldrei as a young girl, shortly after the war.

barbed wire. We were going to the Srodula Ghetto.

Within a few hours, Niania appeared and rustled me away, claiming me as her own child. Subsequently, she sent me to a farm near Poznan, where I remained until the liberation of Poland. My grandma perished in the ghetto. I only had contact with my *niania*.

Later, with the liberating forces, my father came from Russia and found me. He took me with him to live in Bialystok where he was stationed with the Polish army. Soon we moved out of the barracks into an apartment, where his friend Stella joined us. She would become my surrogate mother.

Déjà Vu

It was in the evening, long after I had finished my homework, when Dad brought her in. I'd known she was coming for quite some time. Dad had said so.

Even when Stella had left to make room for my mother, I had adopted a wait-and-see attitude. Although I desperately wanted my mummy, and longed for her to hold me, I was afraid that I might be disappointed again. That evening, Dad entered the room where I was sitting. 'I have a surprise for you,' he announced. 'Your own mummy is back.'

Although Dad said she was my real mother, I had been deceived before. Why should I believe anyone anymore? 'Oh, really?' I thought, ' I've heard that one before!' Then she entered the room. I sat there, and silently watched every movement she made. She looked weird. She had an odd-looking hat and wore a strange suit with a very coarse weave, as if it were homemade. Her eyes were droopy. Her face was long, her cheeks sunken, and her body limp. She was sickly-skinny. To my horror, when she took off her hat, her hair was reddish brown and short. 'She can't be my mother,' I thought. 'This must be another trick, only more sinister. I've been through all this before!'

'Aren't you going to give your mummy a hug and a kiss, Zosia?' asked my father. My mind went into turmoil. 'He's pushing it a bit too far,' I thought. 'What does he think I am? A moron?'

I stood still. The woman approached slowly, embracing me and kissing me. I had a flashback from the time when Stella had introduced me to a Russian woman, an acquaintance of my father, whom she 'mistakenly' took for my mother. I screamed now with the same disgust and horror with which I'd screamed at Stella. 'She is not my mother!' I yelled. 'That's a pack of lies. Take her away from me. You can't lie to me any more. She is not my mother, I know my mother! She does not look anything like my mother!'

Some years later, I recalled how traumatic this meeting was. It was only then that I realised how devastating it must have been for my mother. I was hysterical; she was in a panic. Her despair knew no boundaries. I was weeping, she was sobbing, and Dad was crying. It could have been a vignette from a funeral, not a family reunion after four years of separation.

For some unexplained reason, I felt better after crying. But why were they crying? I knew why I had cried, I knew my feelings were hurt, but who had hurt Dad and this woman? That was not too clear to me. After sitting still for some time, Dad lifted his head and wiped the tears from his eyes. 'Let's go out to a nice restaurant and celebrate,' he said. 'It's silly to cry.'

'No, thanks,' she said. 'I'm not in the mood to celebrate. Of all those years of darkness, this must be the darkest of all.'

'What does she mean?' I thought. 'What does she have to complain about? She's the cause of all this, isn't she? But ... she doesn't admit to having deceived me. Could it be that I'm wrong? No! She isn't a bit like my mother!'

Lying on the sofa, and still in deep thought, I heard a voice. 'Zosienko,' the voice said softly. That voice was familiar. No one had ever called me Zosienko except my mother. 'We must talk,' the voice said. 'I won't kiss you if you don't want to be kissed, but you must talk to me. You seem to be a clever girl. You said that you remembered your mummy, but what you remember *is* really me, as I was four years ago. A lot has changed since. What is it that you remember that is different now?'

'My mummy had long blonde hair. Yours is red,' I answered matter-of-factly. By now, I had calmed down.

'Well, you see,' she said, 'the Germans cut off my hair at Oswiecim. Then, I had typhus when we were liberated. I was repatriated to Sweden by the Red Cross, I have been very ill, and there was a danger that all my hair would fall out. The treatment I received changed the colour of my hair.'*

---

* Oswiecim is the city also known as Auschwitz.

I was not impressed, but I didn't say anything. 'What else do you remember?' she asked. 'I remember everything,' I said, with all the arrogance that only a six-year-old could muster. 'I remember my grandma.' At this, she pounced on me: 'What do you remember about Grandma?'

'Everything,' I said.

'What is it that you remember about her? Describe it to me, describe your grandma; she is my mother, you know that, don't you?'

'She was short and fat and had a walking stick and a foreign accent,' I snapped. 'Yes, that's right,' she said.

'What do you remember about Grandma that I didn't tell you about?' I snapped back at her.

'You can ask me anything,' she said.

I had to think that one over. There had to be something special, something that nobody knew about my grandma except those who knew her well. This was my chance to find out if this woman really knew my grandma as well as she pretended to know her.

'You say that you know my grandma?' I finally said. 'You know that she had a walking stick. What was on the handle of her walking stick?'

A broad smile spread over the woman's face — she must have been worried that I might ask her something she didn't know. Without a moment's hesitation she said, 'A ram's head.' I looked at her in disbelief. She really knew the answer. I was positive that no one could have guessed it, since Grandma had always said that her walking stick was unique. I had to ask her another question, quickly.

'If you are my mother, as you say you are, where did you work before the Germans took you away?'

'In a café,' she said.

'Did I ever come to visit you there?' I couldn't stop asking questions — she answered them all with such decisiveness.

The woman still looked strange, but I had to admit that she

seemed to know everything I knew, and everyone I knew. I had to concede that, regardless of her looks, she might be my mother. How else could she know all this? I had no other explanation. And the voice ... the voice was unmistakably my mother's!

Coming to terms with the changed image of my mother was hard. If not for Basia, my friend, it may have taken a lot longer. She encouraged me to accept my mother and to try to understand and share her feelings. Basia made me feel that I, too, could have the same family as all the other kids in my class. But that was cut short. My parents separated after nine months. My mother moved in with a friend she had made at the nursing school. I had the choice to stay with my father or go with my mother — not an easy choice. After careful consideration, I chose to go with my mother.

PIERRE MEYER
I will always remember

My parents, Paul and Irma Meyer (née Bauer), were from the German port city of Hamburg. I was born there, as Peter Egon-Meyer, on 17 April 1933, only months after the Nazi seizure of power.

In 1939, my parents and I escaped from Nazi Germany to France. After the Fall of France in 1940, we lived in hiding in Lyons for four years. Lyons was part of the so-called 'Free Zone' of France — not occupied by the Germans, but ruled instead by the anti-Semitic collaborationist government of Marshal Pétain, based in Vichy. In autumn 1942, the Germans occupied the Free Zone as well, and Lyons became the headquarters of the notorious Gestapo officer Klaus Barbie. But it was also a centre of resistance, and that helped us to survive.

In France, we were illegals, with no valid French papers; however, we did have plenty of German letters and documents. After the Fall of France, my father took one of those letters and folded it in such a way that the official stamp bearing the swastika and the spread eagle was highly visible. He carried it at all times in a wallet-size mica pocket.

One rainy day, as I was walking down a little street with my father, we saw that both ends of the street had been sealed off, trapping all the pedestrians in a classic Nazi round-up. In order to exit, you had to prove that your identity papers were in order. My father, flashing his worthless letter, walked straight towards the youngest policeman. The young man, a Frenchman, could not read German, and took the letter for a German *laissez-passer*. He stood to attention, saluted, and waved us through. That time, we were lucky. After that, we decided that if we were ever challenged while I was walking with my parents, I would walk on, as if they were strangers to me.

The Antiquaille

One evening in July 1943, my father didn't come home. He didn't come home the next day, or the day after that. News filtered through to us that he was in the prison ward of a public hospital called the Antiquaille, which was run by an order of Catholic nuns in the suburb of Minimes. It was decided that I would go and visit him, on the pretext of delivering him food and clothing.

I was directed to the prison ward and, as I stood facing it, I had a strange feeling. That feeling is hard to describe. I knew I had to act calmly and not cry, but I felt nauseated with the apprehension and tightness in my chest. Then I found myself facing two burly French policemen. After they had checked me, I was allowed to enter the prison ward.

The prison ward had about 15 beds, an adjoining room with another three beds, and a common room with a couple of large tables and chairs. Adjoining the common room were the showers and toilets.

After the typical French-style kiss on both cheeks, my father and I sat facing each other in a corner. He looked pathetic in his oversized hospital pyjamas, and his eyes reminded me of a cocker spaniel's. My message to him was, 'We will get you out very soon. It's only a matter of money and finding the right contact.' Then I asked him, 'Papa, how did you land here?'

He told me, in a very shaky voice, 'I was riding in a tram that stopped, and everybody had to get out and be processed. When my turn came, I used the same tactic, showing the letter in the mica pocket. My luck ran out, and a senior police officer marched me across the road to a police station, where I was searched. They made a phone call to request an interpreter. What could I do? The game was up. So I collapsed on the floor, faking a fainting spell,

In 1930s Germany: Peter Meyer aged two and a half, in the snows of Hamburg (right), and (below) with his mother Irma in 1938, shortly before the family fled to France.

and frothing from the mouth. I actually did hurt my hip during the fall. I lay on the floor, flies were all over my face, it was very hot and, eventually, I was put into an ambulance and brought here. So, what now, son?'

'Well, Papa,' I said, 'you have been very fortunate so far, and we will get you out. How is the food? How are you sleeping?'

My father showed me his bed, and introduced me to Alphonse, the man in the bed next to his. Alphonse was a two-metre, 100-kilo-plus criminal who, amongst other things, had cut off both his wife's ears. That was enough for a first visit! I hurried home, happy to have seen my father, but somewhat confused about his circumstances.

After that, I saw my father almost every day. The days became weeks, and the weeks became months. I tried to reason with him. 'Actually, you're safe here,' I said. 'You're being fed, it's cosy and warm, and the war will soon be over.' He patted me on the head and said, 'I would have liked to have had grandchildren one day.'

Life wasn't easy, whether in the hospital or in the outside world. As time went by, most of the sick criminals were replaced by political prisoners. They were routinely sent to headquarters for questioning, and they came back badly beaten up. They were nursed back to health, only to go through the same ordeal again and again.

My father was the only Jew amongst the detainees, and the nuns were particularly good to him. Whenever the German or French investigators came, they had to report at the front gate. By the time they reached the prison ward, my father was in bed looking very sick, all thanks to a phone call from the gatekeeper.

The courier

By now, I was acting as a courier, bringing mail into the prison ward, and taking it out. My father would give me a note or a small envelope. I had to memorise the address. Using the ward's toilet,

I would conceal the note or letter in one of my socks and put my shoe back on. This was my weekly assignment.

One sunny Sunday morning, I came in as usual, and my father warned me to be wary of a new patient. This man was in a bed almost opposite us. He had red hair and a beautiful beard and moustache. It wasn't long before he called me over.

'Hello!' he said. 'We know each other, don't we?' I realised that I had seen his face before … but where, and when? Dumbfounded, I replied that I didn't know him.

'Let me help your memory, boy,' he said. 'I saw you a few times at the stamp fair where I had a stand and traded on the Place Bellecour.' Actually, this was true. I had attended the stamp fair on a few occasions in the previous six months. I acknowledged that he was right. He smiled and told me that next week he would give me some stamps. But, from that day on, my father forbade me to visit him again.

The very next day, I changed schools to a small Catholic school of about 40 children, located on the second floor of an apartment building.

Within three weeks, I was sent to the countryside to live with farmers. This was organised by an underground cell of the Jewish resistance movement known as the *Union des Juifs pour la Résistance et l'Entraide*, or UJRE. As a ten-year-old boy, I got busy on the farm, attending school, going to church … I enjoyed many new experiences, and especially the plentiful food. My father and mother, although not forgotten, were not my priority.

During those years in hiding, our family was split up several times, as circumstances dictated, and I stayed with several different families. Quite often, I went to bed hungry, wearing torn clothing without underwear or socks. It was disturbing and unsettling being moved around the countryside without warning, and it happened all too often. I'm sure that it is as a result of these experiences that today I am a hoarder, especially of clothes.

Liberation

By the late summer of 1944, I had just been settled with yet another new family, in a village about 40 kilometres from Lyons. For the past two days we had heard explosions and seen a lot of smoke in the distance. The Americans and the 1st Free French Division were approaching from the south.

It was sometime after breakfast that Henri, a boy I had befriended, came running in with great excitement: 'It's happening, it's happening! Quick, come with me!'

So off we ran, heading for the village square. This square was typical of the squares in hundreds of villages all over France. In the centre was a monument to the memory of the fallen in the Great War, 1914–18; around the monument was a circular water-trough for the horses; and around the square stood the school, the church, the cafe, the barber, the tobacconist, and the bakery. The summer sky was blue and cloudless. I could feel a light breeze.

A solemn silence hung over the square, even though there were many people standing around in it. Looking to the right, about ten metres from where I stood, I saw a pile of bodies. They were lying in strange, twisted positions, all piled on top of each other. Clearly, they were still just as they had been thrown onto the heap.

By now, Henri and I were clutching each other's hands in fear, but we still went a few paces forward to get a better view. All the boots and belts had been removed from the bodies in the pile. The body closest to me was a blond man's; he was about 20, with a beautiful face. His mouth was half-open, and his bright blue eyes seemed fixed on me. Right in the middle of his forehead was a neat, round bullet-hole, with blood around it. His uniform was immaculate. His army identification tag was shining on a chain around his neck. I think there must have been at least ten dead German soldiers there, with their limbs outstretched in bizarre positions. Henri had disappeared, but I was transfixed by those big blue eyes, still looking at me.

I moved away to look on the other side of the square. There I saw three ambulances with their rear doors wide open. In each, I could see a stretcher. As I drew closer, I realised that on each stretcher was the body of a French combatant covered by the national tricolour flag.

I could not help but think how unfair it was that even in death, people were not equal! The bodies of the victors treated with dignity and respect, whereas the bodies of the defeated were humiliated. I was 11 years old — how could I reason in these matters?

A few days after the liberation, I was reunited with my father. He told me what had happened after the abrupt end of my hospital visits. As the day of liberation approached, he had become more and more anxious. He feared that the Gestapo would come and dispose of all the patients, especially as they now included some high-ranking members of the Resistance.

Then, one night, *maquisards* — members of the underground — had burst in to rescue their comrades. The two French policemen complied with the orders of the *maquisards*. The operation was well planned, brilliantly executed, and very swift. They had known exactly who each person in the hospital was, and they left the criminals behind. They had taken the stamp dealer, though. He was reluctant to go, and they had to drag him out. He was a spy, planted in the ward by the Germans. The *maquisards* executed him right outside the front gate.

Outside the hospital, transport was waiting for the liberated prisoners, and they were taken to a rendezvous in the hills outside Lyons. From there, they joined a group of Free French underground fighters. Owing to his frail condition, my father was given the job of instructing the new recruits in the maintenance of their weapons. Why was he cut out for this? Because, ironically enough, he had been a German officer in the First World War.

All of this was a chapter in my father's life that played a significant part many years later when, in 1959, he took his own life.

Maison Lafitte

Lyons was liberated in August 1944. I left the last of the families who had looked after me, and went back to my parents.

During the next two years, things got a bit out of hand. With much of France a recent battleground and the economy in chaos, I became involved in the small-time black market. I would go back to the farmers who had hidden me and exchange silk stockings and cigarettes for eggs, butter, cheese, and *marc* (pomace brandy — the same drink that is known in Italy as *grappa*). Back in town, I would sell the food and drink at a profit. The stockings came from American GIs, and I got the cigarettes from senior students who did not smoke but received a cigarette allowance, which they sold to me. I also sold communist newspapers at a bus station. At the flea markets, I had a permanent stand where I sold second-hand shoes, which we got from wealthy Jewish families, and gloves from army disposal stores. My mother and I split the profits — she used to iron the banknotes when I brought them home on Sundays.

My parents separated when their so-called flat — really only one room, with common facilities — was repossessed. I felt like the meat in the sandwich, and it affected me very much, emotionally. I was sent back to school — about my sixth or seventh. Times were tough, so tough that I came to the attention of a social worker, who was introduced to me as a friend of the family.

As things became worse, I was told that the following week I would go to a Jewish children's home run by *Oeuvre de Secours aux Enfants*, or OSE — an organisation that still exists today. I didn't care; but the day before my departure, the little gang I belonged to decided to take me to an air-raid shelter deep beneath a public playground. It wasn't long before I found out that they had 'lost' me inside it, on purpose. It was pitch dark, and they had left me there on my own. I panicked and began to run. I ran straight into a wall and knocked myself out. When I came to, I was lying flat on the ground and, from that angle, I could see the exit. I felt pain all over my body.

Late in the afternoon of the following day, with a badly bruised eye and a label pinned to my chest, I stood at the railway station clutching a small suitcase. A gentleman in a business suit introduced himself to my father, and then off the gentleman and I went on the train. We arrived in Paris in the morning. He took me to his home for breakfast, and his wife got a shock when she saw my face.

Afterwards, we went to head office, and from there, another person took me on a suburban train to the children's home. It was in Maison Lafitte, a township outside Paris.

From the outside, the home looked quite pleasant. It was a small chateau that had been occupied by the Germans during the war. It was getting dark when I arrived, and I was directed to a barber in a room upstairs. He greeted me with, 'You're the lucky last! I've been cutting hair all day.' The floor was covered with hair. It wasn't long before I realised that I was to have all my hair cut off, and I screamed in protest. He called for help, and I felt like crying, but I couldn't. My hair was cut off, and I was too late for dinner. Instead, I was taken to a large common room to meet the other children.

I made my grand entrance — a small, skinny boy with a black left eye completely closed up, and no hair on his head! About 50 children looked up at me from around a huge long table while I was introduced as: 'Pierrot, the new boy from Lyons'. I was in good company. All the children had their heads shaved, for the home was infected with lice. After that, I didn't feel sorry for myself any more. Instead, I felt sorry for the teenage girls who had lost their hair.

I took a chair and sat at the table, wondering what was going on. It was simple: all the washing had come back from the laundry, and the baskets had been emptied at the top of the table. A *moniteur*, or leader, was holding up one piece of clothing after another for all to see. She would call out the name on the label, a child would lift his or her hand, and the item would then be passed or thrown to that child. Again, I felt sorry for the teenage girls, who had personal items such as underwear passed to them.

Those were my first few hours in my new home. About three months and a few adventures later, I was thrown out.

Arriving in Australia

When we arrived in Australia in February 1952, the first port of call was Fremantle. I was surprised that there were no kangaroos or emus running along the wharf — it looked just like a regular town.

A series of officials boarded the ship: immigration, health, banking ... and the police, who arrested and isolated a male member of our group, as he was wanted by the police in Germany.

Later that day, I went ashore with an Australian official, and was introduced to the famous hamburger and milkshake (yum). My parents stayed on board.

The voyage to Melbourne was a nightmare — we had no idea how rough the sea would be across the Great Australian Bight; however, as a result of a complaint to the authorities, the food became cordon bleu. It didn't affect me, as I had been upgraded to First Class earlier in the journey. This was my very worthwhile reward for organising the children on board to perform at the 'Crossing the Equator' party.

Half of our group stayed in Melbourne. The rest of us continued overland to Sydney, changing trains at Albury. In Sydney to meet us were my Uncle and Aunty Benscher. I didn't remember them, as they had come to Sydney years earlier, from Shanghai.

I was filled with apprehension. It was a new world! I hoped it was going to be a successful third start, in a new country, with a new language — but without Dominique, the girlfriend I'd left behind in Lyons.

My first impressions of Sydney, as they flash in front of my eyes now, after more than 50 years, were: the heat, the flies, the mineral taste of the water, how thin the eggshells were, electricity blackouts, shortages of cigarettes, the great size of the policemen,

Bex powders for headaches, home delivery of ice for the icebox, vegetables at your doorstep sold from a truck ... There seemed to be lots of children who had suffered from polio and who wore metal calipers on their legs. The number of healthy young people wearing false teeth was a shock. But the display windows at David Jones, with their food hampers at Christmas, seemed to show an unbelievable prosperity. I was impressed by the virility of beach inspectors and lifesavers; by the open-air 'toast-rack' tram carriages in summer; and by the compulsory standing-to-attention for 'God Save the Queen' before screenings at cinemas. I really enjoyed the

After the war: Pierre Meyer in Lyons in about 1947, and (inset) in 1951 before leaving for Australia.

informality of calling almost everybody by their first names, the luxury of having two showers a day if I wanted to, and having access to a home phone.

I began settling into a routine, with English and Technical College classes, getting a job, and going to work on a bike. On the social scene, I learned to play tennis, and I played volleyball at the YMCA. I joined the bushwalkers and the University of NSW Nagunnagan (friendship) Club, attended the first Sydney Film Festival at Sydney University in 1954, and got involved with the adult and community education organisation the WEA. I spent most weekends at Taylors Bay, a youth hostel in Pittwater.

After a while, I discovered the Jewish youth scene on the steps at Bondi Beach. I was made welcome at regular Saturday afternoons at the home of the late Queenie Davis and her husband John, where I mingled with a lot of boys and girls my own age. I became involved with the Jewish sporting organisation Kadimah, among other groups, and gradually integrated into the Jewish community.

The next few years after this early settling in were not easy — I spent two years working on the Snowy Mountains Scheme — but I was young and healthy, and the future looked challenging.

JOZEF VISSEL

Jozef's story

My name is Jozef Vissel. I am a retired photographer and have lived in Australia since April 1960. However, I was born in Holland and survived the Second World War only because I was hidden from the Germans by wonderful, courageous people.

Holland was neutral during the First World War, and because of that, the Dutch expected to be neutral again during the Second World War. They were therefore totally unprepared for what was to come. On 10 May 1940 — the third birthday of my younger brother, Leo — Hitler launched his offensive in the West. Rotterdam was bombed almost flat, and the Nazis took Holland in a matter of a few days.

Life soon became very difficult, particularly for Jews. In February 1941, on the orders of Heinrich Himmler, 425 Jews were arrested and marched away. The people of Amsterdam then decided to go on strike in protest. Transport, offices, schools, and even banks closed. Large crowds marched in the streets in protest. The Nazis fired at the demonstrators. Some were killed, many were arrested, and severe punishment was threatened if the protest did not cease. The strikers had no option but to go back to work.

During the Occupation, the Germans called for people between the ages of 18 and 40 to volunteer to work in Germany. I believe my father, Jakob Vissel, decided to go, because he hoped his family would then be left alone. Instead, he was sent straight to Auschwitz and put to death on 30 September 1942. This was a shocking deceit.

My mother, Rika Vissel, went into hiding, along with many Jews and others also wanted by the Nazis. Unfortunately, she was betrayed and was put to death in Auschwitz on 28 January 1944. In fact, most of my family died in Auschwitz. Very few of them survived the Holocaust.

My mother must have guessed that she was being watched and, somehow, she found people to hide my brother and me. I was taken by a nurse, Mrs Riettart, to Mr Ebbe de Boer, who was a 'go-between' involved with the underground movement. My name

Before the war: Jozef Vissel with his parents, Rika and Jakob.

was changed to a very Dutch-sounding name, Joop Jan Visser, and, en route, my glasses were taken off to make me more difficult to recognise. I was, of course, not wearing the compulsory yellow Star of David on my sleeve with the word *Jood* ('Jew') in it. That whole experience must have been very traumatic for a little fellow of just seven years old.

Ebbe de Boer took me to a friend of his, Hendrik Pentinga, who was also involved in the Resistance and was in one of the banned Dutch political parties. I stayed with the Pentinga family until the end of the war, and was treated like their own son. I called my 'new parents' Oom and Tante ('Uncle' and 'Aunt'). They had a son of their own called Geert, and during my stay with them, another boy and girl were born. I quote some passages from a letter I received from Oom in 1954:

> When you came to us as a little boy you most likely did not know why and what for, but we knew better. When the first request came to take you into our home, the gentlemen had a plan to hide you in a very dark room [of the house]. I then let the gentlemen know that we would gladly take you into our family, but on the condition that you must have complete freedom as though you were our own son. That is, you could live a normal life and also go to school with our own son Geert like all the other children.
>
> And so you came to stay with us and we often asked ourselves why, and what was the difference between our son and yourself, when you lay in bed at night, both innocent children and both naughty boys by day.
>
> We tried very hard to be a father and a mother for you, despite the enormous dangers such things could bring, and we realised the double responsibility ...
>
> [W]hat does it matter whether we are white or black, Jew or Christian? Everyone, wherever they are in the world, has a responsibility, and that responsibility is to live as a decent human being and be civilised towards other people.

And so, I was free to roam and to go to school as a supposed refugee who had lost his parents in bombed-out Rotterdam. In doing so, I could unintentionally have given them away. I realised not long ago that the Pentingas' home was actually only about 15 kilometres away from my own home, and so I spoke the same dialect as the locals, and not the Dutch of Rotterdam. I now believe that all the locals must have realised this — but they all kept silent. That was incredible, as there was a reward for turning someone in. The dangers and the daring were unbelievable, as all of us — Oom, Tante, the children, and I — might have been shot, had we been found out.

I often ask myself whether, in similar circumstances, I would dare to do the same as they did. I also think of the trauma my mother must have suffered in giving us away to complete strangers. It must have been terrible for her, not knowing what was going to happen to us, whether we were safe, whether we would survive. I am sure it was still on her mind as she was being gassed. I understand that my brother Leo, who was approximately five, had a terrible time during the period he was hidden. He survived the war, but died in his forties, most likely as a result of those traumas.

I was most fortunate and, considering the circumstances, I had a good life. I had freedom, and there was adequate food, because the family lived in a small village in the country. Oom worked on a harvester and so received some grain to make bread, and he rented a couple of small plots of land on which to grow potatoes and vegetables. Just the same, it must have been an incredible trauma for a little fellow. I can hardly remember anything of what happened to me, even after the war. Many years are a haze to me.

Hiding me was not as easy as it might seem. After the war, Oom mentioned that towards the end, he and Tante were mentally exhausted from all their worries. The enemy were everywhere with their rifles and obnoxious deeds. Shells flew overhead from a cannon called 'Big Bertha'. In the roof, he was hiding rifles and ammunition. To top it all off, he was helping other local farmers and people from the underground in looking

Righteous Among the Nations:

Above: A post-war portrait of the Pentinga family, who sheltered Jozef Vissel during the war (left to right: Henk; Hendrik or 'Oom'; Geert; Joke; Jantje or 'Tante').

Below: The van Zutphen family, who ran an orphanage for Jewish boys where Jòzef lived after the war (left to right: Niek, Anton, Nettie, Elly).

after about 50 non-Jewish boys, aged 18 to 20, who were evading compulsory labour in factories in Germany.

At one point, Oom was taken to a German prison and interrogated for about four days. Why, I don't know, but they must have suspected something. However, he had a very strong mind, and obviously did not talk, even though he most likely came under enormous pressure.

That last winter, 1944–45, was the most terrible for the whole nation. It was called the 'hunger winter'. The Germans deliberately starved the Dutch by not supplying food or fuel. I was recently told by an old Dutch Resistance fighter that food was so scarce in the last year of the war that people were reduced to eating tulip bulbs. A small section in the centre of the bulb is poisonous, so they cut that part out first. People would give up their wedding rings, or whatever possessions they had, in exchange for a bit of food.

Shortly before the end of the war, the Allies, including the Royal Australian Air Force, dropped enormous quantities of food parcels over starving Holland, particularly in the Amsterdam/Rotterdam area, in what was called 'Operation Manna'.

Oom and Tante worried about me even after the war. Since a surviving member of my family did not want me to remain in the village after the war, I went to stay with an aunt and uncle who lived in the red-light district of Amsterdam. They had an eating saloon in a narrow but longish street that had more than 40 bars and cafes. At night, it was full of loud music and people laughing, crying, screaming, vomiting, and so on. Oom came to visit me and threatened the powers-that-be that if I was not quickly removed from there, he would take me back home. It was no place for an 11-year-old boy.

I was then sent to an Amsterdam orphanage for Jewish boys. We were very well cared for there. It was managed by a wonderful couple, Anton and Nettie van Zutphen, who had two children of their own, Niek and Elly. The van Zutphens had also hidden Jewish people during the war, and for this they were recognised with the high Jewish honour, 'Righteous Among the Nations', as were Oom and Tante Pentinga. Oom also received a medal from the Dutch government for his work in the Resistance.

To this day, I am saddened by the fact that Leo and I remained separated. A couple — friends of my parents — had promised themselves that if they survived the war, they would adopt a child. The child they adopted was my brother, and they then immigrated to Israel. Although we corresponded, Leo and I lost contact after some time, and I saw very little of him during his lifetime. As a result, I never really got to know him.

When I grew up, I went to Israel for a year, as a volunteer in a kibbutz. It was there that I met my wife, Frances, who came from London. On my return to Holland, I had to do a compulsory year's service in the Dutch army. Then, in 1958, I married Frances in England, and we arrived in Sydney during Easter in 1960. I worked in various commercial and advertising photo studios and also in a film studio, after which I had my own studio for six years. For the 20 years up to 1994, I worked as a photographer at Macquarie University.

A large collection of my commercial and creative photographic work, along with manuscripts, ephemera, news cuttings, and textual records, is now with the State Library of New South Wales.

Since retiring, I have been involved with an organisation called Courage to Care, talking to schoolchildren about the Holocaust. We use this as an example of extreme bullying, trying to make schoolchildren understand that it is an awful experience for the person on the receiving end. Our question is: 'Are you brave enough to do something about it, or are you a bystander when you see bullying occur?'

Postscript

A schoolgirl once asked me, during a talk I was giving, whether I cried for my mother when I was sent into hiding. Unfortunately, I can't remember.

A survey shows that when children are told to behave — not to play up or cry, etc. — because there is danger, they instinctively obey, and seem to realise the seriousness of the situation.

Recently, I was asked by a schoolgirl whether I missed my parents. I cannot remember my answer, as I was completely bowled over by the question. After some 65 years without my parents, they are somehow almost daily in the back of my mind, particularly as I am getting older and have more time to reflect.

One of the schoolchildren thought I must have had a terrible mother, because she gave her children away.

MARIA LACHS

Recollections of a hidden child survivor — Mimi

My mother, Rose Glazman, was born in the small *stetl* of Miedzyrzec (in Yiddish, Mezritch) near Warsaw on 16 February 1914. She was the youngest of four daughters, among nine siblings.

During the wedding of one of her sisters, a gang of hoodlum Cossacks disrupted the festivities and created terror for the wedding party and guests. One of her grandfathers was beaten and injured, and suffered the indignity of having his beard and side-curls cut off. That incident prompted Rose to try to leave Poland as soon as she was able to do so.

By 1938, Rose was being taught tailoring in Warsaw, making suits for both ladies and men. She was in love with a young man, and she suggested that they should emigrate together. He, however, refused to leave either his family or Poland. That was the end of that courtship. But Rose discovered that one of her co-workers, Richard Szeps, also wanted to emigrate. She persuaded him to take her with him. Her family would have forbidden her, as a single young woman, to leave home, so she convinced Richard to speak to her parents and assure them that he would marry her 'on the way'.

Having little money when they left, Rose and Richard were forced to find work to survive on their trek. It took them over a year to get to Belgium. By then, Rose was pregnant. With the German invasion of Belgium looming, they moved on to France, where Rose's baby was born in June 1940. I was that baby.

After the Fall of France, Richard left to join a special French Underground unit consisting wholly of foreigners who had escaped to France. Rose had found work at a Paris inn, the Maison Bleue, which fed and housed her. But now she had to fend for herself.

When anti-Jewish measures were introduced under the German Occupation, it became too dangerous for the innkeeper to house Rose and me openly. So, in lieu of wages, Rose's employer paid the rent for two different rooms for her, at two different addresses. One

War baby: Maria Lachs in Paris, in about 1942.

Mother and daughter: Left, Rose Glazman and Maria on the balcony of the Maison Bleue; right, in the park after registering with the Paris police.

address was declared to the police, to whom, as an alien, she had to present herself regularly. The other room was where she actually stayed after work, and this address was not disclosed to the police — hence it was not registered. That is how she managed to escape being picked up during the infamous *Rafle de Paris* on Thursday 16 July 1942. On that day, the gendarmes of Paris, acting on behalf of the Nazis, raided Jewish homes to round up the occupants and send them to huge holding depots, such as the Vélodrome d'hiver, prior to sending them on to concentration camps.

Rose was now extremely scared. Not only did she have me to care for, but she was also pregnant with her second child. She contacted Richard by messenger to ask for his help, and he returned on several occasions to help her move. It was thanks to him that Rose (now in her seventh month) and I were smuggled across the barbed wire at the border into Switzerland.

Once in Switzerland, Rose and I were placed in the Lausanne labour camp for mothers and babies, where Rose and other refugees sewed sheets and uniforms for hospitals, nurses, and doctors. It was there, on 2 October 1943, that my brother Henri was born.

Rose noticed that a lot of the other women were so traumatised by their recent experiences that they were unable to breastfeed their babies. Baby food in those days was not what it is today, and 11 babies died in this camp during the month after our arrival. When their babies died, the mothers were deported back to the parts of occupied Europe from which they had escaped. That meant almost certain death for the mothers as well.

Rose quickly realised the importance of breastfeeding, both for the survival of her own baby and for her capacity to remain in the camp. She also realised that if she could breastfeed another baby, she would save two other human beings — the baby and its mother.

During my mother's confinement, I once tried to take her place at the sewing machine, which I could hardly reach when I stood on the treadle, and which I certainly could not see, as it was above my head. The needle pierced my finger, and I let out a loud scream. To avoid another mishap, the camp supervisor put a young nurse in charge of me during my mother's hospitalisation. She took me with her wherever she went, even when off-duty. On one excursion to a haberdashery shop, the shopkeepers were so enchanted by the little three-year-old describing her accident and its subsequent treatment that they offered to keep and look after me, if my mother was willing. Rose was willing! Later, when they offered to foster 11-month-old Henri, Rose was delighted, because was worried that if her milk ran out and she could no longer breastfeed, she might be sent back to her country of

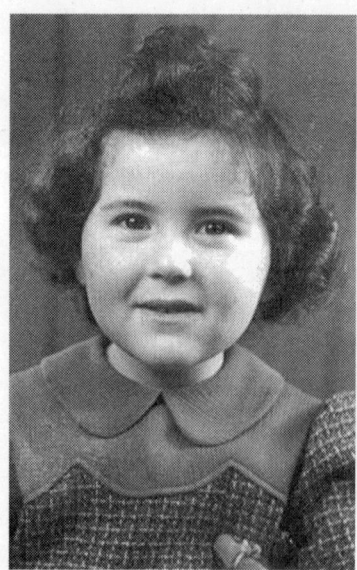

Maria Lachs in Switzerland, aged three.

origin, and probable death, as had happened to other mothers whose babies had died (because Switzerland declared itself to be a neutral country and only saved young babies and their mothers). This way, Rose could at least be sure that her children would be safe.

Rose had become so skinny that she had hardly any bust, but she still had an adequate milk supply. In this, she was aided by the extra rations given to her by grateful mothers whose babies she was feeding. She devoted herself completely to the task of saving as many as possible, breastfeeding five to eight different babies daily, depending on which of them looked the most needy. She went on doing this until the war finally ended and the camp closed.

After the war, Rose returned to Annemasse, France, (near the Swiss border), and attempted to pick up the threads of her life with Richard. But she noticed that he had changed: he was now a heavy smoker and a heavier drinker. Within weeks, that relationship failed, and Rose left him and went back to Paris with her children. There she worked extremely hard to house, feed, and clothe Henri and me. Sometimes, she would bring home huge bundles of clothing, far bigger than her, and later carry them back to her boss. She would be completely doubled over beneath the weight, in all weathers, sometimes slipping in the snow.

Even though Rose worked late into the night, there was never enough money. And sickness was always hovering. In 1945, just after our return from Switzerland, Henri caught the measles, and I caught them from him. He improved quickly, but I failed to improve. I was diagnosed with pulmonary tuberculosis and sent to a sanatorium, where I remained for almost 18 months. Rose no longer had anyone to 'help look after her baby', so she sent Henri back to the foster parents who had cared for him in Switzerland. He remained there until 1950.

Rose herself had five consecutive operations, over a three-year period, for a severe case of mastoiditis. It would have healed up much faster if she had been able to afford a better diet.

Because of my stay in the sanatorium, I was very late in starting school. When I finally did start, I was two years behind the other students, and my teacher thought I was a dunce. She did not strain herself with me, as 'you can't teach an idiot,' she would say. She was also quite anti-Semitic. In my class, there was a Jewish girl whose family had brought her up as a Christian. To escape the curse of a Jewish name, they used to pronounce their surname 'Itman' (in French, the 'n' is not pronounced, as in 'Can-Can'), but the teacher insisted on revealing her Jewish background by emphasising the 'n' and calling her 'Itmanne'. The little girl repeatedly asked the teacher to call her by her correct name, and eventually the parents came to repeat the request. The teacher refused, and accused the family of 'trying to hide their Jewishness'.

Once, when the headmistress entered the classroom to make an announcement, the same teacher thumbed her nose behind the

Henri, Maria Lachs' younger brother:
A picture taken in Paris, spring 1945.

headmistress's back. On another occasion, after our electricity had been cut off due to non-payment of bills, in the dark of a winter morning, I put on two different-coloured socks, one blue and one green. The teacher made fun of me, repeatedly, all day and for several days afterwards.

The following year, I had another teacher. Still not understanding arithmetic, I made guesses at the answers to my problems. Of course, most of my results were wrong, and I got no marks. But one fateful day, I actually guessed the correct answer, and I was so pleased to get some marks at last. I decided to try to repeat this event by asking the teacher what I had done 'right' to deserve my marks. She quite rightly asked me how I had obtained my result. When she found out, she had the patience to explain that one solves all problems in arithmetic by adding, subtracting, multiplying, and dividing. It was a life-altering revelation for me: from then on, I was able to solve most problems correctly, and became a 'good student'. I not only got marks, but sometimes high marks, and I became interested in my studies. I gained a prize at the end of each year, from that year on. But my mother was never able to come to prize-giving days, as she was so busy trying to meet her deadlines with the sewing.

At my primary school in Paris, we often played hide-and-seek during recess and lunch breaks. We would count down from 20 to one, and then yell loudly, 'Babi Yar!' This meant that we were about to look for the hidden children. Not till many years later did I learn of the atrocities committed at Babi Yar, which was a site of German mass executions of Jews in Ukraine. I don't know how this name came to be used in this innocent childhood game. But, obviously, someone had needed to yell it out, and had trained us all to do it.

My best friend at school was Elise Slivinska, who had survived Auschwitz. Upon arrival at that camp, her family had refused to be separated, and she had witnessed her father being shot dead before her eyes. One day during class, we had to read aloud excerpts from a book entitled *Hors du Nid* ('Out of the Nest'). Elise had to read the portion where the father is lying on his deathbed, surrounded by his family members, to each of whom he gives wise advice. While my friend was reading, her voice became more hoarse, less controlled, and I knew that it was a very difficult passage for her to read. As her voice became more quavery, I put my hand up, desperate to attract the teacher's attention and ask her to spare my friend from reading any more. The teacher, not wanting to interrupt what she thought was an emotional reading, ignored my gesticulations. My friend's voice completely changed, her face turned white and, with tears in her eyes, she roared, 'Why couldn't my father die like that!' And she stormed out of the room to sob against the school wall, away from prying eyes. I ran after her to console her.

The teacher did not understand what had happened during the class … and she never asked either of us.

One day, when I was aged seven, I came home with the *prix d'excellence* (which was second only to the *prix d'or*, or gold prize) and received a book as a prize. I was still downstairs in the courtyard when I heard loud sobbing. The sobbing became louder and more heart-rending as I climbed the stairs to our second-floor apartment and, at times, I thought I could recognise my mother's voice in the weeping. I rushed inside and found my mother slumped over her sewing machine, crying bitterly, completely oblivious of my presence, her shoulders and trunk shaking with each sob. In her hand, a letter trembled in time to her sobbing. It took me a long while to gain her attention. I asked, 'What's wrong, Mummy? Are you sick? What's the problem?'

My mother dissolved into tears all over again. I let her weep, and put my hand on her shoulders and neck. I could see that she was physically all right, so I waited for the deluge of tears to stop. I started telling her about my prize, emphasising that it was a most excellent prize and that she should be happy for me.

Mother looked me in the eyes and, between sobs, told me, 'I have just received a letter. All my family are dead. Even my parents' house has been razed to the ground. It doesn't exist in the street any more … From now on, Mimi, you'll have to be my father, my mother, my grandparents, my sisters, my brothers, my cousins, my aunts, my uncles, and all my best friends, because they are all dead — my parents, my siblings, my family, and my friends. From now on, I have only you.'

I was overwhelmed by the enormity of the request. I knew that I couldn't do it all. That was too much to expect from me. But to be her best friend … yes, I thought, I could do that. And that is what I always aimed to be, and what I saw myself as — her best friend. I helped her by sewing buttons on the clothes she had to sew for her boss. I progressed to sewing buttonholes by hand, something I did better than my mother, because she tried to make them too fast. Later, I even sewed some of her boss's suits and overcoats on her sewing machine after school. I tried my hand at preparing meals, cleaning our home, painting a room, making her a dress — the things a best friend might do.

In 1948, my mother found out that her two younger brothers had survived in Russia. She brought them over to live in her tiny flat in Paris. The younger brother, Simon, soon found himself a French wife, and their marriage was a happy occasion. The older of the two, Nachman, was already married, and had a baby and another on the way. He soon left us to fight for Israel in its War of Independence — 'a country for his children'. Rose found another distant cousin, Shimon, who was extremely depressed because of the loss of his wife and two children in the crematoria of a concentration camp. For him, Rose took on a mother's role, eventually finding him a wife with child, and organising their wedding.

When my mother was having her operations for mastoiditis, I was sent to various children's homes. Almost all of them were horrible, with lice, fleas, outbreaks of impetigo, and bad food. But the last home was an exception. This one was first rate. The Château de Laguette, as it was called, was a small castle belonging to the Baroness Rothschild. She had made it available for wealthy German Jews to send their children to, so they could live in safety whilst their parents 'tidied up their affairs before leaving Germany'. What actually happened was that the parents' assets were confiscated, and the parents themselves were not allowed to leave Germany. In time, they became victims of the Holocaust, leaving their children orphans.

The Château de Laguette effectively became a true (though unexpected) orphanage for these children, and also a refuge for those French children who, like me, had only one parent.

On Sunday mornings, a bus would come from Paris, and those children who were lucky enough to still have a living parent would wait at the large metal gates in the front yard, amongst the trees and bushes of the huge property, or watch from the lounge room to see if their parent had arrived.

I did have my mother but, because she was always short of money, or either ill or working, she could not come to the chateau to visit me. On the rare occasions when she had enough money, she would send me a small parcel with coloured pencils or a packet of lollies, which I would share with my best friend, Marcel Frydman,

Maria Lachs at the Château de Laguette:
From a picture mounted in the back of a mirror.

who shared my seat at school. So I did not expect my mother to visit, but I enjoyed watching the excitement of the children whose parents did come. I made a point of not watching the parents' departure on the afternoon bus, as it was always so sad.

Because I never really expected my mother to come, I was able to observe the behaviour of the other children. Several times I had noticed a little redheaded boy hiding behind tree trunks or bushes in the garden when the bus arrived. His name was Bernard, but he was nicknamed Bébère. He was a 6-year-old, with a congenitally dislocated hip that gave him a severe limp, for which he was often teased. This made him short-tempered and quick to get into fights, both to defend his honour and to assert himself.

One day, I was at the lounge room window, watching all the people gathering around the bus arrivals in the front garden. I felt a bit envious and lonely, thinking I was alone in the room. Then I noticed a pair of small black shoes at the bottom of the huge curtains surrounding the picture windows. The owner of the shoes was completely enveloped by the curtain, but the shoes had feet in them. I quickly unfurled the curtain and recognised Bébère. He was holding a piece of paper in his hand and looking intently at the incoming visitors. I was ten years old and bigger than Bébère, and I grabbed the paper from him. It was a photo of a woman. I quickly realised that this might be his most valuable possession and returned it to him, asking him who the woman was. Of course, at first he refused to tell me. But after he had made me promise to keep his secret, he told me it was a photo of his mother. When I asked him what he was doing with it, and why on other days he would hide with it behind tree trunks and bushes, he turned quite red and told me, with tears in his eyes, 'It's a very long time since I last saw my mother, and if she came to visit me, I might not recognise her. So I check every female visitor against my photo to see if it is my mother.'

I was totally overcome with feelings of compassion and sadness for Bébère. Being older, I realised that his mother was not coming back. He had been there since he was a baby, and since the war — this was now 1950 — most children had been sought and found by their relatives. I felt so sorry for him that when next I saw my mother, after she had succeeded in bringing my brother Henri back from Switzerland, I asked her to adopt Bébère, because he badly needed a family. She burst out laughing, with tears in her eyes, and told me, 'Mimi, the only reason you are here is because I am not able to look after you and Henri, and I have to work to earn money to have my mastoiditis treated. I have too many problems to even consider adopting another child.' I was deeply disappointed, but I promised myself there and then that when I grew up, I would adopt a child who needed a family, in memory of Bébère.

Sadly, I have never been able to find out what happened to Bébère, or what he became. I often think of him and wish him well. I have adopted a child in his memory. His name is Jaime, which means 'I love' in French.

My mother, who had brought Henri with her on this, her only, visit, left Henri with me in the Château de Laguette for the next three months. There was quite a story behind his reappearance. Having decided to immigrate, Rose had requested Henri's Swiss foster parents, the Meyers, to return him to her. She suffered much anguish when they refused to send 'their' adored child back to her, after so long. She had to go twice to Switzerland and involve the police before the Meyers would give him up. But finally, in 1950, we were reunited — Henri and I were together again.

Mother had begun to make arrangements for our family to immigrate to Australia. As she expected the papers to be completed soon, she took us out of the Château three months later to live with her, and we both attended schools in Paris for a short while. I was then in high school.

In 1951, our little family immigrated to the nicest country in the world: Australia. There, food was plentiful and affordable and, with plenty of work, Rose was able to save for a bed, a wardrobe, and a first home of our own. Henri and I were now older, easier to manage, and capable of helping. We were both able to get a good education: I studied medicine; and Henri studied engineering and, his passion, acting.

Eventually, the times of struggle ended. Rose had fallen in love with another man, Maurice, whom she married in Australia but later divorced — although they reunited, several years later.

Both my brother and I did well, and Rose often introduced us with the fond words: 'These are my wealth, my pride and joy.'

Rose's hard work, reliability, and persistence enabled her to rear and educate her children in the face of enormous odds. She never allowed herself to be stopped by a refusal or a closed door. While she often felt like giving up, she claimed it was her children who gave her the energy and courage she needed to keep going. But it was also her own great resourcefulness and industry that allowed her to save herself and her children, when most of her family perished in the Holocaust.

PAUL DREXLER
Under arrest

I was born in 1938 in the village of Špačince, in western Slovakia. Slovakia was an ally of Nazi Germany during the Second World War, and from 1941, it had its own version of the Nazi Nuremberg Laws. The 'Jewish Code', as it was called, aimed to exclude Jews from public life and, ultimately, to deprive them of any place in society. Most of Slovakia's Jews were deported for 'resettlement in the East' — a euphemism for extermination — in 1942.

My father, Eugen Drexler, was exempted from these measures because of his professional expertise. My father was an expert in wheat, and he represented the wheat growers of our district in their dealings with the flourmills.

By mid 1944, the exemption had run its course. My father's business was taken over by a so-called *Arizator* — one of the trustees appointed by the fascist Slovak government to 'Aryanise' a business belonging to Jews. This meant that my father was no longer involved in the running of his own business. A well-dressed man from Trnava, wearing a similar grey suit to my father's, came every day for about a week, and had long meetings with my father about the change in ownership. Shortly afterward, this man, his wife, his three children, and his mother moved into our house.

My father, my mother, Helen, and I were forced to live in the apartment attached to the house. Previously, it had been occupied by my father's mother, Regina; she now moved out to stay with her other son, Josko. The apartment was very much smaller than the main part of the house. It consisted of a living room with a small kitchen at one end, and a bedroom where my parents slept. I slept on a settee in the living room.

From my memory, the changeover was very civil. I enjoyed playing with the youngest son of the family, who was my age. The older son, aged eight, and the ten-year-old daughter sometimes joined us when we played hide-and-seek. For me, the benefit of the changeover was that my father, no longer attending to his daily business needs, was able to spend more time with me. He would sit with me as I did jigsaw puzzles and, now and then, he would put a piece of the puzzle into the right spot. That gave me a good feeling, as if we were doing the puzzle together. He would read to me and, best of all, we would kick my big red ball to each other. His warm, calm, and caring nature, together with his sense of humour, made him a wonderful father. I worshipped him.

My father did all he could to maintain a calm atmosphere, but I sensed that something wasn't right. In the past, my parents had often spoken to each other in German when they didn't want me to understand what they were saying. They were now doing this more than ever.

At this time, my mother would prepare a picnic basket, and my father and I would go on bicycle outings, with me sitting in front of my father as he pedalled. The weather was beautiful; the sun shone every day. My father showed me the different grains growing in the fields. He also pointed out the sunflower seeds, and the most interesting ones of all — the poppy seeds. He broke off a poppy-seed pod so that I could dissect it. It was a lot of fun. It was only

Eugen Drexler: A portait of Paul Drexler's father from about 1942. Together with 2000 other prisoners of the Nazis, Eugen Drexler was executed on the shore of Lübeck Bay, northern Germany, five days before the end of the war in Europe.

years later that I learned the real reason for these picnics: to avoid the ever-present threat of arrest.

I had turned six on 29 June 1944. The year before, when I turned five, I remember there was a big party with my uncles, Josko and Max, my grandmothers, and various family friends coming from Trnava to celebrate with me. This birthday, there was no celebration.

In September, I began school. The school was on the other side of the creek, about ten minutes' walk from our home. I didn't realise it at the time but, under the Jewish Code, Jewish children were not allowed to attend school. However, the headmaster was a good friend of my parents, and in my case, he turned a blind eye. I was fortunate, as he was the teacher for my grade. Most of the first day was taken up by showing the girls and boys where the toilets were! In Australia, many years later, the same thing happened when my daughters began school.

My school life in Špačince was short. It lasted only a week, for, late in August, the Slovak National Uprising broke out. Twenty thousand Slovak partisans, aided by 60,000 soldiers of the rebel Czechoslovak army in Slovakia, mobilised to overthrow the Slovak People's Party government and free Slovakia from its dependence on Nazi Germany.

The uprising depended on the Soviet army invading Slovakia through German lines on two fronts. However, the Soviet government regarded the Slovak resistance as politically suspect, and so did not inform the Slovaks of a change in Soviet strategy. Gradually, the Germans suppressed the uprising and, on 27 October, they captured the rebel headquarters of Banská Bystrica. This city, the administrative capital of central Slovakia, lies in a valley where three major mountain ranges intersect. The rebels retreated to these mountains, and continued with guerrilla warfare until the liberation. About ten per cent of the partisans were Jewish.

The rebels reminded me of Jánošík, a Slovak hero who fought injustice and oppression, and who symbolised justice and truth. I would listen to my father for hours as he read the stories of my favourite hero over and over again.

In the summer of 1944, after crushing the uprising, the Nazis ordered the remaining Jews of Slovakia to report to the authorities. My father didn't do this. Instead, we left the apartment, and went into hiding with a local farmer.

It was probably in early November 1944 that we were forced to go back to the apartment. The farmer we were staying with had become very nervous about the number of German soldiers in the area. We were only back in the apartment for two days before my father had made arrangements for us to go into hiding again. This time, however, my mother and I were separated from my father. We hid with one farmer and his family, and he hid with another. But, after only two weeks, my mother and I were forced to return to the apartment after the farmer heard our names broadcast on the local radio with a warning that the penalty for hiding Jews was now death. His own safety was more important than any money we could pay.

My father was still in hiding, and we were unable to contact him. My mother became even more nervous at not being able to let him know that we were back in the apartment. However, she had heard that a man in Trnava who had several motor vehicles was involved in smuggling Jews out of the area.

I remember very clearly my mother and I leaving the apartment in the frosty early hours, sometime after midnight, to walk to Trnava to contact this man. We were dressed in heavy overcoats with hoods for the cold. It was dangerous to take the main road, and so we set out through the wheatfields. We could hear the Nazis driving on the main road in their trucks and in motorbikes with sidecars, which had a piercing siren sound. It was very frightening.

It was seven kilometres from Špačince to Trnava, and I grew very tired along the way. There were various haystacks in the fields, and my mother suggested that I curl up against one of them and have a sleep. I don't know how long I slept for, but when I woke up I got a terrible shock, as I couldn't see her anywhere. I was very frightened, and quickly walked around the haystack. To my relief, I found her on the other side, keeping an eye out for Nazis on the road. From our vantage point, we could see a convoy of military trucks.

We arrived in Trnava at daybreak and made our way directly to the home of the man who was said to be smuggling Jews out of the area. The man told my mother that he couldn't help us. She was distraught, as the district was now fully occupied by the Nazis.

I remember being puzzled by what she did next: she walked towards a church. She knocked at the side door, and was greeted by a clergyman dressed in robes. He let us in, my mother did a lot of talking, and he asked a lot of questions. Then she gave him money, and he gave her what looked to me like official papers. Later, my mother told me that he was a Protestant clergyman. He had supplied us with papers to certify that we had been baptised and were members of the Protestant church. She was desperate for our safety.

I can't remember exactly how we returned to Špačince, only that we did not walk. By now, the Nazis were everywhere in the village, and they were actually billeted in the larger homes. This my mother found out in the most frightening way. Late one night, she left the apartment to cross the courtyard to use the toilet. To her surprise, a tall man in a black SS uniform came out of it. On seeing my mother, who was terrified at the sight of him, he asked simply: 'Jewess?' She told me that all she could say was 'yes' and, at the same time, she wet her pants. The Nazi shouted, 'By the time I've finished with you, you'll more than wet yourself!' Then he stormed off back into the main house.

Many years later, my mother told me that she became so desperate after this incident that, in a panic, she decided to take her own life. She had swallowed a whole bottle of aspirin, she said, when she suddenly remembered that I was asleep in the other room. Further panic went through her mind. Hurriedly, she got some warm milk and drank it, in order to vomit up the aspirin. She was successful, but it left her very weak.

The following night, my father was also forced out of his hiding place, because of the penalties announced over the radio. He returned to the apartment, and it made my mother feel better to have the three of us together again. But now, we were trapped in the apartment, and my parents were constantly talking together in German. They did their best to prepare me for the events that were to follow. Patiently, they explained that we would soon have to leave the apartment. We would be taken by policemen to a big place where there would be a lot of Jewish people, they said, assuring me that we would all be together.

It happened the next night. There was a loud knock on the front door. My mother quickly told my father to hide in the wardrobe, as she had the idea that it was only my father they were after, and not the women and children. She opened the door, and was confronted by two Gestapo men, very tall and broad, and two members of the local police. I got such a shock at seeing these four men at the door that no prior preparation could have prevented my reaction. I vomited.

The first thing that the men asked about was the whereabouts of my father. At that moment, my father stepped out of the wardrobe. The two Gestapo men announced that we were now under arrest, and that we should pack two small bags. Meanwhile, one of the policemen went to fetch Miklós, our coach driver. When he arrived, Miklós was ordered to get the coach and horses ready as our transport. One of the Gestapo men also ordered him to change clothes with my father. Both Miklós and my father were wearing three-piece suits, but Miklós' suit was baggy and well worn, whilst my father's was elegant and tailor-made. Miklós was extremely distressed at this order. My father calmly took his arm and told him that it was all right to do as they'd been ordered. Quietly, they exchanged clothes.

My mother packed the two small cases with our clothing. In addition, she took two little blankets of mine, which she attached to the outside of one of the cases. One of those blankets has remained in my possession to this day.

As we were being arrested, my other grandmother, Maria, suddenly appeared at the door. She had been being cared for in a nearby house, and she had been arrested at the same time. I remember that, whilst my parents remained calm, Maria was shouting loudly in protest.

We were all ordered to get into the coach. I had never been in this coach before. I was very frightened. Miklós, feeling most uncomfortable in my father's suit, was ordered to get up at the front and take us to the local police station.

When we arrived at the police station, my grandmother and I were ordered to sit in a room, whilst my parents were pushed into an adjoining one. I heard a lot of shouting at my parents, and then a kind of lashing sound. I was frightened. Later, I found out that my mother and father were stripped to the waist, and then whipped on the back by a policeman with a horsewhip. The police wanted to know where they had hidden their valuables. Did they hide them with Shulko, our neighbour and friend? They denied this. When my parents came out of the room after this harrowing experience, they appeared to be exceptionally calm.

We were all ordered back into the coach, and then Miklós took us to a police station in Trnava. The two Gestapo men escorted us in their car. On arrival at the Trnava police station, the four of us were pushed into a cell, where we stayed for the remainder of the night. My mother made me comfortable on the only bed in the cell, wrapping me in the two blankets she had taken to keep me warm. I was completely exhausted and slept until morning.

Next morning, we were given some coffee and bread. The Gestapo then escorted us to the railway station. On the platform, there were other families looking as forlorn as we were. They too were clutching small cases. We stood there for a long while. Eventually a passenger train arrived. Everyone was ordered onto the train. I sat between my parents, who made conversation with the people on the seat opposite. My grandmother, who sat next to us, was silent.

The train went to the nearby town of Sered. When it stopped there, everyone was ordered off, and we were marched to the Sered labour camp. The next thing I remember was that we, and lots of other families, were put into a large dormitory with double bunks. We were allocated one bunk per person. Soup and bread were distributed.

People began to change into their nightwear. I got such a shock when my parents took off their shirts and I saw their backs — they were completely black and blue from the beatings that they had endured in the Špačince police station the night before. Other people around asked them what had happened. My parents got into one bunk together. I was in a bunk opposite them. My grandmother slept in a bunk in front of me. I remember thinking it must be uncomfortable sleeping together in one bunk. And I fell asleep.

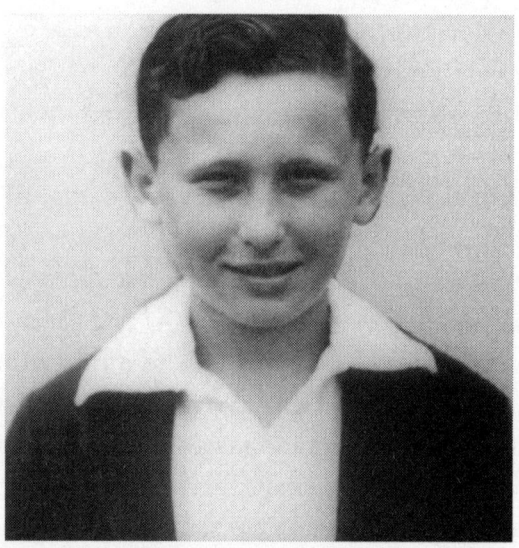

Paul Drexler, aged nine: A picture taken in 1948, Paul's first year in Australia.

This chapter has been adapted from Paul Drexler's book *In Search of My Father*, Sydney Jewish Museum, Sydney, 2006.

WALTER LACHS
Walter's story

When the *Anschluss* absorbed Austria into the Third Reich in March 1938, I was living in Vienna with my father, my mother, and my younger brother. The Nazis entered Austria unopposed, and when they marched into Vienna, much of the population welcomed them.

My father, Josef Lachs, who was 52 at the time, was one of 200 consulting engineers in Vienna. He had a professional status that is hard to conceive of today. If he was required to make a technical report in a matter for litigation, his report was accepted without question or cross-examination — a stark contrast to the practice of our present courts. He was addressed as *Herr Ingenieur* and, as a matter of course, my mother, Ellen, was addressed as *Frau Ingenieur*, even though she had no qualifications herself.

We lived in one of the apartments in a building owned by my father. It was in the centre of Vienna, five minutes' walk from St Stephen's Cathedral.

Late in 1938, the Nazis legislated to prohibit Jews, including my father, from following their professions. The new laws also transferred to the state all their valuable possessions, from buildings, paintings, and works of art to bank accounts and insurance policies. My family was also obliged to share our apartment with two other Jewish families who lived in the same building.

This is a record of three incidents that occurred between the *Anschluss* and my family's departure from Vienna for Australia in March, 1939.

First incident

I had just turned six when the Nazis marched into Vienna. On that day, my family and our relatives were on the third floor of a building that lay on the route of the German procession.

I can still vividly recall my mixed emotions on that day. When I first heard the sound of the approaching military band, my reaction, as a six-year-old, was a feeling of excitement at the coming spectacle. However, I sensed even more strongly the anxiety and fear of all my adult relatives in the room. Although not a word was spoken, this feeling completely overwhelmed my elation at hearing the marching music, and completely arrested my impulse to look out of the window.

I have never before or since experienced such a strong dichotomy of emotions.

Second incident

We lived a short walk from a Jewish school, which I attended for the first time in the latter half of 1938.

I had finished my classes and was walking away from the school, when a pupil from a higher class — a girl of eight or nine — followed me out of the school's front entrance. As she came out onto the street, she was harassed by four young boys who were shouting rude, anti-Semitic remarks.

Attracted by the commotion, I turned to look, and was horrified to see that not one of the many adult bystanders made any attempt to intercede for the helpless girl. What was unfolding before my eyes conflicted with what I had been taught: to respect adults and acknowledge their greater wisdom. In retrospect, this incident shows how the repressive regime had so cowed the community that not a single individual had the moral fortitude to protest. It also demonstrates the underlying anti-Semitism that prevailed in Vienna.

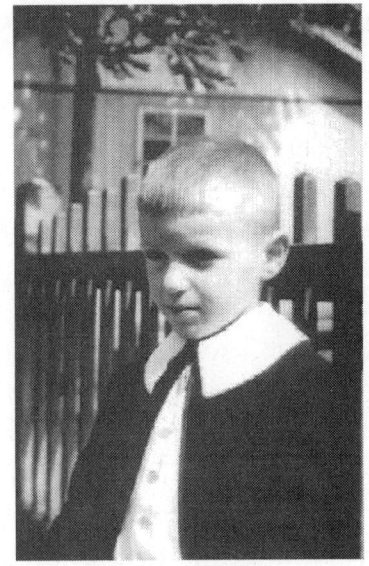

Walter Lachs as a boy in 1930s Austria.

Third incident

Shortly before my family left Vienna for Australia, my father received a phone call from Adolf Eichmann, a senior member of the SS whose activities were well known to my father.* Eichmann began abruptly, with a single word: 'Lachs?' My father corrected him: '*Ingenieur* Lachs.'

Eichmann had phoned to 'request' the membership list of the Jewish University Graduates' Group, of which my father was the president. My father refused point-blank to give him the list, knowing full well that the SS would be sent for him. He had faith

---

* Adolf Eichmann was the architect of Hitler's plan to exterminate European Jewry. He was captured by Israeli agents in Argentina in 1960, tried in Jerusalem in 1961, and hanged for his crimes.

in the delayed actions of the clerical staff.

His presidency of the Jewish graduates' group and our entry permit to Australia were both due to his exceptional ability as a fencer.

My father had been active in a Zionist organisation, the Jewish Bund, from 1910, the year he began his engineering degree at Vienna University. At that time, many Prussians of the officer caste attended the university, and their particular pleasure was to challenge Jewish students to a fencing duel. My father invariably fought on behalf of the Jewish students who were challenged, and not once did he lose. As a token of their gratitude, Jewish former students elected him as graduates' group president.

My father's fencing activities were cut short by the First World War. On completing his degree in 1914, he joined the Austrian army as an engineering officer, and when the war came to an end, he devoted most of his energies to developing his engineering career. Nonetheless, at the age of 37, he became the Austrian fencing champion. He was selected for the 1924 Olympics; but, in that year, instead of participating in the Olympics, he married my mother.

After the Nazi occupation of Austria, my father was one of the 200 active Zionists who received an entry permit for Palestine. At the same time, he received an entry permit to Australia from an ex-university colleague, one of those for whom he had fought a duel. Knowing that war was inevitable, he decided on Australia, as 'Australia was far away from Europe' — the same reason that many Holocaust survivors chose Australia as their home after the war.

After several harrowing months fronting up to the Nazi bureaucracy, not knowing each time whether he would be arrested as a Jew, my father succeeded in having all our departure visas stamped. Eichmann's call came just after he had booked our passage to Australia on a Dutch ship that was departing from Rotterdam.

The next day, my brother and I were diagnosed with measles, and the family was quarantined in our flat for five days. My father must have been distraught. Fortunately, we were still able to embark at Genoa, as the ship, the *Alten Barnefeld*, took five days to sail there from Rotterdam.

I remember the voyage to Australia as a new and exciting adventure for a seven-year-old. The family had to stay three days in Colombo, before boarding a second ship, the *Ormonde*, which arrived in Fremantle on Anzac Day, 1939, and then in Sydney, the port where we disembarked, on the first of May.

My father had only been allowed to take with him 100 Australian pounds, our clothes, and some furniture. We had arrived, but my father was unable to get a job, as his qualifications were not recognised and Australia was in deep depression. He and my mother, as their only way of earning money, had to hawk clothing provided by Jewish Welfare from door to door. I can imagine the insults they received for their broken English.

After our arrival, we received a letter from the caretaker of our apartment building in Vienna. He told us that two hours after we left our Vienna apartment for the last time, the SS had arrived to arrest my father.

It was my father's courage and foresight that allowed our family to avoid the horrors of the Second World War in Europe. For that, I will always be grateful to him.

PETER NASH (BORN NACHEMSTEIN)
Belongings

I was born in Berlin in 1935, two years after the Nazis came to power. That was the year the so-called Nuremberg Laws imposed drastic restrictions on the rights and citizenship of Jews in Germany. But my mother's father, Isidor Lewin, had served for Germany in the First World War and, as a war veteran, he believed that no harm would come to his family under National Socialism. So the family made no move to leave Germany.

Then came *Kristallnacht*, the 'Night of Broken Glass', 9 November 1938. All over Germany, synagogues were put to the torch, property owned by Jews was destroyed, and many individual Jews were attacked and imprisoned.

Soon after *Kristallnacht*, my family received an eviction notice. As Jews, it said, we could no longer live alongside 'Aryans'. The deadline for getting out was 31 December 1938. My father, Herbert Nachemstein, tried to get entry visas for both Australia and the United States; however, in each case, he was turned down. But word was spreading among the desperate Jews of Germany that you didn't need a visa for the Chinese city of Shanghai. Shanghai was an 'open port' — all you had to do was to get there, and you were accepted. My parents and my maternal grandparents, together with Heinz Lewin, my mother's brother, decided to make for Shanghai.

On the first stage of our journey, we left Berlin by train and travelled to Genoa. Then, on 26 April 1939, we boarded a ship — ironically enough, a German passenger liner, the SS *Scharnhorst*. Right to the end, Grandfather Lewin had been very reluctant to leave, and shortly before our departure, he suffered a heart attack. When we landed in Shanghai, after a voyage of three weeks, he was still quite ill. Sadly, he died just a month later.

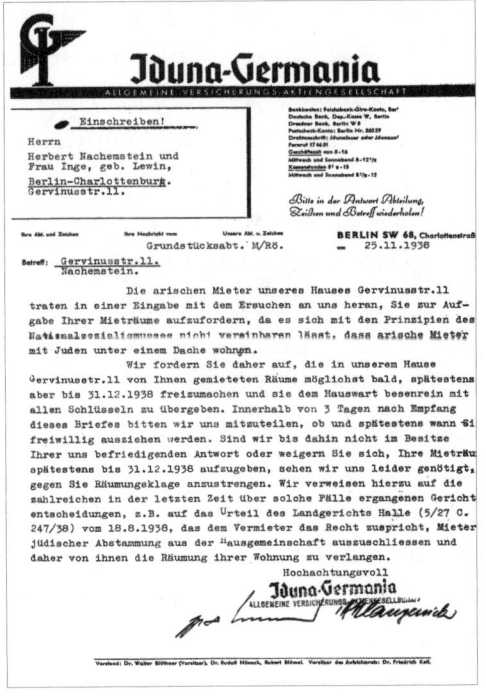

Notice of eviction: The notice, addressed to Peter Nash's parents by the insurance company that owned their apartment building, begins: 'The Aryan tenants of our building at 11 Gervinusstrasse have requested us to ask you to give up your rental tenancy, since it is not acceptable under the principles of National Socialism that Aryan tenants live under the same roof as Jews.'

Shanghai, home to generations of Jews, had a strong Jewish community. It was founded by a few Sephardic Jews who came from India in the 1850s. By 1920, thousands of Russian Jews fleeing persecution had joined them. By 1941, 20,000 Jewish refugees from Central Europe had also made their way to Shanghai, including about 8000 from Germany.

My family arrived in Shanghai with very little by way of goods or financial assets. We lived in Hongkew, a dilapidated area just north of the city centre that was the main district for refugees.

Initially, we depended on welfare. Every day, my mother would go and pick up our main daily meal from a *Heim* — a dormitory-style camp that accommodated about 100 people in quarters with double bunks and no privacy. But we didn't live in the *Heim*. We were lucky enough to have a room to ourselves in a kind of terrace house, with a stove, a sink, and two beds. It had four levels, with three rooms and a shared toilet and bath on each level. It was very basic, with no sewerage system. The effluent was collected daily.

My father could only get work for short periods. Because inflation was high, with prices rising every day, he had to go out hawking things like coal, coffee, and *wurst* (sausage). Eventually, he managed to start his own carrier business.

In November 1940, we were joined by my mother's sister Ruth, who had travelled, with her husband, via Moscow and the Trans-Siberian Railway.

Hongkew was part of the International Settlement — an autonomous, foreign-controlled section of inner Shanghai. It wasn't a very pleasant place: the streets were filthy, there were no trees, parks, or beaches, and unemployment was high. On the other hand, our education was quite rigorous. It was based on the Cambridge system, with lessons in English. The British were the most influential power in the International Settlement at the time, and that made English the universal language for the foreign nationalities. We never mixed with the Chinese. In my daily life, I only came into contact with other refugee children.

Apart from the International Settlement, the whole of Shanghai was occupied by the Japanese, who had been at war with China since 1937. After Japan attacked Pearl Harbor in December 1941, the Japanese marched into the International Settlement as well. Their German allies then insisted that they take action against the Jews, so Hongkew — the place of refuge — was turned into a ghetto. All Jewish refugees not already living in Hongkew were forced to move there, and movement in and out was controlled. At the same time, the Japanese language became a compulsory subject at school.

Most of the refugees thought of Shanghai as a place of transit. They had no intention of remaining there once the war finally ended. But when the war did at last end, my father's carrier business was doing well. The economy picked up, and baggage-transport, and the related area of customs handling, was the right sort of business for the times. For some time, we didn't push the idea of leaving.

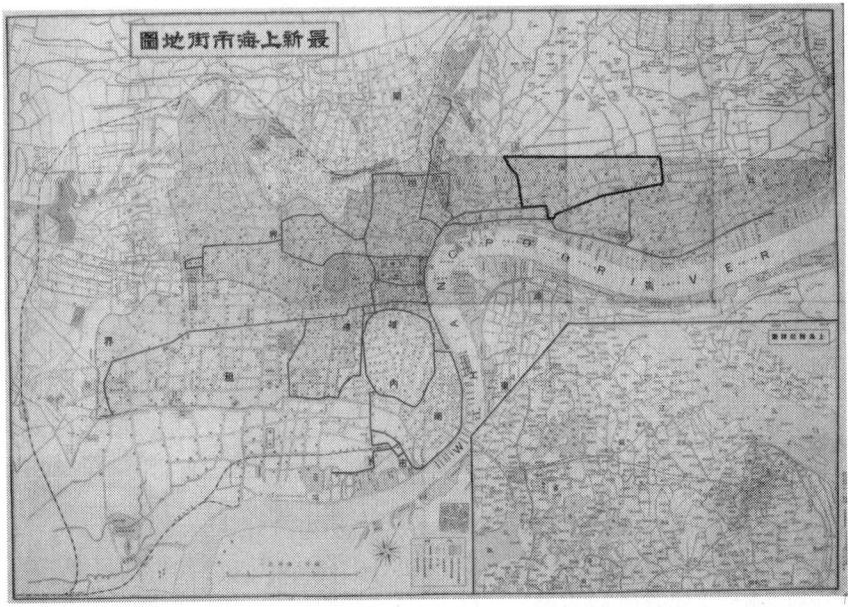

Japanese Shanghai: Headed 'Latest Plan Map of the City of Shanghai', this wartime map shows the location and districts of the International Settlement. The Hongkew Ghetto is outlined in black. (Source: http://en.wikipedia.org/wiki/Image:Shanghai_ghetto.jpg)

But soon, dark clouds were hovering once again. Mao Tse-tung's Communist movement was stirring sufficiently to cause a lot of concern about the future. That forced the issue of once more finding somewhere to go. We decided to immigrate to Australia.

There were many restrictions placed on Jewish refugees immigrating to Australia. Appointed public servants carefully examined the refugees in relation to their eligibility and fitness. There were restrictions on the number of Jews per shipload, and they could not exceed 25 per cent of any passenger load, irrespective of numbers sailing. The application form for immigration, Form No. 40, stipulated: 'Cross out whichever does not apply: Jewish, non-Jewish.' It made no reference to any other religion. Nonetheless, my father found a former business colleague from Berlin who had immigrated to Australia in 1938. He was prepared to sponsor us so we could get an entry permit.

In July 1948, six months before our departure, I had my bar mitzvah. There was only one Chinese guest: an employee of my father by the name of Umbo, who presented me with a gift of two silver vases. I still remember him explaining their significance: he told us that they signified the friendship between the Jewish community and the Chinese.

On 15 February 1949, we sailed to Hong Kong on the SS *General Meigs*, then switched to the SS *Changte*, which had just sailed from Japan with quite a number of de-mobbed Australian servicemen. Towards the end of our voyage, as we were heading down the Queensland coast, we stopped in Cairns, where I had my very first milkshake.

Soon afterwards, on a sunny day with clear blue skies, we arrived in Sydney. We sailed through the Heads into a beautiful Sydney Harbour, and docked at Circular Quay. My mother instantly fell in love with our new home.

Friends arranged accommodation for us in a rented room in a residential hotel. Later, we moved into a flat in Kings Cross.

Many of the refugees were in the garment trade, either making

Bar mitzvah in the Kadoorie School, Shanghai: Peter Nash is in the centre; his father, Herbert Nachemstein, is third from right; and their Chinese guest, Umbo, is on the far right.

clothing or retailing it. Initially, my parents worked as employees in a retail business, but within a year, they opened their own women's sportswear shop, Piccadilly Ladies Wear, in the Piccadilly Arcade, Pitt Street, in the city.

In June 1949, I started school at Randwick Boys' High. There were already quite a few migrant boys there, and the numbers continued to grow. That created such a competitive environment — the standard became very high. I had classmates who couldn't speak a word of English when they arrived, and one of them was top in English at the end of his first year! I was a good student, too, and did quite well; but the social side was difficult for me and, as an only child, I was often alone.

In spite of the high numbers of refugees, I experienced a general anti-'reffo' sentiment in society. My personal refuge was sport, and I achieved a high standard in soccer and table tennis at the Hakoah Club, a Jewish club in Sydney that sponsors a range of sports. From the age of 14, I worked my way up with the Hakoah Soccer Club, and by the time I was 20, we were in the top league.

Nowadays, when I meet up with my friends from Shanghai, we find we're like a clan. Ex-Shanghai Holocaust survivors are a unique community. Looking back, wartime Shanghai was a terrible place to live. But we survived — and only because of Shanghai! We were saved because we were able to immigrate there. And then, we had to start all over again, coming to this beautiful sun-drenched country, particularly to Sydney.

I am now a volunteer guide at the Sydney Jewish Museum. I do this because of the devastation the Holocaust wrought on my family — I have submitted testimonies to Yad Vashem, the Holocaust memorial in Jerusalem, for no less than 50 of my family who perished. My wife and I are keenly involved with genealogy. I've discovered family who also survived the Holocaust, and I help people find former Jewish residents of China. I feel I'm contributing to an important aspect of Holocaust history, for so few people are aware that Shanghai was a place of refuge.

Vases from Shanghai: The silver vases that Umbo presented to Peter Nash in 1948.

My greatest joy is my family. Our three children and five grandsons secure the Jewish descent and heritage that Hitler tried to destroy. I love the Australian way of life, and always feel there is no better place to live.

With no first cousins, I've made a point of meeting my second and third cousins all over the world. These 'reunions' have been very special for me. I still feel very emotional when I take groups around the Jewish Museum and tell them my story.

My parents brought their Chinese furniture with them to Australia, and I always have Umbo's vases prominently displayed upon it. They are a constant reminder of the strange and awesome journey that brought me here.

When I consider the impact of being kicked out of Germany, finding refuge in Shanghai, and then finding a place in Australia to grow up and develop, I want to share the story. I have to tell people that this is what happened.

RUTH RACK
Return to Leipzig

In June 2001, I visited Saxony, in the former East Germany. My first stop was Dresden, where I saw the famous singer Olaf Baer in a memorable production of *Tannhäuser* at the Semper Opera. But I wasn't visiting Germany as a music lover, nor was Dresden my final destination.

The day after *Tannhäuser*, I caught the intercity express from Dresden to Leipzig. The journey took just over an hour. In that hour, I relived another rail journey — one I made in 1939. I was then an 11-year-old girl leaving Leipzig, and fleeing Hitler's Germany, on a *Kindertransport*. The memories flooded through me with startling clarity. As I stepped onto the platform at Leipzig and waited to be met by a representative of the town hall, I was very nervous. I doubted my judgement in accepting this invitation from the German government to revisit the city of my birth.

On the platform, a tall, handsome man stepped forward to greet me. As he presented me with a single long-stemmed red rose, I couldn't hold back my tears. Then, as we left the station, I could see poles decorated with blue-and-white 'Shalom' signs in Hebrew and German. They were part of the preparations for Leipzig's Jewish Week, at which I would be a guest. I was filled with a mixture of curiosity and dread as to what lay ahead, for I would be talking to teenagers at school, in German, about my experiences under Hitler in this city, where both they and I were born.

Leipzig's location in the very centre of Europe made it an ideal base for business, and since the Middle Ages it has been known for its trade fair, the *Messe*. But it was largely because of the city's wealth of music and culture that my father, Bernhard Landesberg, chose to settle there. Leipzig had been host to many famous writers and composers, including Goethe, who based some scenes in *Faust* on a Leipzig tavern known as 'Auerbach's Keller'. The city also had associations with J.S. Bach, Schiller, Mendelssohn, Wagner, and Schumann.

Welcome to Leipzig: 'Shalom' signs welcome visitors to the city's Jewish Week in 2001.

Until the early 1930s, my father was a successful opera singer. He performed in the Vienna Opera, among others, before the First World War. In that war, he fought on the German side, and was decorated with the Iron Cross. He was captured by the Russians, who gave him special privileges when he sang for them.

After the First World War, he resumed his opera career. But in 1933, when Hitler came to power, Jews were banned from performing, and my father was thrown off the stage. He became, instead, an honorary cantor in Leipzig's Etz Chaim synagogue, and he went into business as a furrier in the Brühl, the main commercial street of Leipzig's old town. He did well as a furrier, and — in spite of the threat from the Nazis — he was able to provide for his family: my mother, my three older siblings, and me.

Nevertheless, the times were dangerous. In 1936, aged eight, I was expelled from the public school because I was Jewish. Bands of Hitler Youth roamed the streets. I was afraid whenever I was away from the sanctuary of home.

Then in November 1938 came *Kristallnacht*, the 'Night of Broken Glass'. Our home was smashed to pieces by the Nazis, Papa was taken away to Sachsenhausen concentration camp, and synagogues all over Germany were burned to the ground. In the streets of Leipzig, I witnessed murders and beatings, and hostile crowds screaming abuse, including the German woman from the lolly shop whose children had been my friends. We took refuge in the Villa Ury, which, in those days, housed the Polish Consulate. I remember the relief that flooded my body after the gate was shut behind us; I thought it would shut out that menacing crowd. Soon after we got there, I collapsed. I remained unconscious for a long time, and I still have no clear memory of the succeeding months.

In September 1995, the Survivors of the Shoah Visual History Foundation — a Steven Spielberg initiative — was recording and filming survivor stories in Sydney. I was invited to take part in this worldwide project. My interviewer was David Spicer, a young man who is now an ABC television news presenter. When David

Bernhard Landesberg as Wagner's Flying Dutchman, in about 1907; robed as a cantor; and leading the singing in Leipzig's Etz Chaim synagogue. Men singers are left and rear, with boy sopranos in the lower right.

Before the storm: Ruth Rack (in front of pram) with siblings and local children in Leipzig, in about 1931; on her first day at school, 1934; and with her mother, Anna Landesberg (below, right), and her mother's sister, Gina, in about 1936.

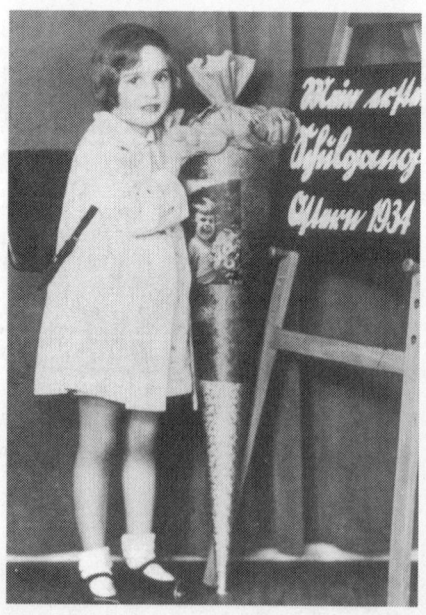

read the notes that I gave him prior to my Spielberg interview, he came back to me with this question: 'There is a gap in your story between November 1938 and May 1939 — what happened in those six months? That is, between *Kristallnacht* and the day you left Germany on the *Kindertransport*?' I had no idea — what is too painful to remember, we choose to forget.

Kristallnacht was a full-scale pogrom and the beginning of the Holocaust. We were never able to return to our home; we had to go into hiding.

So it happened that, in May 1939, my mother took me to Leipzig's railway station. From there, I was to be transported via Holland to England. It was the first time I had travelled anywhere alone. It was frightening. My mother promised to follow in a few weeks, but we never saw each other again. The *Kindertransport* saved my life; however, it was at the expense of my mother's life, for

Family wedding, Leipzig, 1936: The children in the front row are, from left, Ruth's cousins Bruno Richter and Puppy Kalfus, Ruth Landesberg (later Rack), and cousins Rita, Lotti, and Manfred Kalfus. Except for Ruth, all of these children perished in the Holocaust.

she chose to remain until all four of her children were safely out of Nazi hands, before attempting to save herself. When the war broke out, she was trapped. I felt guilty for benefiting from her supreme sacrifice.

At the hotel, I met other former Leipzigers who had come from Israel and the United States. I was the only representative from Australia. My daughter Roslyn had flown from Sydney to be by my side, but some of the other guests were accompanied by two generations of their families. It seemed that these descendants mostly knew nothing of their mother's or grandmother's early lives, and had had no Jewish upbringing or education. Some were wearing crosses. But the mother of one happy, united family remembered my own family — and she remembered *me* as a baby. When she addressed me by my childhood nickname, Rutele, which no one had used since I left Germany, I literally screamed with joy. I ended up sitting on her lap!

In the course of Jewish Week, we attended official functions in the town hall, where we listened to music and speeches by dignitaries. By arrangement with Rotary, local residents were our hosts for dinner. We also went to concerts at the Gewandhaus, where the Leipzig Synagogue Choir sang and played Jewish songs and music. These professional musicians, who are not Jewish, devote themselves to preserving Yiddish and Hebrew songs, and they perform them all over the world.

The program included a visit to the restored Brody Synagogue, the only one of Leipzig's nine synagogues to survive *Kristallnacht*. All the others were burned down by Nazi mobs, but the Brody Synagogue occupied a floor in a building that was shared with non-Jews, and so escaped the flames. It did not escape unscathed, however, for the Nazis still desecrated the interior.

I followed the Brody Shabbat service note for note and word for word, and it was a lovely experience. I noticed that the congregation was not all Jewish, and also that I was the only woman who could follow the service. This I owed to my Orthodox upbringing, and to my longtime membership of the professional choir at the Temple Emanuel, in Woollahra, Sydney.

Our guide took us to Pfaffendorfer Strasse, where my family had lived. Roslyn was fascinated to enter the building and see the spacious top-floor apartment, now beautifully restored. It was from that apartment that we fled during *Kristallnacht*.

We also visited the Villa Ury, our refuge on *Kristallnacht*. It has a small garden area all round it, where we hid in 1938. Today, the Villa Ury is a guesthouse, with a small plaque commemorating its role as a sanctuary. Visitors must wonder how 1300 people managed to find shelter on such a small plot of land. It's certainly consistent with my childhood memory of stunned, silent, traumatised people squeezing into a tiny outdoor area.

It is remarkable how accurate my memory of those traumatic days turned out to be. The Karlebach Schule, which was ransacked during the pogrom, is now a library for the blind. I have vivid memories of my schooldays in that building, when it was a Jewish school named after the Karlebachs, a famous family of rabbis.

We were taken to visit both of Leipzig's Jewish cemeteries, and I was able to locate the graves of my paternal grandfather and an uncle, one of my father's older brothers. They both died of natural causes, and were buried in conventional graves, and the inscriptions on their tombstones are still legible. Remarkably, this old cemetery withstood both the Nazi destruction and the bombing of Leipzig in the Second World War.

In the Old Jewish Cemetery, there is a large memorial to concentration camp victims, some of whom are buried there, under tiny stones. We were not able to identify the stone that covered the ashes of my father, but I know from witnesses' stories that in 1940 an urn containing his ashes was delivered to my poor mother, who had stayed behind in Leipzig in case he needed her on his return from Sachsenhausen. The story goes that she buried the urn in the Jewish cemetery, and it gave her a degree of comfort.

Anna Landesberg: Ruth Rack's mother as a young woman.

By then, she was a prisoner herself. After *Kristallnacht*, conditions grew worse and worse for her. First our home, then her liberty, her furs, and all her woollen and warm clothing were taken away. All her personal possessions of any value were stolen. She was forced to live in a *Judenhaus* (Jewish house), and to toil as a slave labourer in Leipzig's Children's Hospital.

My mother spent three cruel years living like this. Then, on 10 May 1942, 50 women and children from Leipzig, together with 196 men, were put on a transport to Belzyce, near Lublin in Poland. My mother's name appears clearly on this list. In Belzyce, they were all shot by Nazi execution squads and left for dead or dying; only one man survived to return to Leipzig. I know this from a recently published book, *Menschen ohne Grabstein** (*People without*

---

* Ellen Bertram, Passage-Verlag, 2001.

Gravestones), which records the fate of every Jew from Leipzig who has no grave.

During our visit, we attended an inter-faith service at the famous Nikolaikirche (Church of St Nicholas), with local Germans singing Jewish songs, and standing and holding hands with the Jewish visitors and new Jewish migrants from Russia. Jewish children, all girls, took an active part in the ceremony.

The service was very moving, and I was tearful, but I could not fully trust the emotion I felt. The girls and their families had come from the East, from Russia; in Germany, they found a comparative paradise, and their mothers were grateful for the higher standard of living. But my mother's father also came from the East. He settled in Leipzig around 1903 in order to escape persecution in Poland. He brought with him his wife and his firstborn child, Anna, who would become my mother. He came, as he said, to 'raise his family in a civilised country'.

Those words rang in my ears as I looked at the Jewish families in the Nikolaikirche. My grandfather fathered 16 children. All of them except my mother were born in Leipzig, and he himself was buried there in 1924. Five of his children died in infancy, but he never dreamed of the horrors that would shortly overwhelm the remaining 11 and their children. Only his three youngest — Sam, Sally, and Gina — survived the Holocaust. Gina, 93, is the only one still alive today, and she lives far away from Germany, in New York City.

Of my generation of the family, I am practically he only one who was lucky enough to escape from Germany and live to tell the tale. So, while we visitors were treated with every consideration during our visit to Leipzig, I cannot trust what the future holds for the little girls I saw in the Nikolaikirche.

Among the synagogues destroyed during *Kristallnacht* was the Great Synagogue of Leipzig. By the 1990s, the site had become a square that doubled as a car park. A worldwide competition was held to design a memorial for the site, and that memorial was

Outside the Leipzig Opera House: The Japanese tourist asked to have his picture taken with this Jewish girls' group, apparently thinking it was a Nazi youth group. Ruth Rack's older sister Charlotte is the group leader; Ruth, with hand raised, stands in front of the tourist.

consecrated during our visit. It consists of rows and rows of bronze chairs, out in the open, arranged just as the congregation's chairs stood inside the synagogue prior to 1938. There is one chair for every murdered member of the synagogue, with an empty platform in place of the *bimah*, the platform upon which the person reading the Torah stands.

This memorial was consecrated by the local rabbi, local dignitaries, and representatives from Israel and the United States. It was a moving service, with teenaged schoolchildren reading words of hope and reconciliation. These were followed by *Kaddish*, the prayer for the dead, and by a trumpeter whose music stopped mid-note, just like the lives that were snuffed out so many years ago.

The elderly locals in the working-class flats surrounding the square leaned out of their windows to watch. Now they have a permanent view of the memorial.

Empty chairs: The memorial to Leipzig's Great Synagogue, destroyed by the Nazis on *Kristallnacht* in 1938.

For me, the most important event in my return to Leipzig took place at the Rudolph Hildebrandt High School, where I was invited to address the students on my memoirs, *Book of Ruth: memoirs of a child survivor*.† This is what one female student wrote about our meeting, in an article for the local newspaper. I received it in the mail after I had come home:

> My interest is in the 'Living Conditions of Youth in the National Socialist Period' generally and also in this 'open instruction program'! This involves what is known as 'oral history' and here the eyewitnesses take centre stage ... The students and teachers involved with the project discussed it at great length. It could not have been otherwise — how else could anyone understand that period? The highlight was the visit of a Jewish woman from

---

† Southern Highlands Publishers, Dickson, 2000.

Australia. Ruth Rack, born in 1928, was a guest at our school and shared her memories from that time with us. It was a moving account and the emotion gripped each one of us. Hearing what Mrs Rack experienced touched us very personally, certainly, because we also knew that she was born here and the setting — Leipzig — is very familiar to all of us. When Mrs Rack returns to Australia, she takes with her all our thanks and our good wishes, but we keep a part of her memories here with us.

On my return to Sydney, I was driven by a strong desire to do something positive. It became important to me to erect a proper tombstone for my late father. By communicating with Hubert Lang, a young German lawyer working for Jewish restitution, I located the position of my father's urn, and had a proper stone put up. Now, future generations of the family, when they wish, can see that Bernhard Landesberg — their grandfather, their great-grandfather — lived. He will never be forgotten.

Anyone who knew my mother, Anna Landesberg, remembers her as a gentle, kind, generous, hospitable woman. She had a heart of gold. Gina says of her, 'She was beautiful inside and out.'

I only had my mother for the first ten years of my childhood. I am grateful for those years; they were full of love.

Throughout the dark years of air raids and war in England, when I was living with many different strangers, dislocated, abandoned, ostracised, and separated from the Jewish community, it was the traditions of home, the remembered synagogue music, and the beauties of nature that sustained me.

But the love of my mother, Anna, has nurtured me throughout my entire life.

EVA ENGEL, OAM

The other side of the moon: Vienna to Auckland, 1938

My father, Fritz Stern, came from an emancipated Jewish Viennese family involved in the Social Democrat Party. In Vienna, he had a successful business making aluminium kitchenware. My great-grandfather Friedman was once chief rabbi of his congregation in Vienna. His daughter, Ursula Friedman, became one of the first Jewish women to graduate in medicine from the University of Vienna. Another daughter, Frederika, graduated with a PhD in psychology and worked with Alfred Adler and Carl Jung. She was one of the first government-appointed social workers in Austria. Their brother, Theodore, was the first honorary lawyer to the Austrian Social Democrat Party.

Our family was always politically involved. Before the *Anschluss* — the German annexation of Austria in March 1938 — my father was highly active in Austrian politics. Much later, in Australia, I learned just how involved he was, and that he always went armed to political functions. My mother was a worker behind the scenes who made things happen, often sticking her neck out to right wrongs.

Proud parents: Markus and Gisella Czopp with their daughter Margarethe (Grete), in about 1910. Grete Czopp would become Eva Engel's mother; both Markus and Gisella died in Auschwitz.

We had a beautiful second-floor apartment. It had three bedrooms, a maid's room, and a living room; but it was in my bedroom where the family always met and talked. I suspect that my parents had the modern notion that children should not be isolated but should rather be incorporated into all the family deliberations. So I have vivid memories of the range of feelings that are found in all families. The radio was a constant source of news at this time, and everyone came to my room to listen. But I was unaware of what was so important. I only sensed the anxiety. It was, after all, 1938, and I was only six years of age.

My room also had the main source of heat for our home. This was a beautifully tiled Dauerbrandt oven that stood on four legs

 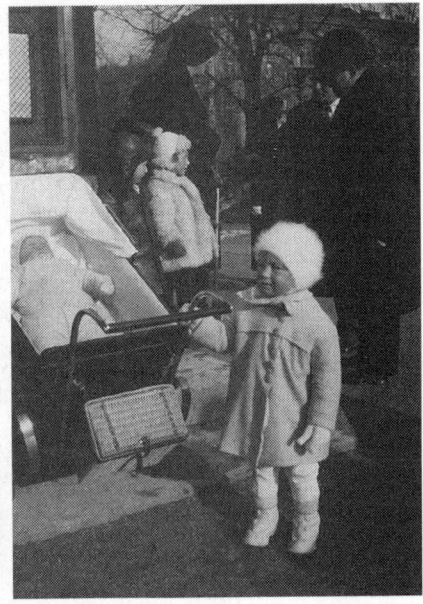

Vienna scenes: (Clockwise from above) Eva Engel in her pram at the Strauss memorial; Eva in a Vienna street; Eva's father Fritz Stern (in white coat) with an aluminium 'Zeppelin' he had built to promote Alumetag, his kitchen-products firm. The Zeppelin was pulled through the streets of Vienna in the heyday of the airship, the late 1920s and early 1930s.

in the corner, tall and elegant and only a few inches from the wall. We had a little dog named Rollie. He was a dachshund, commonly known as a sausage dog in Australia, or a *dakl* in Austria. He often slept in the warm spot behind the stove. How often on our return home did we hear the joyful thumping of Rollie's tail — although he did not think it necessary to actually leave his warm spot to greet us.

This clever little dog hated boots, notably those of Nazis in uniform. This gave me a terrifying moment one day, when my non-Jewish babysitter took Rollie and me out for a walk. We went downstairs as usual, with Rollie wearing his muzzle, because of a rabies scare. When we emerged onto the street, we found ourselves facing a group of men in boots coming towards us. Hundreds of patriotic booted Nazis had suddenly appeared in the streets since the *Anschluss*, and the instruction throughout Europe's Jewish communities was: 'Remain inconspicuous.' But Rollie knew nothing of this. He went berserk, and nothing we could do would stop him barking. Far from remaining inconspicuous, we were the most noticeable people in the street. I picked up the barking Rollie, and we ran for our lives. The fear of that event remains with me. We never again took him out in the daytime.

In July 1938, we fled Vienna for Switzerland. Before we boarded the plane, we were searched extremely thoroughly by the Nazis. What were they looking for? On arrival in Zurich, we took part in an informal lakeside gathering of exiles from Vienna. The adults were anxious. All their talk was of the Evian Conference, where it had just been decided that few countries would accept Jews as refugees.

But the children had no such worries. The focus of their attention was my watch, a little ornamental watch that I had pinned to my suit. It was the only luxury I had been able to bring with me, and everyone wanted to see it and hold it. Inevitably, one child dropped it into the lake, where it sank to the bottom. Disaster! My tears and the cries of the other children broke into the adult

Margarethe Stern's Austrian passport: Though issued by the Republic of Austria, it was stamped 'J' for *Jude* (Jew) following Austria's incorporation into the Third Reich.

conversation. How to find a small watch at the bottom of a lake in Zurich? Well, somebody did. The relief within me was wonderful. It was carefully wiped and re-pinned onto my jacket, never to be removed again, at least not on that journey. It has travelled the world with me since. There are still some rust marks from that misadventure, but the watch is with me to this day.

After making our way to Marseilles, we sailed for Australia aboard the P&O electric ship the *Strathaird*, landing in Sydney, where we spent 11 months. My father bought a petrol station; but in September 1939, war was declared, petrol rationing was introduced, and severe restrictions were put on private motoring. So when a certain Mr Littlejohn offered my father a job in an Auckland factory that made aluminium cooking utensils, we moved on to New Zealand, where I was educated. By then, I was seven.

There were not many refugees in New Zealand, but nobody would dare to talk about 'those Jews' or say anything 'politically incorrect' within hearing of my mother — she would give the speaker an earful that could be heard a block away!

Immediately after our arrival, our English was still very poor. We mixed socially only with other German-speaking Jews. At one of these gatherings, my mother met a woman who had escaped the Nazis by obtaining a work permit to become a housekeeper for a single 'gentleman' in New Zealand. Though beautiful and cultured, she now found herself in an untenable situation. My mother became her confidante.

We had thought we were far from the scene of the Nazi horror, but it turned out that we were not, for the New Zealand man was a key organiser of the clandestine Nazi Party in Auckland. His home was the printing and distribution centre for Nazi propaganda and the venue for secret meetings. The unfortunate woman had been an unwilling witness to all of this, and she didn't know what to do. Her employer was a harsh man, and if she said or did anything, she didn't know what might happen to her visa, or what effect it could have on her circumstances. She was living in terror.

My feisty mother came to the rescue. She needed to find an official who would keep her friend's confidence and have the power to do something. Where did she go? She went to the top, straight to the office of the Lord Mayor of Auckland! The Lord Mayor was conscious that any inquiry would have had to be conducted in complete secrecy, so that no suspicion would fall on the housekeeper. So he began by sending some officials from his office to visit the house. Two days later, the woman's employer committed suicide.

It was only much later, in my adult life, that I became aware that those years were fraught with anxiety for my family. Even so, I was an only child, and throughout my younger years I was always fearful of separation from my parents.

In New Zealand, life became far more normal than it had been in Vienna. I made friends readily, and I had a carefree life with few tensions. I joined the Zionist Youth League (ZYL) and was happy at school. But the anxiety about abandonment never left me.

It was when I was about 13 that a singing teacher singled me out to suggest that I join the school choir and also a separate group of madrigal singers. I was flabbergasted. I could not believe that she thought I was good enough. I was not a confident child, and had been convinced that I could not draw, when everyone else seemed able to. Now I found it amazing that I was chosen because of my voice.

At this time two things happened that had an important effect on me: displaced persons, as they were called, began arriving from Europe; and some other children asked me to the ZYL summer holiday camp. Young boys of only nine or ten, the children of displaced persons, also came to the camp, and the senior *madrich* (leader) asked me if I would be their friend and help look after them. I had no idea why I was chosen, and felt enormously complimented.

Looking back, I now realise that these two events boosted my morale to give me confidence to embark on many later adventures. I was aware of my parents' vitality and strength. I now became aware of my own strength and abilities.

Our escape from Vienna was instigated by my father's non-Jewish business partner, who was working in an enameling plant in Zurich, Switzerland, a branch of my father's Vienna-based aluminium business. The Swiss partner arranged a fictitious business conference in Zurich in August 1938. It was 'essential' that my father attend. He therefore had a legitimate reason to leave Austria for a short period of time. He went, and my mother and I accompanied him.

While in Zurich, my father sent job applications to many countries. His type of engineering qualification was rare and sought after around the world. Australia was the first to offer him a position that included refuge for my mother and me.

I recalled this period of my life when I worked with young people in the late 1970s and early 1980s. During that period, I was instrumental in establishing groups that raised awareness among young Jewish people who were not active in the community — the outreach approach. It was a time during which the awareness of the Holocaust experience became more public. In 1987, together with Professor Sarah Moskovitz, a doctor of psychology at University of California who was pioneering the study of second-generation and child survivors of the Holocaust in the US via so-called 'rap' groups, I created a gathering in Sydney of people who had been children during the Hitler regime and survived the Holocaust.

When Professor Moskovitz returned to the US, it was left to me to keep the group together. Over the years, the original people became the core of a support network that continues today. I am proud and honoured to still be an active member of that bonded group.

CHARLES KESSLER
A memoir of Lingfield House

My name is Charles Kessler. I was born in Vienna in 1937. All through the Second World War, I was hidden on a farm near Brussels. My father died in Auschwitz and, after the liberation, my mother could not afford to look after me. So, in 1946, the Belgian organisation AIVG (*Aide aux Israélites Victimes de la Guerre*, or Aid for Jewish Victims of the War) took me into one of their homes, a chateau called Profondsart, about 25 kilometres from Brussels. I stayed there for three years. In 1949, I was moved to Isleworth in Surrey, west of London. There, I began a six-year stay at Lingfield House.

Lingfield House — at 42, The Grove, Isleworth — was officially a Jewish orphanage for children who had survived the Holocaust. However, it did not feel like an orphanage; it was more like one big happy family. Alice Goldberger was officially the matron, but to us she was as close to a mother as could be. There were 20 children in the home, with three ladies — Gertrude, Suzy, and Sophie — who looked after all our needs.

Sophie was the miracle woman. She did all the cooking, and made some wonderful meals out of nothing. She was very practical, especially in making and repairing clothes, and she was very kind and sympathetic. I'll never forget when she 'unofficially' took me down to the Odeon at the bottom of our street to see a double-feature program of *Simba* and *Destination Moon*. I hope she didn't get into trouble.

Gertrude was the strict one, but she had a good heart.

Suzy loved music and played the piano. We were invited by a friend of hers, the conductor Walter Susskind (who had come to Britain as a refugee from Prague in 1939), to see him conduct a concert at the newly opened Royal Festival Hall in London. Through him we were introduced to the leading British conductor of the day, Sir Thomas Beecham.

My early years in Isleworth were very happy ones. We had wonderful summer holidays in Seaforth, Worthing, and Brighton, and I recall them with nostalgia. There was always something to do. Some of us played musical instruments. To keep us company, we had rabbits, guinea pigs, chickens, cats, and Teddy the dog. The garden was a wonderful one-acre plot where we could ride our bikes and look after our own individual gardens. There were also lots of fruit trees. We liked to pick the odd piece of fruit to eat, even though Sophie used to worry, as sometimes there was not much fruit left on the trees for her to make her wonderful desserts!

As I approached adolescence, I grew less happy, as I began to wonder what would happen to me. I guess if I had been in an ordinary family, I might also have grown unhappy at that stage, but at least I would have known that my home would still be there after I reached the age of 16. Lingfield House, by contrast, closed in 1957. Fortunately, Alice and Sophie acquired a flat in West Hampstead, and it was a great relief to us all. We were always made very welcome whenever we felt the need to see them, and it became a wonderful meeting place.

In 1961, I married Tanja Muench, who had been one of my

fellow 'inmates' at Lingfield House. In 1965, we immigrated to Australia. We have four children and six grandchildren, and live in happy retirement in Sydney.

In 1978, Alice featured on the British version of the television program *This is Your Life*. Thames Television spared no expense to have as many of Alice's 'children' as possible on the show. It was very moving to watch her reaction as we came in, one by one, from Israel, the United States, Belgium, Germany, Italy, and Australia.

The following year, the American academic Sarah Moskovitz began writing the book *Love Despite Hate* on the Lingfield House children, dedicating one chapter to each child she interviewed. Sarah travelled many miles to carry out these interviews; little did she know how attached we would become to her. Sarah became very involved with Holocaust survivors and, not surprisingly, started a survivors' group in Los Angeles. She was invited to speak to a group of Jewish survivors in Sydney. In her introduction, she mentioned the book in detail. In the audience was Litzi Lemberg, who was also a Lingfield House child. Sarah encouraged Litzi to start a survivors' group in Sydney, which she did, and she has been running it very successfully ever since. Tanya and I were informed about the group by Sarah, who suggested that we join it, which we did.

Alice, Sophie, Gertrude, and Suzy are with us no more. But in 1997, when Alice would have reached her 100th birthday, had she lived, Denny Muench (who was my wife's brother and also an 'inmate' of Lingfield House) suggested that we should do something to mark the occasion. It was decided that we would hold a reunion to celebrate her life. It was a wonderful party, held in Denny's flat in London. Sadly, Denny died two years later.

A few years ago, I visited the Beth Shalom Holocaust Memorial and Education Centre near Sherwood Forest, in the north of England. I was very impressed. The exhibitions are first class. I listened to a survivor called Paul Oppenheimer give an account of his life in Belsen. I watched the audience of children, who looked very interested in what Paul had to say. I spoke to the mother of Stephen D. Smith, Beth Shalom's founder, and learned about the reasons and the struggles behind the building of this house of peace. Tanja and I feel honoured and privileged that a small corner in Beth Shalom will be dedicated to the children of Lingfield House.

MAGDALENA LANGER

Silver city to bronze casting: the long journey of a child

I arrived in Sydney on the SS *General Harry Taylor* on 22 July 1949. My foster-family and I had come from the Glassenbach Displaced Persons Camp, Austria, via Naples. I was five years old. Having been very seasick, I was happy to set foot on dry land. We were taken first to Bathurst, and then on to Greta Camp, in the Lower Hunter Valley, where we would stay for several years.

It was a very hot summer in our new country, Australia. The sun was shining on the corrugated iron walls of the Nissen huts. The heat seemed to rattle the metal walls. They were too hot to touch. The ground was too hot for my bare feet, and the nauseating smell of communal cooking was all-pervasive. My guardians found it hard to adjust, for the heat was so intense, and discontent mounted in the huts. The difficulty of coping with the new rules and regulations, and the language barriers, were often stressful to them. They made constant plans to leave the camp by some secret method. But I don't recall sharing their discomfort. I think I was too relieved to be off the ship, on which I had been very sick.

I remember the isolation and the ostracism. And my household chores seemed to be endless, even at that young age. I don't recall speaking or understanding any previous language, and I learned English very quickly. That made me something of a translator for us all, albeit a limited one.

We never felt we could mix with anyone else. We left our hut only to get food or to go on some important errand. Of course, it was forbidden to converse with anyone — or so we thought. For fear of being overheard, my agitated, angry guardians always spoke to each other in whispers. To them, it seemed the normal way to communicate.

At night, the lights went out early, so I often lay awake nattering to my brother, trying to guess what was going to happen the next day.

The best thing about the camp, I recall, was the names, which are with me even now. The huts in one part of the camp were called Silver City; in the other, they were Chocolate City. One name was very shiny, and the other very yummy.

My first term at school in Australia was fantastic. At Greta Public School there was a wonderful teacher, big, fat, and jolly, named Mr Davies. I loved to learn, and was top of the class. But I had a competitor named George. This boy always taunted me for being a 'New Australian'; but this only reinforced my keenness to learn. I didn't want him to beat me, maybe because I was increasingly frightened of having to share Mr Davies' attention, which I craved so much.

One unforgettable day, we had to write about our family weekend. I don't remember what I wrote, only that there was a big kerfuffle as a result. I was devastated. My guardians transferred me to another school, which broke my heart. I tried, unsuccessfully, to cope with this. To this day, I still think of Mr Davies and miss that good man.

By the time I was in third grade, the family had become very dysfunctional, and things deteriorated rapidly. Inevitably, I developed the classic Cinderella syndrome. My intense loneliness and yearning to be loved were a constant interruption to my life. I remember being sick very often, isolated in hospital very often.

I turned to a big old oak tree for love, and I thought it loved me in return. It became a mother to me. I would hug 'her' and climb her branches, swinging on them, seeing the world upside down. I would take a leaf, and put it in my pocket so I could have her beside me. But at school, if I had to write to a parent, I would try to speak, but couldn't remember how, nor how to cry. It would read something like this: 'Oh dear Mama, do you remember me? Do I look like I belong? Have I the face you'd like to know? The skin you'd like to touch? Do you hear the pitter-patter of my little feet, the sound of my voice, my trembling body? Can you recall how I slept with my eyes open? Do you hear my soul whisper to you? The echo of my voice, the tears on my cheeks for you to wipe? In my heart is always you. I don't know who is me.'

My life changed a lot in my formative years, and for the worse. When I was 16, I left home, got married, and had children.

The turning point in my life came a few years ago when, with help, I addressed some major issues. I am now able to deal with the huge, painful journey that I went through as a child.

Clutching the documents from Austria's notorious Archives of Displaced Persons Camps and finding out what had happened to my missing mother gave me a sense of honour, as did obtaining the documents from Australia guaranteeing my right to stay. They affirmed that I, Magdalena Langer, needed this important certificate to allow me to be a citizen of Australia. They also stated that I was an International Refugee Organisation Alien person, to arrive in 1949 on 22 July, which also happened to be her birthday.

The photograph

It must have been summer. I remember the hot corrugated metal walls, the bleak light hanging over the kitchen table with a portable radio on it. The radio was the main focus. For fear of someone knocking on the door, we kept it on, softly, all the time — that way no one could hear us. National news time was, I think, 5 or 6 p.m., and 'God Save the Queen' was always played beforehand. We would stand up, and the paper blinds were pulled down so we couldn't be seen. I had to stand on a chair so that, if anyone checked, they could see my silhouette on the blind.

I don't remember any friends, or even conversing with anyone, except with a very few select people. One of them was a photographer. My guardians wanted him to take a picture of my sister and brother. The session was arranged for Sunday. The photographer had started to set up when he spotted me and asked who I was. 'Surely you are not with them?' he asked with surprise, as I was very dirty and uncared for.

'Well yes ... no ...' I didn't quite know how to answer.

'Well,' he said, 'if this is your sister, why aren't you having your photo taken also?'

I was aghast, and panicked. 'No, no, I am too ugly. My sister is beautiful. I will spoil the photo.' I was very scared at that moment, because I thought I was going to be punished for talking to him. But the photographer turned to my guardians and explained quite clearly that he would only take the photo if I were included.

They were pretty furious with me and tried to explain to him that they had dressed my sister especially for the occasion.

'I see that,' he told them, 'but next week I'll be back, and you can dress Magdalena also, and I promise you the photos will be beautiful.'

I don't remember the week passing, just the Sunday morning, as my hair was curled and pulled off my face to have a big white ribbon put in it. Tears were streaming down my cheeks, and I was beginning to wonder if I actually wanted this stupid photo taken, anyway.

I think it was early afternoon at Greta Camp when the photographer arrived and all the excitement started. This person was speaking to me, and I forgot for a moment that I was supposed to be ugly. I felt almost normal. My sister looked beautiful, and so did my brother; but, for me, the big moment came as I had my photo taken, just the same as my sister. I felt a great sense of equality for the first time.

The photographer lined me up with the big open space. He was just about ready to take the photo when I started to scream and cry, 'I can't have this photo taken. I haven't got a doll like my sister! It won't be any good.'

'Don't worry,' said the photographer, 'We will just borrow hers.' To my sister's horror, he took the doll and placed it in my arms.

There was an immediate reaction. I beamed, filled with all the excitement I could ever have expressed. On the other hand, my sister was furious, but nothing could dampen my excited little spirit.

'So, here's the big moment. Are you ready?'

I was so ecstatic that I nearly wet my pants. 'Yes,' I called out. The photographer pressed the shutter release and took my photograph. I didn't quite understand what had actually happened, but he promised to call with the results the following week.

The long-awaited days dragged by until Sunday. There he was, as promised. But when he showed me the picture, I couldn't believe it. It was as if my whole world had fallen apart. It was a long shot, and you could hardly see me! Of course, my immediate response was to feel shattered. I was desperate to tell the photographer that he too thought I was ugly, and that was why I was so tiny in the picture — so you could not see my face.

Alarmed by my reaction, he promised to fix it and prove to me that it was not so. He would bring it back the following Sunday.

By this time, I didn't believe him; but, when he came back, he sat me down and said, 'Now tell me you think you are ugly.' Frightened to cast my eyes on the photograph, I gingerly took a peep with tear-filled eyes, thinking I would prove him wrong. Instead came a shriek of absolute joy. I think it restored my trust in friendship. I remember that man so fondly for bringing acceptance and joy into my life for a moment.

Many years went by, and I never saw that photo again. I actually forgot about it until my foster-mother's death. Among the rubbish at her house was a dirty plastic bag ready to be burned. Something drew me to check this bag and, to my amazement, I found 'little me'.

The memory of this incident will remain with me forever. Now I honour this brave little girl by featuring her as a logo on all my important documents, business cards, and advertisements. That little photo brings me such joy. I remember, over 50 years later, that it was the only picture taken of me. I see her face in my photos in the 'Going Out' pages of the *Jewish News*. She is alive in me always, giving me courage and hope and a sense of belonging.

The sculptor

In 1990, I was introduced to the medium of clay. Originally it was a way of putting words to my silence. At first I was dubious, associating clay only with making mud pies as a child and sloshing my bare feet in it after a rainy day. Still, I felt very connected with the earth when I did it.

My first class consisted of learning to understand clay, and making a few household items. But I soon internalised the possibilities of this wonderful substance. I began to understand the spirit and language of clay, a language that has no words. Breaking all the rules (because there are no rules to break) was cathartic for me, enabling me to express and support my memories.

My first significant piece was a very large plate. It had a big centre representing a mother, and around the edges were little children carved with awkward little feet and bodies, hands holding tightly to each other.

Acknowledging this plate brought me to a high pitch of emotion. With tears streaming down my face, I picked up the unfired object and instinctively crushed it against my chest. In that emotional meltdown, I broke the plate into small pieces. Shocked, I rushed to rescue the child-pieces, and from them I spontaneously created 12 sculptures representing myself at an early age. So a dialogue of its own began to take shape, unveiling the silence that is universal, hidden, withdrawn.

In the spirit of clay, I found an internal language: sculptures that attempt to express the pain and horror of silence, that reflect fear, and that make a statement about the fragility of life. A narrative of my childhood was completed, each piece wrapped in its own momentum.

My experience with clay was limited then, but what counted was to express my memories. It became vital that I gave myself permission to express my memories in this way. The sculptures showed my experiences, tense and defined: some had vacant and empty eyes streaming with tears, some were hardly developed, and some were left unfired when they were too painful to complete.

The dialogue in these pieces is universal. It created its own language in clay.

My sculptures are now cast in bronze. I exhibit them proudly in my own gallery, the Gallery Magdalena, for the benefit of the Sydney Jewish Museum. My greatest honour came when Yad Vashem, the Holocaust memorial in Jerusalem, requested one of my sculptures, 'Mother & Child', for their permanent exhibition. This was the turning point that empowered and liberated the adult in me.

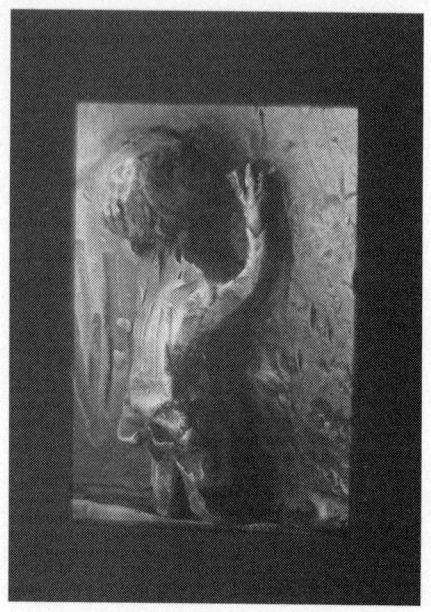

Three bronzes by Magdalena Langer.

NORA M. HUPPERT

Untimely journeys

The year is 1933. It is a typical cold, bleak European March day. I am not yet five years old; my brother Fredi is all of two and a half. Our lives up to this point have been very normal. After today, however, nothing will ever be the same again.

We're on a train with Mama's girlfriend, Tante Milochka, on our way to our grandparents in Kovno, the capital of Lithuania, the best part of a day's journey. As we stare at her, the train clatters and sways out of Berlin's central railway station, the Hauptbahnhof. Mama has told me that, as I am the big sister, I am to take care of my brother, because he is only little.

Mama has looked very worried since Papa suddenly disappeared a few days ago, without even saying goodbye. She told us that he went on a plane to Holland, and promised us that we would all be together again soon. As she waved *Auf wiedersehen* at the station, I wondered where Papa was, and whether he would come to Kovno to take Fredi and me back to Berlin.

Thinking of Mama, I look across at Tante Milochka. Her eyes

are closed, but I don't think she is asleep. Her lipstick is smudged on one side. I like this Russian lady, with her smart little hat complete with a short, spotted veil. She is fashionably dressed, like Mama, with high-heeled shoes and shiny silk stockings, and she is different from the other Russian lady I know. My teacher at the Montessori kindergarten is a very quiet little lady, gentle, but not as pretty as this aunty, and she always wears thick stockings with heavy shoes, and an apron over her dark dress. I wonder whether she or the other children will notice my absence and miss me, or remember me when I come back.

Next to me, Fredi is sleeping peacefully, and I remember the first time I saw him in the hospital. He was just a bundle with a small pink face. When Papa proudly asked what I thought of him, I replied that I thought it was a silly place to deliver him, and that I did not want such a helpless baby for a brother. 'This is not the playmate I wanted and was promised,' I said. Fredi was not much use then. He slept a lot, and I always had to be very quiet. I did not realise how he would grow and sometimes cause me much amusement.

I have no idea why we have to leave our home, or of the terrible events leading to our exodus. I will learn of them much later. For now, I am concerned with the present, with our trip to the home of my maternal grandparents and the place where Mama grew up. Fredi wakes up and asks where Mama is. I believe I have to know everything for him, so I make up some stories about the two cousins we are soon to meet. I hope some of these stories will come true. He sleeps some more, until eventually we arrive in Kovno.

While I know little about my mother's family history, I do know that her family fled westward from Russia around 1918, and acquired the house we were going to. The front of the house had an imposing position at one end of the main boulevard, Ozieskienes Boulevard, a wide street with a tree-lined footpath down its centre. Although the property spanned three house numbers, architecturally it was rather plain, with small, symmetrical windows and a gabled roof. Inside the roof was a spacious attic, allowing for much storage and for drying of clothes in winter. The attic was a wonderful space for children to play; but, sadly, it was out of bounds most of the time.

Grandfather and his brothers had been victims of Czarist pogroms and were sent to Siberia for some years. Their crime was being Jewish. Mama used to talk about sending them parcels to

Nora Huppert as a child:

Above: Nora with her mother, Anita Benjamin, in Berlin, about 1930.

Right: with her mother and Fredi, her younger brother, on holiday in Lithuania in 1933.

help them survive. Years later, during and after the Second World War, I would watch my Aunt Rosa do the same for her brother Fawa and his family. They too were sentenced to Siberia. Their crime was being capitalists and owning property.

My grandfather, Moshe Yitzechak ben Chanoch Zvi Dawidovitz, known as Isaac, lived in the Kovno house with my grandmother, Gittel. She was known as Olga, and was the daughter of Mordechai Aaron Rosenblum. My mother, Anita Benjamin, was born on 24 November 1898. She and her three siblings all lived in the Kovno house with their parents.

Anita was the middle sister and the most adventurous. Well read in classical literature and the arts, she left Kovno as a single woman around 1922, and found employment at the Russian Bureau of Trade in Berlin. In Berlin, she met my father, an idealistic young journalist who had dealings with the Russian authorities. The story goes that he had to marry my mother in order for her to learn proper German from him.

After sending Fredi and me, for our safety, to her family in Kovno, Mama cleared the apartment, and dispatched everything she could to her parents for safekeeping. Having done all that, she left Berlin, never to return.

Mama and Papa soon joined us in Kovno. The family was reunited, if only temporarily. But life was very different among my argumentative Russian-born, now Lithuanian, relatives. They had many intense discussions about the rising anti-Semitism. Some of them believed that Papa's passionate political activities and writings were somewhat excessive, and the danger vastly exaggerated. They thought he was a scaremonger, and believed that, as citizens, they would be protected. It was ridiculous, they said, to leave prosperous businesses, employment, friends, and families for an unknown future. It was Papa, they insisted, who was on Hitler's blacklist for his anti-Nazi political activities, not Mama's relatives.

I don't know exactly how long we stayed in Kovno. Papa needed to make contact with people where he could continue the campaign against Hitler's anti-Semitic ideology and activities. We left as a family, and I was glad of that. The year was 1935.

History was to be repeated for my Russian relatives, victims of a fate beyond their control. They were deported several times, and exiled in Siberia, with hardship beyond belief. Hoping one day to reclaim their property in Kovno, they survived, only to be hounded out again by the post-war Communist regime. They ended their days in Riga.

Bombs over London

On 21 July 2005, our Sydney newspapers carried the dramatic headline 'Bomb Explosion in London', which triggered a flood of memories in me. I remembered 1941, when German bombers dominated the night sky over England. By then, I was a ten-year-old refugee living with Mr and Mrs John Balentine and Susie McNair and their children on a fruit-and-vegetable farm in Kent. The farm was 20 miles south of London, and lay directly beneath the flight path of German bombers en route to discharge their lethal cargoes over London and beyond. As soon as the German planes reached the coast of England, air-raid sirens would begin to blare — the signal for people to move to the nearest air-raid shelter. In my case, the shelter was the cellar of the farmhouse, a sixteenth-century building called 'Hockenden'.

It was 18 months since I had been flown out of Czechoslovakia on a *Kindertransport* aircraft, leaving my family behind in German-occupied Prague. By the time I received my first diary — a present for the Christmas of 1940 — I had already acquired a sizeable English vocabulary. The diary was foolscap, with pink blotting paper separating the pages and hard covers proclaiming in bold print: 'Boots Scribbling Diary'. It was a good book to draw, scribble, or doodle in, and I decided to use it also to record daily events, the weather, and what we ate.

Nora Huppert in Prague: An identification photo taken in February or March 1939 for her evacuation to England.

On January 1941: 'all the windows are blacked out each evening with heavy wooden shutters or thick curtains and air raid warnings every evening and night.'

Typically there was a warning siren around 6 p.m., and an 'all clear' siren a couple of hours later.

For me, it was a regular pattern to go to bed in the cellar, taking a candle or torch with me, as there was no electricity down there. I did record the odd occasion when the pattern varied: 'I was allowed to get undressed upstairs in the bedroom and went to bed in the cellar.'

In the school holidays and at weekends that January, there were also many occasions when I had breakfast while wearing my winter coat — a reflection of the restrictions on winter fuel at the time.

On 15 January: 'it started to snow and we had bacon and eggs for supper.'

A few days later, before going to school: 'we had sardines on toast for breakfast.' After school, afternoon tea was in the drawing room: 'bread and butter and sponge cake.' The sponge cake was home baked every Friday.

February was 'very cold', and the night raids continued, as well as more daytime air raids. Lessons were often conducted in the school's air-raid shelter. This consisted of narrow underground corridors made of concrete and connected in a zig-zag pattern beneath the school sportsground. We sat on narrow benches on each side, with a space between just wide enough to pass one another. The teachers did their best to hold our attention as we sat in the chilly gloom, with the only light a single globe at each end of the zigs and zags. As we sat, we listened anxiously to the muffled sound of aircraft engines in the sky above us ... was that one of ours, or one of theirs? It was not unusual to have air-raid sirens all morning, from around 9.30 a.m. to 12.30 p.m. After that, we would return to our classrooms and resume normal lessons.

In spite of all this, there was always milk for us at morning break and a wholesome cooked meal at lunchtime: sausages followed by tapioca apple for pudding, or egg with bacon rind, followed by chocolate pudding. In the evening, at Hockenden, it was: 'grilled herrings and bread and butter with cheese or jam for supper.' By the end of the month, the raids were of shorter duration. I recorded: 'a warning siren at 8.20 pm and an "all clear" 20 minutes later; then again a warning siren at 9.03 pm and an "all clear" 20 minutes later at 9.37; another warning from 10.11 pm to 11.26 pm.'

On 19 February: 'incendiary bombs fell all down the lane and 2 HEs [high explosives] in Chaplins fields opposite. Mum Mc. came down the cellar and brought me and Lilly a cup of tea.' Lilly was the housemaid; she was soon to leave us to join the armed forces.

March was 'cold and misty'. Food must have been scarcer, as there are frequent entries mentioning eggs from the farm hens for breakfast or supper, and rabbit for midday dinner. In spite of all this, I was often allowed to join friends for a Saturday matinee at the local cinema. All are faithfully recorded, although few remain memorable — 'Conrad Veit [sic] in "Escape"; Ginger Rogers in "Kitty Foyle"; Charlie Chaplin in "The Great Dictator"; and "49th Parallel" with Leslie Howard and Laurence Olivier.'

May was 'still cold with brighter sunny days'. Air raids continued, though of shorter duration, both by day and at night. 'On the 21st I was told if there are no raids for a whole week I could sleep in my bed upstairs; and so it happened.'

August was school-holiday time, and it must have been chilly and cold, as I recorded: 'I sat by the fire in the drawing room, reading and knitting and we had lentil rissoles for supper; a full moon and I watched the searchlights in the sky tracking the planes — our planes, making for the coast, hoping all will return.' I do not remember ever thinking what their mission might have been, either then or later, when hearing on the radio news that a number of planes had not returned from a mission.

Arthur Askey was the popular radio comedian preceding the nine o'clock news on Friday nights, and I was allowed to stay up for this. At

The refugee: Nora Huppert in June 1939, three months after her arrival in England — a picture that was taken to be sent to her mother in Prague.

harvest time, all hands were enlisted, and I also helped with picking beans or fruit, then packing apples. Each one was first wrapped in a square of thin tissue paper, and then neatly packed into round bushel baskets ready for sending to the market in London early the following morning. I remember receiving a pay packet from the foreman at the end of the week. My first earned money — the amount is not recorded.

I revisited the district over 40 years later, on 22 December 2002. I was driving with Sue, a McNair granddaughter. 'Would you like to drive past Hockenden?' she asked impulsively. Feeling excited, I replied: 'Would I ever — I'll take a photo.'

The car swung off the A20 into Hockenden Lane — no paved footpaths here, but a few houses along the winding, hedge-flanked lane. One mile on, we turned into the Hockenden driveway, to be halted by a high, imposing metal security gate. Sue pressed the buzzer and waited for a hidden voice to ask who we were; no voice came, but the gate swung open. We drove round the oval driveway, now missing the large lime-trees I remembered, to the front porch, where a casually clad man with a friendly manner wondered who we were. Sue explained that her grandparents had once lived there, and that I had, too, during the 1940s.

We spent the next half-hour being shown around the house, which now has a National Trust listing. It has been beautifully restored, with modern heating, bathrooms, and draught-proof windows. The new owners operate a children's day-care nursery in part of the house and garden; they expressed an interest in knowing about the people who had once lived there. I paused in front of one of the many identical doors to say, 'You know, I slept many months down there, in the cellar.' Our host was intrigued as he asked, 'You slept down there? Would you like to see it?' And he opened the door.

The uneven stone steps felt familiar under my feet, as did the smell of fresh, cool, dank earth. The emergency exit to the garden, once a coal-delivery chute, was boarded up; outside, spring bulbs were beginning to press up through the soil. Gone were the old iron

'Hockenden', Kent, in 2002.

bedsteads, benches and chairs, emergency rations, candles, matches, gas masks, and first-aid kits. Our host had turned the cellar into a bright, neon-lit workshop, with shelves and pegboards along the thick, whitewashed stone walls. They now displayed electrician's and carpenter's tools, brushes, and pots of paint. I mentioned how it was when I slept there, listening to the drone of engines in the sky and anti-aircraft guns and explosions, some distant and others not so distant, as a bomb or a plane hit the ground.

Outside, the garden looked cared for as we took our leave in the drizzle and the chilly winter mist. It was a nostalgic experience for both of us: Sue recalled happy visits to her grandparents, and I recalled the security I experienced at Hockenden with the McNair family, in spite of the wartime conditions. Both of us felt pleased to see yet another family with children open their home to other young children, and to see the house maintained in the style and manner befitting its heritage.

August 2005: 'Further alleged terrorists responsible for the London bombing have been arrested,' the morning radio voice announced. I am somewhat reassured that, just as the skies were eventually made safe from enemy attacks in 1941, so the streets of London will be made safe once again.

Spreading my wings

London had still to shed much of its wartime scarcity and shabbiness. Yet by 1948, I was, for the first time, fully self-supporting, paying my rent for an attic bed-sitter on the fourth floor, with a gas ring for cooking, a washbasin in one corner, and a bath and toilet on the floor below. I had a magnificent view overlooking busy Bayswater Road and the quieter Hyde Park. I spent 45 hours a week working for a ladies' garment manufacturer, producing new designs and samples every six months. I enjoyed the atmosphere and the teamwork, all for the princely sum of one shilling an hour, with no thought of being exploited.

My social life was full and exciting, with a budding new romance. I had been invited to spend Christmas with Peter Huppert, who was living in Zurich with his sister Inge and her husband, Louis. Peter had started a medical degree in Vienna before the war. Now, with Britain crying out for doctors to staff the newly introduced health service, he had gained a place at Zurich University to complete the degree.

I was excited about Peter's invitation, even though my Aunt Rosa struck a warning note: 'He is too old for you, and he's back from the war and studying. What prospects does he have?' Yes, he was well over 30, and I was a starry-eyed 20-year-old, in love and very excited. I booked the cheapest rail and ferry ticket possible from London to Zurich, and then rang my bank manager to make sure my fare would be covered.

'I hope it's a sound investment, m'dear,' was the comment when I told the manager why it was important, and that I might need just a tiny overdraft for a wee while.

The sheer elegance of the shop windows in Zurich's Bahnhofstrasse amazed and delighted me. 'Quite out of this world,' I wrote to Auntie Rosa in London. Franz Carl Weber, the huge toyshop, displayed toys the like of which I had never possessed, including an array of beautifully dressed dolls, toy soldiers in a variety of smart uniforms, tableaus from German fairytales and literature, mountain scenes of the Swiss Alps with Santa Claus appearing from the clouds, gnomes and fairies, wood-carved castles, and villages with neat railway stations and trains endlessly running through tunnels and over bridges.

Further along the wide street, with trams clanking along the centre, the aroma of fresh coffee and chocolate wafted from the confectioners, with their artistic window displays of tastefully packaged chocolates. Towards the Limmat Quay, the air was clear and crisp, and church bells were ringing as dusk turned into night. Inge and I had been shopping at the market and the Migros food department, buying mind-blowing delicatessen items for days of feasting.

'You will enjoy New Year's Eve,' she said. 'We always have a big party with *Bleigiessen*.' This was an old custom where lead symbols, such as a cloverleaf, heart, horseshoe, and such like, were melted down and tipped into cold water to form new shapes, which were subsequently interpreted to forecast the person's fortune for the New Year. I loved parties, and I felt intrigued. 'I have to be at work on the first of January, though,' I replied. 'It's the annual stocktaking day.' Inge looked at me in disbelief. 'But you can't be serious?' she said. Rashly or otherwise, I sent a telegram to my employers, believing that they were also my friends; I was so sure they would understand if I came back a day or two later.

The party was great. Inge, a lovely, vibrant hostess, was popular with her friends and adored by Louis, a Swiss businessman 21 years her senior. They were generous hosts, with a wide circle of interesting friends. The food was always lavish, and accompanied by top French wines. The conversation was often very political and very familiar to my ears. However, what was new to me was the open, passionate discussion about suicide, which was treated as a criminal act at that time in England. 'Was this fair, or should it be legalised?' How would I know? I had hardly reached voting age, and these things never entered my head. It was many years before

I understood the implications of that discussion — only when I learned more about the family history and its three generations of suicides. Peter and Inge's grandparents (both their mother's and their father's parents, who lived in Vienna) had died at their own hands, when their post-First World War old-age pension in Austria could not even buy them a loaf of bread. Peter and Inge's parents did escape to Italy, following the Nazi annexation of Austria, where their father, fearing the worst, could see no way of surviving and, similarly, died at his own hands. Their mother found sanctuary in a convent with a group of nuns, and survived the Holocaust to enjoy some good years with her daughter, living to see her two grandchildren. Both Inge and Peter were to die at their own hands, sufferers of prolonged medical conditions.

Meanwhile, Louis had realised that I was an inexperienced party drinker, and advised me to stick to whisky diluted with soda water, with perhaps a little white wine or champagne with the meal later on. He assured me I could keep that up late into the night and still have a clear head the next day. I have been eternally grateful for this advice.

A day or two later, I boarded the train, having considerably overspent my budget, and fronted up at work, still basking in a holiday after-glow. The greeting I received was cold, to say the least. I was informed that my job was terminated, since I had let my employers down and behaved most irresponsibly, and they 'could not possibly retain anyone so unreliable'. I collected my large cutting shears, tape measure, and other tools of trade, together with my employment cards, and was shown the door. I walked to the bus stop feeling rejected and despondent, and uncertain as to how I would find another job and pay my rent — and the wee overdraft.

However, it had been a truly memorable New Year's Eve, and time would tell if it had been a good investment. As the hour struck midnight, the church bells had pealed all around, and we'd opened all the doors and stood on the balcony to welcome in the New Year. I had hugged Peter and sipped French champagne. We had cast our fortunes for the year. I'd held the spoon with my lead thimble over a flame, and watched it melt, forming strange new shapes as it splashed into a bowl of ice-cold water. Inge was the expert at interpreting the newly cast lead. For me, she had predicted travel, as the shape looked like a ship or train, and the little drops on it meant money was coming my way. I was pleased with such good news ... until she added, 'Sometimes it also means tears or sorrow.'

The ring

I inherited the ring, my one and only piece of family-heirloom jewellery, a thin thread connecting me to past generations of loyal, much-loved Jewish women. As jewellery goes, this piece is totally non-ostentatious and, hence, hard to describe. Some would call it almost insignificant: a thin, well-worn gold band, a shade thicker towards the front, with a raised centre-stone of vivid turquoise less than half a centimetre in diameter, held in place by a thin white-gold ring. This in turn is encrusted with a scalloped circle of 16 tiny diamonds, each held in its own claw-setting of white gold with a yellow-gold base.

For a woman, every ring has a story. This ring once belonged to my Aunt Toni, a much-loved woman, who received it from Hugo Bing as a token of friendship early in their relationship. Toni and Hugo were married in Berlin towards the end of the First World War, in 1917 or 1918. Toni was the eldest of four children, and she and Hugo were considered by all her extended family in Berlin, and by the assimilated Jewish community, to be 'a very good match'.

Hugo was a respected, rising financier with a seat on the Berlin Stock Exchange, where many of his Jewish colleagues had had their services abruptly and unceremoniously terminated.[*] He adored his young wife Toni, a petite, vivacious, if somewhat dumpy, lady

---

[*] Gordon, Sarah Ann, *Hitler, Germans, and the Jewish Question*, Princeton University Press, 1984, p. 12.

with regal bearing and progressive ideas. Prior to her marriage, she had worked as a personal secretary for a solicitor. For much of their marriage, Hugo lavished beautiful, exquisitely designed and crafted items of jewellery on her. These pieces, I am told, became quite legendary, and attracted comment in magazines and the daily papers whenever Toni and Hugo were seen at a concert, the opera, a play, or a government reception.

Toni and Hugo's home was elegant and tastefully furnished with dark, solid, carved Jacobean furniture. Persian carpets adorned the floors, and original oil paintings hung on the walls. They had two children: Bubi, the favourite, and Ruth, nicknamed *der Krümmel* (the Crumb).

Bubi and Ruth, my cousins, were aged around 16 and 14, respectively, when the family's first disaster occurred. Hugo made one big mistake that cost him his career: he made a high-risk investment using not his own funds but clients' funds that had been entrusted to him for more conservative investments. This was, of course, totally illegal by the rules of his profession and position. Hugo lost the gamble and could not cover his debts. The story broke, and Hugo was used as example to justify the dismissals of Jews at the Berlin Stock Exchange; the Nazi press and media made the most of the scandal. Hugo was disgraced and singled out, to justify the dismissals of all Jews working at the Berlin Stock Exchange.

Toni stood by her man. She requested an interview with the director of the Berlin Stock Exchange. Taking her jewellery box with its precious contents, she placed it squarely in front of him on the desk, and respectfully asked: '*Herr Direktor*, please tell me, will this cover my husband's debts?'

It did. However, before handing over the box and its precious contents, she removed one ring — the one of least value, a single turquoise stone, insignificant among the large diamonds and crafted rubies, the sapphires and emeralds set in gold, silver, and platinum.

Although Hugo's honour was restored, it made no difference and was of no interest to any news editor. But the crisis affected his health. Toni now had to find ways of supporting the family, and this at a time of rising anti-Semitism. As an accomplished hostess, she decided to extend her hospitality skills and take in well-heeled boarders. Hugo supported this as best he could, loving and admiring his Toni. It must have been a hard adjustment for both of them.

Disasters often come in multiples, and another blow fell when Toni and Hugo's favourite child, Bubi, contracted meningitis at the age of 17. No antibiotic or other remedies were available when Bubi died in 1935. His sister, Ruth, recalled weekly family processions, led by Toni, bearing flowers. 'The pilgrimage to Bubi's grave,' she called it.

Hugo never recovered his robust health and energy. He died of a heart attack in 1940, aged 63. Both Hugo and Bubi are buried in the Jewish section of the Berlin cemetery. Ruth, the only survivor, was sent to England in 1938, hoping her mother would soon join her. She went equipped with a trunk full of household linen, silver Sabbath candle holders, a complete Rosenthal china dinner set for 12, a few family photographs ... and this ring from her mother.

Toni never made it out of Germany. She was deported, we know not where, as were many other Berlin Jews, to end up as victims of Hitler's Holocaust.

Ruth married and immigrated to Sydney, where she enjoyed more peaceful times and became instrumental in my coming to Australia. She died in 1981. And I inherited the ring, my one tangible link to generations of loyal, much-loved women. It is my good fortune to count myself among them.

Full circle

Like many child survivors, I often asked myself, 'Why me?' Why was I destined to survive, and not anyone else from my entire family? How did I come to be on that first *Kindertransport* from Prague on 14 March 1939, just 24 hours before German troops occupied all of Czechoslovakia without a single shot being fired?

There were no answers. I stopped asking, and got on with life as best I could. For many years, I did not return to Berlin or to Prague, the scenes of my childhood, although these questions haunted me periodically over the years.

A decade of widowhood and a new partner, a much-travelled New Zealander, led me to a chance visit to Prague in 2002. My partner had never been there, and wanted to visit a female relation who had lived there for many years. One of her friends, the New Zealand Honorary Consul, asked me, over a meal in a good restaurant, 'What brings you to Prague?'

Somewhat shyly, I replied, 'I used to go to school here — the German school.'

The lady looked surprised, and I continued, 'I left 24 hours before the German *Einmarsch* — on a plane with other children.'

The lady's eyes twinkled and, with a broad smile, she announced, 'Why of course, you must be one of Nicholas Winton's children. Your name would be on the list.'

I had never heard of this man, and felt confused. All I knew was that my mother had gone to every organisation she could find to put her children's names on their lists, in the hope of getting them to a place of safety. I never knew who or what organisation was instrumental in this, only the name of the family I joined on my arrival in England. At that time, the only question I was interested in was, 'What has happened to my mother and all the others?'

By the end of lunch, I knew all about Nicholas Winton and his rescue operation of some 669 children. The first of them were flown out on the same plane as me, and the others were rescued in a series of seven rail transports in the months leading up to the outbreak of the Second World War.

I was determined to meet my rescuer. In December 2002, I did so, at the British premiere of the film *The Power of Good*. The film told the story of this amazing man who has received honours and accolades from many countries. I could not help but ask him, 'What *made* you do it?'

He pondered, and humbly replied, 'I was there, and it needed to be done. No one was doing anything about the children ... I was just there, you see.' I cannot recall his exact words, but the meaning is clear enough: It is not enough in today's world merely to lead an exemplary life and do no wrong. It is incumbent on each one of us to actively take responsibility and to care for the less privileged and the disadvantaged. It was a moving, memorable meeting with a significant *mensch*.

Rescued and Rescuer: Nora Huppert visits Sir Nicholas Winton at his home near Maidenhead, England, in 2006. (Picture: Vera Gissing.)

'Spreading my wings' and 'The ring' are edited excerpts from Nora M. Huppert, *Holocaust to Haven: five countries, five migrations*, self-published, 2002.

HALINA ROBINSON
Survivor

Sitting in a sun-drenched lounge room, I gaze at ocean waves pounding Manly beach. The view from my window is beautiful; but my thoughts are of the days following the end of the Second World War. Then, I felt like a traveller from outer space who returns too late to find any of his contemporaries alive.

My maternal great-grandmother had 142 descendants. I knew and loved them all. By 1945, it seemed I was the sole survivor. My schoolteachers and classmates had vanished as well. All the institutions and familiar structures of my early life had ceased to exist.

In that vanished world, the world before the Holocaust, I attended the Jewish primary school in Kalisz, in western Poland. I completed five grades. Then came the German invasion. Jews in occupied Poland were stripped of everything but the bare minimum of personal effects. From early in 1940, we were herded into ghettoes, where we faced a slow death from starvation and disease. For Gentiles, harbouring a fugitive from a Jewish ghetto

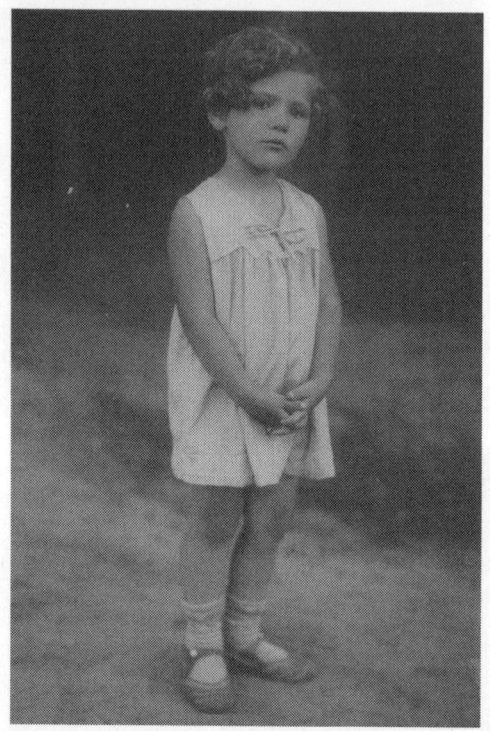

Halinka Trachtenberg (later Halina Robinson), aged four:
A portrait for her maternal grandmother.

carried the death penalty. So did offering even the slightest assistance to a Jew. In occupied Poland, and only in occupied Poland, the penalty often extended to a benefactor's whole family or even to the entire neighbourhood.

I spent almost two years in the Warsaw Ghetto. At one point, the regulations said that no one younger than 16 or older than 60 was allowed to remain there. I wasn't yet 16, but my documents were altered to allow me to stay.

Towards the end of my time in the ghetto, I worked the night shift in the 'shop' run by the German textile firm Walter Toebbens. The work was sheer drudgery. We would be thrown a bundle of German uniforms that had come straight from the Eastern Front. We had to inspect them thoroughly. If there were parts missing, we threw them into a box to be given to tailors who would sew on new collars, pockets, or cuffs. If they were in one piece, we just sewed on any loose buttons or made loops for fastenings.

The uniforms were heavy. Often they were wet, stained with blood and excrement, or infected with lice. Working through my daily heap of clothes, I could see what contempt the people in charge must have for us, their workers. They didn't even have the uniforms cleaned before they gave them to us.

We sat in a large hall, on rows of chairs with attached desks. The chairs were placed quite close together, so if one wanted to go to the toilet, it was necessary to find a way of negotiating the piles of uniforms on the floor.

For the first few nights, I didn't lift my eyes from the job at hand. I had never been good at needlework, so I had to concentrate on what I was doing. Most of the other workers were much older than I was. Guards in German uniforms walked among us, but I just sat quietly in the corner and never had anything to do with them.

Every morning, I returned home exhausted and went to bed straight away. At least this way I didn't have time to think about how much I missed my beloved stepmother, Jaga Sander, who had been taken from the shop and sent to Treblinka. Grandma Sander often sat by my bed with a fly whisk, trying to keep the flies off my face. She also picked out the bed bugs and drowned them in a mug of water.

In June 1942, the Germans commenced the liquidation of the Warsaw Ghetto. Six to ten thousand people a day were despatched to the death camps of Treblinka and Auschwitz. On top of that, Latvian, Lithuanian, and Ukrainian auxiliaries roamed the ghetto, shooting people indiscriminately on the streets, in courtyards, and on stairways.

After the first few nights at the shop, I noticed that I had a new neighbour. This girl, who appeared to be three or four years older than me, began telling me all sorts of news about what was going on. Apparently, the numbers in the ghetto had dwindled to 40,000.

Underground fighters had attempted to assassinate the head of the Jewish police, Szerynski. There had been no round-ups in the previous two days. One of the guards, the one the girl referred to as 'Bulldog', gave her a dirty look and, once or twice, told her to shut up. But it cheered me to have a new companion, and her whispering made work less tedious and prevented us from dozing off.

The next night, the girl was even more talkative. I noticed that some of the other workers seemed to have had enough of her 'blabber', and were looking at her askance. In the early hours of the morning, Bulldog came round patrolling the hall. Again, he told the girl to shut up. She stopped talking for a moment, but then started again, compulsively. She was in the middle of a funny story when Bulldog reappeared. He pulled out his revolver and shot the girl in the head. Her blood and bits of brain and shattered bones splashed all over me as I turned away in horror, not able even to look at the dying girl as she slumped down from her chair and lay motionless among the heaps of uniforms.

That morning, I carried my bowl of soup home with trembling hands. How much more of this could I stand? Instead of going to bed, I went through the basement tunnels to see Iza, my best friend. We sat together and talked and cried.

We decided to search for a phone and, in an empty apartment, we found one. Mercifully, it worked. I rang a friend of the family outside the ghetto. 'Pani Loda,' I whispered into the receiver. 'I can't take this any more. I have to get out. Jaga is gone. I'll tell you more when I see you. The only thing I can do for her now is to try to save her mother and sister. Please help.'

We agreed that I would ring again in two days. Then I returned home and fell into an exhausted sleep.

Going back to the shop the next evening was one of the most difficult things I have ever had to do, but there was no alternative. I sat sewing, propelled by nervous energy and ignoring those around me.

On the third day, I rang Pani Loda. She told me what she had

Halina Robinson aged 11: From her ID card at her Jewish day school.

arranged: at 3 p.m. on Thursday 27 September, I was to go over the ghetto wall with a group of smugglers. We would make the crossing in Sliska Street.

When the day came, I returned from the shop and went to bed as usual. But Grandma Sander woke me up and dressed me in many layers of clothes. These were the only things I could take with me. I asked her not to see me off. I just embraced her, and kissed her pale face many times. 'Don't fret, Granny,' I said. 'I will see you soon on the other side.'

I went to Sliska Street with only Iza for company. She would be able to tell the others if I got away safely. A tall, heavily set man approached us and said: 'You're Halina? I nodded. 'Listen, sweetie,' he said gruffly, 'I'll put a ladder up against the wall. You must run to it as quickly as you can. There'll be another ladder on the other side. Clear?' I nodded again, kissed Iza, and flew up the ladder.

But when I got to the top, there was no other ladder. Instead, I could see five or six German guards pointing their machine guns towards me, so vulnerable and visible on top of the wall in my beige overcoat. 'Jump, you stupid skunk!' the man called. When I froze in fear, he quickly climbed the ladder, and threw me down like a kitten. Then he jumped down next to me. Pulling me by the hand, he ran after two women who were loaded with heavy parcels and bits of furniture. I took some of their load, and we marched in a heavy silence until we reached a dilapidated shack.

They put their loads in the corner. One of the women started to make some plank beds. 'Where is the toilet?' I asked. The woman just gave me a torch and pointed outside. With the torch in my hand, I eventually found a brick outhouse. I squatted in it awkwardly, in disgust. How I disliked this set-up, the place, the people, and the atmosphere. To me they looked like people who might take money from Pani Loda to smuggle me over the wall, and then, in the morning, hand me over to the Germans as an escapee. They would get a kilo of sugar as a reward.

The people lay down on their beds of rags and, as soon as the light was switched off, I could hear their heavy gasps of tiredness. I kept the torch and, soon after, ventured towards the doorway. I didn't need to use the toilet again, but I wanted to get some idea of how I might escape. I didn't trust those people one bit.

The women next to me on the floor said huffily, 'Why are you so fidgety? Can't you settle and keep quiet? People want to sleep.'

'I'm terribly sorry,' I apologised. 'I need the toilet. I can't do it here, can I?'

'Just try not to make such a racket,' said the woman, turning towards the wall.

I pretended to go to the toilet a few more times. When I finally decided that everyone was asleep, I ran out, and kept on running, at first through backyards, then through a place that appeared to be allotments cultivated by apartment residents. There, I found a summer-house and dozed off in it.

When I was woken by the cold air of dawn, I was grateful for the layers of clothes that Grandma had put on me. I was sure they had also saved me from injury when I was thrown from the three-and-a-half-metre wall.

I straightened up my coat and tried to do something with my hair. Since I didn't have a comb, I covered it with a scarf.

Next I found myself wandering totally unfamiliar streets. I joined queues, not even asking the people in them what they were waiting for. I drank water from fountains, and marvelled at the grass and trees. It was years since I'd seen any.

Around midday I gathered up my courage and curtsied to an old lady. 'Excuse me, madam,' I said. 'I'm not from here. I seem to have lost my way. Are we very far from Hoza Street?'

The old lady smiled and said, 'If you don't mind walking slowly with me, we could go together part of the way, and then I will show you the quickest route. Which part of Hoza do you need?'

'The place very close to the Ambulance Service,' I told her.

'That's easy. I'll point you in the right direction.'

When we parted I curtsied again, thanking the old lady profusely. 'God bless,' she said.

I shall have to ask Pani Loda what that expression means and whether I should use it, I thought, eagerly checking the numbers along Hoza Street.

Eventually I found my destination and rang the doorbell. 'Where have you been?' asked Pani Loda, taking me in her arms. 'Have you eaten?' My cheeks were wet with tears, and I shook my head. 'What's wrong?' she asked.

I tried to smile. 'Nothing. I'm just so tired.'

Pani Loda went to the bathroom to prepare a bath for me. She returned with a nightgown and a bowl of hot gruel and milk.

'Take off all your clothes,' she said. 'And before you go to bed, remember, you are now Halinka Gorska. Your guardian is a ranger in the Kampinos Forest who was taken by the Germans for interrogation. He gave you my address and you arrived last night, falling asleep on your feet. You have never seen me before in your life. Can you remember all that?' I nodded my head. The food was warm and soothing.

Pani Loda, who organised my escape from the ghetto, was Mrs Loda Komarnicka. It was also she who arranged my first two hiding places after my escape. Later, I learned that she helped over 100 Jews in this way. Sadly, just before the end of the German Occupation, this courageous woman was caught and executed.

In the 23 months I spent in hiding, following my escape, I had to pass through 13 locations with four sets of false documents. That means that close to 100 other Righteous Gentiles risked their lives to save just one Jewish teenager.

To live even a semblance of normal life in occupied Poland, every person aged 16 years or more had to have an identity card known as a *Kennkarte*. To obtain a *Kennkarte*, one had to prove that there were no Jews in one's ancestry, back to the third generation. Having even a single Jewish grandparent put one in grave danger of being classified as a Jew oneself, so it was no easy matter to provide me with four different non-Jewish identities. But, each time, I received the necessary documents and explanations of relationships, the maiden names of mother and grandmother, and such like.

None of this vital assistance fell from the sky. I would like to pay tribute to a unique organisation — the underground Council for Aid to Jews, known by its code-name 'Zegota'. Zegota was founded in Warsaw in October 1942, just after my escape from the ghetto, and I surely had assistance from Zegota that I knew nothing of at the time.

Zegota was the only organisation of its kind in German-occupied Europe. It was initiated by Catholic democratic organisations, but eventually involved a broad spectrum of groups that included two Jewish organisations: the Jewish National Committee and the Bund. Zegota received up to 10 per cent of the entire budget of the *Delegatura na Kraj*, the underground arm of the Polish government-in-exile in London.

I know only what happened in Warsaw, and even there I know only a part of the story. It provided small emergency sums of money — for example, during the Warsaw Uprising in August 1944, my current guardian applied to Zegota for financial assistance, and it was promptly rendered. Sometimes Zegota also supplied false documents or medical help. It took care of children who had been orphaned, or who were unable to be hidden with their parents. Its most difficult challenge was finding Jews a place to live, especially those whose appearance, mannerisms, or accent could be easily recognised as Jewish. It even resorted to sending Jewish women and girls, with false papers, to do forced labour in Germany, where they were less likely to be recognised as Jews.

Zegota also denounced anyone it discovered who was trying to blackmail Jews or their saviours. The underground Home Army had clear orders to court-martial such people. I knew of a number of perpetrators who were sentenced and executed.

The organisers had to do all this in the certain knowledge that, even with the greatest sacrifice and effort, they could save only a minute percentage of the pre-war Jewish population. But it is estimated that Zegota assisted 40,000 to 50,000 Jews, including around 2500 children who were saved. This last figure is confirmed by the number of Jewish children who eventually found their way to Jewish orphanages, immigrated to Israel, or were reunited with surviving relatives in other countries. Years afterward, in Sydney, I met two other people who owed their survival to Zegota.

In the ghetto, and in hiding afterwards, I had short periods of education with various tutors, none of whom were teachers by profession. My only formal education at this time came when I attended a secondary boarding school run by nuns, from October to mid-December 1942, and from mid-January to February 1943. Under the German Occupation, even this innocuous activity had to be clandestine, for the authorities had banned secondary and tertiary education for Poles. Under certain conditions, however, they still permitted vocational training. The sisters took advantage of this to conduct their school in the guise of cookery and patisserie training.

I was still in Warsaw when I was liberated in September 1944. Fortunately, I happened to be on the eastern side of the River Vistula rather than the western side, for that bank remained under German Occupation for almost another four months. Upon my liberation, I wanted to join the Soviet-backed Polish army, in order to fight the Germans and make my own contribution to victory. However, the recruitment officer pointed out that due to the decimation of the Polish intelligentsia by the Nazis (and, let it be said, by the Soviets), every individual who was capable of attempting higher education should pursue this goal.

For the time being, I was assigned to the Brigades for the Reconstruction of Warsaw. Since much of Warsaw lay in ruins, this was the hardest physical slog that I have ever done. At the same time, I clung to one of my guardians from the Occupation. I was finding it very difficult to start a new chapter in my life. Everything I had ever known before the war was gone — everything, with one exception. I discovered some months after the end of the war that a cousin of my mother's had also survived. He had immigrated to Palestine just before the war began.

My guardian, Maria Jiruska, must have guessed what was going in my mind. One afternoon, she said to me, 'Hala, it's time to decide what are you going to do. If you want to go to Palestine and try to find your mother's cousin, I could use my contacts with Hashomer Hatzair. If you would prefer to stay here with us, we would be very pleased.'* But then, she added, 'If you do stay, however, I suggest you keep your assumed name and identity.'

I hit the roof. 'It was all right for the seven generations of my

---

* Maria was a pillar of the Polish Girl Guides movement, so she had contacts at Hashomer Hatzair, a socialist Zionist youth movement involved with camping.

family that I know about, and for many more before them, to live in this country under names that didn't sound Polish! And I can't stay in my own country unless I change my birth name? Why?'

She took me in her arms. 'We love you. We want you to forget the atrocities and be happy here with us. But what people went through in the war changed people's outlooks and the way they think. We can't be sure what lies ahead of us.' In the end, she turned out to be right. But I never wished, even for a moment, to live anywhere else.

Then it happened, entirely by chance, that I encountered a family in need of a governess for three girls aged five to 11. I accepted the position. My duties included supervising each of the girls' piano practice and engaging them in French conversation. The father of this family, an orthopaedic surgeon of high repute, was appointed a professor and given the task of helping reclaim the old German university city of Breslau. This city, which returned to its historical name, Wroclaw, was a part of the so-called 'regained territories' given to Poland by the Yalta Conference.

In the midst of the expulsion of Germans from Wroclaw and the influx of Poles from territories lost to the Soviet Union, I settled down to prepare for public examinations that would allow me to matriculate. I was lucky enough to become a student in the Faculty of Medicine at the University of Wroclaw.

Yet the war and the Holocaust had taken their toll: after two years, I was obliged to break off my studies. My thyroid gland was overreacting. The doctors said it might require surgery; but they also suggested that surgery might not be necessary if I moved to the Baltic seacoast, where the air was rich in iodine.

Having no way to support myself at the Baltic Shores, I applied to do a hotel management course there. I was offered a place in the student hostel in Sopot, with generous credits for my previous studies. I completed the course, and began work not as a doctor but as a catering officer, in the mountain resort of Karpacz in the Sudeten Mountains (which are nowadays known as the Karkonosze

Mountains). By correspondence, I also resumed my studies, pursuing a degree in psychology.

By the beginning of 1953, I had a BA in Psychology. I had a husband, Edward Czernuszyn, a two-year-old daughter, Joanna, and a baby boy, Vitek. I was working as a broadcaster for Polskie Radio, the state broadcaster, where I had my own program for schoolchildren. I had by then started reading for a Master's degree.

Meanwhile, a friend of mine — a prominent Communist — had been given the task of editing a periodical that would help revamp the Polish Boy Scouts into Soviet-style Young Pioneers. Unknown to me, he demanded that I should be assigned to help him. The order came through from the Central Committee of the Polish Workers' Party that I should lose my job in Polskie Radio; and then, the periodical didn't go ahead. I was furious, but the officials would have lost face if they'd had to restore my position. Instead I was offered, and had to accept, a job as an editor in the state publishing house Nasza Ksiegarnia.

It was my husband Edward, a Roman Catholic Pole, who decided that he wanted to leave Poland. In 1956, he asked me to seek the help of my mother's cousin. This cousin, Janek, was a former member of the Haganah (a Zionist Jewish paramilitary organisation fighting against the British Mandate of Palestine), and a fighter in Israel's War of Independence. Janek, by this time, had reached the rank of *sgan-aluf*, or brigadier-general, in the Israeli army.

Thus by December 1957, the family had landed in Israel. I spent three months in an *ulpan* to revive my dormant Hebrew, then worked for 16 months as an instructor in a training centre for newly arrived adolescents from Morocco and neighbouring countries. After that, I taught cookery for a year at a state school in Kyriath Nazareth.

Our travels were not over, however. Soon I was contacted by an uncle, 'Poldek' Hartman, who had survived in Australia, and by Michael Hartman, the brother of my maternal grandfather, who had long ago immigrated to Florida. I felt that both of them were

Halina 'Gralewska': Left, groomed and dressed to look very Polish on the German *Kennkarte*, issued under the assumed name of Gralewska; above, as a medical student at Wrocław University, 1946.

rather paranoid about the need to whisk me out of the 'danger zone' I was living in. But, in their eyes, we were the best hope for continuing the family line, for I was the only member of our destroyed family to have had children.

So it was that we boarded a ship in Haifa to sail Down Under. Our daughter was then aged ten, and our son was eight.

The family arrived in Sydney in July 1961. In the beginning, it was tough. Overwhelmed by the strangeness of this place, not knowing much English, and lacking qualifications for employment, I made for the place I knew best, the one place that at least smells the same all over the world, the hospital — to be specific, the Randwick Chest Hospital. While working there, I attended courses leading to the quaintly named position of State Enrolled Nursing Aide. But when I found no further progress was possible by this route, I began preparing for registration with the Library Association of Australia. Upon passing the first two exams, I applied for a position as a library assistant. That launched me on a library career.

Forty years later, I'm hardly able to count my vast family. Our two children blessed me with six grandchildren. One grandchild grew up to be a filmmaker, another a doctor. The younger ones also show good promise and are each a light in my life.

The relatives of my first husband, Edward, scattered across Poland, Australia, Hong Kong, and the United States, are in close contact, despite the 30 years that have passed since his death in 1976. There are three generations of them, almost 20 in number. They inform me of their doings, they send photographs, emails, and good wishes. They come for visits, and they invite me to visit them.

In 1979, I met a man named Les Robinson, whom I married later on. Then, in 2003, I was widowed for the second time. The support I received from Les's family was overwhelming. It occurred to me that if I invited all of the well-wishers to the funeral and added some friends, I would have had to hire a town hall.

Life is so strange. In 1945 I was just one survivor of my large family. Sixty years later, there are 70 people calling me 'Aunty'. My late second-husband, Les, said, a few days before his departure, 'You'll be all right, you're surrounded by love.' I can feel these waves of love touching me now, and I think, even in my grief, what a lucky person I am.

DASHA CAMINER

Journeys

My phone rang insistently, and I ran from my garden to answer it. It was a friend, to tell me that she had heard on the radio that an inquiry was being made into the whereabouts of Dasha Caminer, who had moved to South Africa in 1954. Any information was to be passed on to a certain Ruth Finch in England, who was searching for me.

My mind was racing as my friend spoke. I was wondering who it might be, and what the urgency of the message was. The only person I knew by the name of Ruth was someone with whom I had shared a few years in a children's hostel during the war. Those were traumatic years for me. They had begun in May 1939, when I was seven years old. Suddenly, many thoughts and painful experiences, which I had pushed to the back of my mind, began to re-emerge.

My father, Richard Deutsch, was an antique-clock collector. Many of his clocks were museum pieces. Before the war, one whole room in our house in Prague was dedicated to them, and they all chimed at different intervals. When I think of our family home,

At the Rialto Bridge: Dasha Caminer's parents, Ruth and Richard Deutsch, in Venice, September 1925.

I remember a special clock on our living-room wall. Its beautiful white enamelled face was adorned with fine Roman numerals, and its melodious chimes could be heard throughout the house striking the hour. It had a large hand-beaten brass pendulum that always attracted my attention as it swung from side to side. The casing was an azure blue, embellished with gold and topped by a golden crown. I felt it was truly fit for Maria Theresa, Empress of Austria, who, my father told us, was given it for her 18th birthday. Just before the war, a number of these clocks, together with three family albums, were sent to London to be cared for by a friend.

It must have been early in 1939 that I recall going with my father into a forest near our home. He carried a large object wrapped in a bag, and he held my hand tightly. He made me promise not to tell anyone what he was about to do. He dug a hole in the ground and buried the bag, which contained a gun. For the next few weeks, I could sense my parents' increasing anxiety. We would look out of

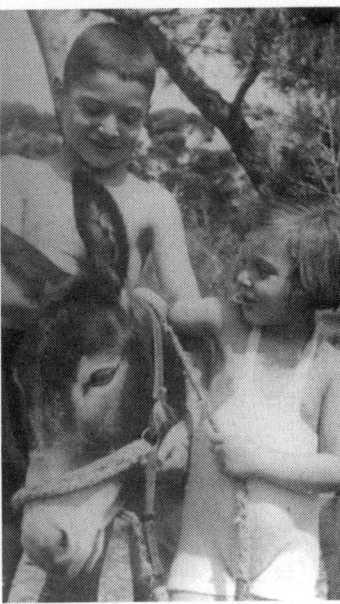

From the album: Top left, Dasha Caminer's parents in the 1930s; Dasha and her brother Jára pose with a donkey; and Dasha in a park in Teplice in August 1934.

our windows to see the Germans with their metal helmets, grey uniforms, and armbands bearing the dreaded swastika. All kinds of preparations were being made at this time.

The next thing I remember was going to the railway station, where a label with a number was tied around my neck. My brother Jára and two other girls, who were daughters of my parents' friends, shared our compartment. My mother was crying bitterly, and for me, the feeling of being abandoned was the most horrible experience of my life. At that stage, I did not understand the implications of our parting. Now that I am a mother myself, I can well imagine the utter despair and helplessness that my parents must have felt, seeing their two young children — their only children — leaving in a *Kindertransport* for an unknown destination, somewhere in England. But it is understandable that they chose this way for us: the shadows of war hung over all of Europe and they feared for our safety.

As the train pulled out of the station, we were filled with anticipation about the journey ahead. Initially, I was frightened at being torn away from my parents, but I still felt lucky to be with my brother, who was five years older than me. The only thing I remember about the journey is getting out of the train to be searched, in Holland.

The security of being with my brother did not last long. As soon as we arrived in England we were parted, and the memory of that fateful farewell still brings tears to my eyes. I do not recall my arrival at the hostel in Tynemouth, but I was with the two friends with whom I had travelled, and we were together for three months, able to communicate with each other in Czech. All the other girls at the hostel spoke German. At school, English was spoken, which meant I had to learn English and German at the same time.

The hostel was supported by a group of Jewish people who had thought it would be a temporary refuge for children fleeing Nazi persecution. It was hoped that the children's parents would join them, and this did happen in the case of my friends. But, unfortunately, the outbreak of war meant that the hostel had to become an orphanage, and we had to be supported for the duration of the war. Two elderly ladies were appointed to look after the 25 girls, whose ages ranged from four to 18.

Coming from a loving family home, I found it hard to adapt to sleeping in a dormitory and being regimented into the routine of marching to school in a crocodile line. To a seven-year-old child who could not make herself understood, it was traumatic. I was miserable, and cried at the least provocation. The boredom at school was endless. Added to all this, the German bombing began, and the shrill sound of the sirens became a nightly routine. We were awakened at all hours, and herded into underground air-raid shelters, where we had to stay for hours. In the daytime, at school, there were constant drills in which we had to learn to put on claustrophobic rubber gas-masks.

At the Tynemouth hostel, summer 1939: Dasha Caminer (with arms folded) is in the back row, centre. Her friend Elfi is third on her right; Ruth Finch (née Oppenheimer) is standing in the foreground, second from the right.

The arduous hours at school seemed endless. In the classroom, I could not understand anyone, or any of the lessons. But there were flowerbeds surrounding the asphalt playground. It didn't take me long to learn the phrase, 'May I be excused?' It was my passport to freedom from the mindlessness of school. I used to escape into the garden. Much later, I learned that the headmaster had enquired of the matron if I was suffering from bladder problems!

In 1940, the bombing became more frequent, and it was decided to evacuate the whole hostel to a safer district in northwest England. Windermere was to be our home for the next four years. By now, I could speak some English and German, and could communicate with the other girls. Some of the older ones began leaving to join the Land Army, the nursing profession, and other occupations.

After that, there were only two groups of us left: the 'little ones', of which I was one, and the 'middle ones'. Our matrons at Windermere were very strict, and performed their tasks in Germanic, controlling ways. Probably overwhelmed by the job, they chose to discipline us using hours of silence and physical chastisement. We were intimidated and afraid of these women. Often, they shouted at one or other of us for very small misdemeanours. We were slapped just for leaving a sleeve turned inside a coat. When we cried, after such irrational punishment, it was the older girls who comforted us. It was the 'middle ones', not the matrons, who gave us the warmth and compassion that were so lacking in our lives.

Members of the committee came to see us from time to time. When this happened, we were obliged to parade in dreary cast-off clothing that members of the committee had sent. We hated this parade, as they looked at us like so many cattle at an auction. Naturally, we had to smile and say the right things when a committee member addressed us.

A weekend task was to collect firewood in the woods. It served the dual purpose of keeping our fires burning and getting us out

Windermere, c. 1943: Dasha Caminer is on the far right; her friend Elfi is on her right in the back row.

of the house. In summer, the ground was covered with a mantle of bluebells: I can still recall their fragrance. It was during these outings that we could shout, laugh, dance, and talk of our hope of being reunited with our families after the war. It was this hope and these dreams that kept our spirits alive.

At school, we were taught to knit socks and blankets for soldiers. Occasionally we were permitted to crowd around the radio to hear the news. Every time, we hoped to learn that the war was over.

In 1944 I was moved once again, this time to Wales, where a Czech school had been set up. It was decided that I should regain the use of my mother tongue, which I had forgotten by then, in case I should rejoin my family. At this school, all the classes were conducted in Czech. Once again, I could understand very little, and had to learn what felt like a new language and make all new friends.

The war in Europe finally ended in May 1945. The Czech

school closed, so I was placed in yet another hostel. It seemed a very long time until a decision was made about my future. I was sent to another hostel, this time in London, with a new school and new faces. I was given an allowance, out of which I had to clothe and feed myself and save whatever I could.

By this time, all the girls in the Windermere hostel had found relatives somewhere in the world who could care for them. By the time I was 13 years old, the names of survivors were being circulated. The dream of finding my parents had never left me, and I frequently went to Bloomsbury House in the hope of seeing the names Richard and Ruth Deutsch, my mother and father. As the lists grew shorter and shorter, I slowly realised that my dreams would not be coming true; that I was on my own and had to think of my future.

By September 1945, the war in Europe had been over for four months. There was still no news of my parents or relatives. I was overwhelmed with grief, but I tried desperately to accept the situation. As it was Jewish New Year, I decided to look for solace in the synagogue, especially to join in the *Yizkor* prayer for the departed. On my arrival at the synagogue, however, I was refused entry, because I had neither a head-covering nor an entry ticket. I was devastated. To this day, although I am proud of my heritage and still feel totally Jewish, that experience has influenced my thoughts on religion and its true meaning.

I had been reconnected with my brother, who was studying at Oxford, and I visited him frequently. He became my mentor. I looked to him for guidance, and considered his opinions seriously. We became very close after the separation caused by the war. I also had an aunt and uncle in London, whom I visited a few times. We corresponded, and they sent me parcels of clothes, for which I was grateful.

In about 1946, the London hostel also closed. I seem to have been a problem for the Czech Trust Fund, which had now become my guardian. A new home had to be found for me and, as no Jewish home could be found for me, I went to stay with a Christian family with two small children in the West End of London. There, I went to Burlington Grammar School, not far from Hammersmith Hospital. I did some household chores and looked after the children. This remained my home until I managed to get a bursary to become a junior school teacher, specialising in art and craft.

Teaching was my only choice, as there was no other career I could pursue without financial backing. I would rather have satisfied my artistic leanings in a profession such as fabric or interior design. I had also considered nursing, but I rejected that idea after helping for some weeks in a Hammersmith Hospital ward and learning that I would have to live in a nurses' home attached to the hospital. By now, having spent so many years in institutionalised communities, I needed my own space and my independence.

At this stage I was 17 years old, but I could not be accepted for the teaching course until I was 18. There was an opening for a

Dasha Caminer in April 1946.

pupil teaching position at Montessori Boarding School in Great Missenden, Buckinghamshire. There I stayed until I entered college in London and became a resident. I took various jobs during college vacations, picking fruit, working in a canning factory, cooking at a farm camp, and working as a receptionist. Finally, I qualified with a Diploma in Junior School Teaching, and was able to earn a salary and take my own lodgings. I was now about 20, and independent at last, with 30 pounds a month for total upkeep. I was very happy about this, although I was lonely, too, on my own and making decisions about my future.

In 1954, I married Claude Caminer in South Africa. During our 47 years of marriage, he gave me love, security, and understanding, all experiences that were sadly lacking in my formative years. The political problems in South Africa prompted yet another journey, to Australia, with our younger son, in 1984. Our older son had made the move two years before us. I now have two daughters-in-law who are as close as daughters, and two adorable grandchildren.

The memorable phone call from Ruth was about a 50-year reunion of the girls from the London hostel, in 1989. Unfortunately, I could not attend that one. But it led to a series of contacts with girls from the hostel, and in 1992, I met Ruth and another friend, Elfi, in Amsterdam. We spent a wonderful two days talking about our times together in those hard years of our lives.

People often ask me how I feel about the events of my life, and how they have affected me. I believe I survived the traumas of my youth successfully because the various experiences strengthened my character and my attitude towards my fellow human beings. Reflecting on those years when most children feel the security of family and belonging, I inevitably get a lump in my throat. I was always the one with the accent, the one without the home, the one who was laughed at when reading a passage aloud from a book. Later, when I lived on my own, I was the girl without parents, without a family. I always felt ashamed.

I feel no bitterness or hatred and, to avoid being a bore, I do not dwell on the past. I am very fortunate to have an innately positive and happy disposition, and I have not allowed my early disappointments and losses to affect my dreams for the future. My experiences have taught me that it is not necessary to look for material wealth in order to find enjoyment and happiness. The simple pleasures of nature and my awareness of things around me have been my inspiration. At times of loneliness and desolation, I turn to creating: in art, or the garden, or cooking, or pottery. I have always been intrigued by how things are made and where they come from. The world is an endlessly fascinating place, and there are always meaningful opportunities to be taken along the path.

CELLA BARUCH
My 'sister'

'And suddenly the memory revealed itself. The taste was that of the little piece of madeleine which on Sunday mornings at Combray (because on those mornings I did not go out before Mass), when I went to say good morning to her in her bedroom, my aunt Léonie used to give me, dipping it first in her own cup of tea or tisane.'
— Proust, *Remembrance of Things Past*

Like any other family, my very extensive family had its own legends and secrets — and some skeletons, carefully locked in sealed cupboards. Sometimes children would listen to the grown-ups' conversations, or rush into a room where the 'old ones' would be in the middle of an animated conversation. Then, the elders would suddenly fall silent, and tell the children to go out and play and not bother them.

I was one of those children. A few words would linger in my mind, registering in a layer of consciousness that only Freud would recognise. But I was immersed in my own awakening, and carried away by the catastrophic events that overtook all my generation. I paid no heed to any chance words that came my way.

There was one snatch of hushed conversation that I overheard in my very early childhood whose meaning I never knew until many years later. By then, I was on a kibbutz in Palestine. There, just as things past returned to Marcel Proust when he dipped the famous madeleine into his milky cup of tea, my buried memory found its catalyst. It happened during the most dangerous period of the war in the Middle East. Tobruk had fallen, the British 8th Army and its few allies had retreated to El Alamein, and Rommel was expected to arrive in Cairo at any moment. In Jerusalem, the ad hoc Jewish parliament was discussing ways to save the Jewish settlements near the Egyptian border. All this was known and decided in Jerusalem, but the people on the land, including myself, were blissfully unaware of the imminent danger.

It was a very hot day. I remember that there were a lot of people on our kibbutz, and the atmosphere was highly festive. The day before, a group of around 50 children had arrived. Some of them had wandered out of Eastern Europe after their parents had been taken to the Nazi death camps. The children, some as young as four, had been left to fend for themselves, and had been wandering in bands, like packs of wolves. They were gathered together in Iran by a legendary woman, Henrietta Szold, who had brought them to Palestine, where they were to be placed in different agricultural settlements. I particularly remember that a lot of cakes were baked for that extraordinary event. For me, this was of the utmost importance, because I was always hungry, especially for cakes.

Whatever happened around us — whether joyful events or world-shattering ones — the cows had to be fed and milked, and the stables had to be cleaned. That was my job at that time. I had just finished my work in the stables, and was on my way to the showers to get out of my smelly overalls and quickly change into

Cella Baruch at Ayanoth Agricultural School, Palestine, 1941.

my one and only clean pair of slacks. Feeling rather mangy as I tried to make my way through the festive crowd, I was hurrying in the direction of the building that I lived in when one of my friends stopped me. Very excitedly, she told me that my sister had just arrived! I growled at her that she was seriously mistaken: I had no sisters, only two brothers.

'Don't be stupid,' she said. 'She's your spitting image! Nobody could miss the fact that she is your sister.' She would probably have continued to make her point, but she was overcome by the strong whiff of cow manure that was emanating from me, and she left. As she went, she urged me to hurry up and get to the dining room where Ruth, my 'sister', was eating cakes and drinking tea with friends from her kibbutz.

The idea that all the cakes would be finished if I didn't get there in time was a great incentive. In record time, I galloped to the dining room, where the excitement was growing. Our very formidable leader was speaking, welcoming the guests from other kibbutzim around us, and letting the little group of 'Teheran children', as they were called, know that they were our beloved sisters and brothers. They didn't understand a word of Hebrew, and didn't seem very impressed by her lofty speech.

I was even less interested. I was trying to push my considerable bulk forward and get as near as possible to the tray of cakes, where only some pitiful bits remained. Brutally, I repelled another hand — a feminine-looking one — that was trying to grab the few crumbs. I turned my head to whisper a few well-chosen words about robbing a hard worker of her due, and — my eyes practically popped out. I was looking at my own face! Eventually, when my eyes cleared, I realised that the double image was better than the original. Nevertheless, in a sort of trance, I felt I was looking at my double.

The shock put me off the crumbs I had fought so hard for and, somehow, I managed to ask her where she came from. I found out that her name was indeed Ruth, but in her kibbutz, she was known as 'the Gentile' because her grandfather, a Russian, was not Jewish. Something clicked in my bewildered brain; I told her that it had been nice meeting her, or something to that effect, and left very quickly, forgetting all about the miserable crumbs of cake.

Floating upwards from the deepest layer of my subconscious was a fragment of gossip exchanged between my grandmother and some of her numerous sisters concerning one of their cousins. After this cousin had been married for some decades to a Russian fugitive from the Tsar's army who had been taken for a Jew by the head of my grandmother's clan, he confessed that he was in fact a good Greek Orthodox man. Meanwhile, he had provided his wife with a considerable number of children, and probably thought it was high time to tell the truth.

The truth was, he was a Sabbatarian, a branch of the Orthodox religion that strictly followed the Bible and recognised Saturday, not Sunday, as the holy day. The Russian clergy considered this sect even more sinful than the Jewish religion, and that was why he had landed in the little Moldovian town, to be integrated under false pretences into my grandmother's huge family. He finished by leaving his wife and numerous descendants, and went on to fulfill every worthy Sabbatarian's dream: to die in the Holy Land.

But the pure air of the holy city of Jerusalem invigorated him no end, and he thought it would be a good idea to start a new line of descendants. He married a lovely young virgin some 30 years younger than himself. Eventually, satisfied with a mission well accomplished, he decided to die, and was buried, according to the precepts of his religion, in the holy city of Jerusalem.

Somehow, all these events reached the avid ears of the Romanian tribe, and a tiny fragment of the saga remained in my tortuous memory, until I met my 'sister' Ruth. Through some incredible scramble of genes and frenetic sexual appetites, I had come face to face with the result of some forgotten Russian Sabbatarian's rampant desires, whose misdeeds were the basis of hotly whispered gossip in my grandmother's house.

JENINE CIBULKA
Jenine's story

Until I was 11 years old, I lived in a happy and loving family in the rue de Flandres, in the 19th Arrondissement of Paris. My father, Paul Faigenbaum, was Polish born, and had immigrated to France in 1925 at the age of 27. He was a businessman, running a men's clothing shop. My mother's family, the Krosts, had come from Lithuania in 1905, when she was a six-month-old baby. My mother, Anna, was very French — coquettish and always elegant. We were not a religious family. I had a brother, Marcel, whom I adored. At the age of 18, he ran away to join the Free French forces in Africa. There, he became a paratrooper with the French SAS — a French unit within the British army — and fought the Germans.

In 1941, well into the German occupation of France, my father was imprisoned for making false documents for Jews and other people on the run. Then, on 16 July 1942, came the *Rafle du Vel' d'Hiver*, when the Paris gendarmes rounded up the city's Jews and locked them in the Velodrome, the cycling stadium. In our case, however, the policeman assigned to the task warned my mother to

Mother and daughter: A pre-war studio portrait of Jenine Cibulka in gypsy costume, with her mother, Anna Faigenbaum.

leave our flat, as he was duty-bound to return and arrest both her and myself.

Meanwhile, in prison, my father had befriended a man known as Grand-Jean, who was due to be released. My father had recommended to my mother that, should she ever need help, she should contact Grand-Jean. Thus, we stayed in hiding at the home of friends of Grand-Jean for one month, from 16 July to 16 August 1942. Then Mother decided to go and share a flat with her girlfriend Odette. She put me into a boarding school for girls, La Pension Jeanne d'Arc, where I stayed for about three months.

As we were still in the summer holidays, I used to take the Metro every day to visit my mother at the flat. I also used to bring her my laundry. But one day, Odette appeared decidedly glum when

I arrived with my laundry. She seemed uneasy and uncomfortable with me, and she seemed to be withholding something. She told me to just leave my laundry, and my mother would come and meet me at the boarding school. She was too ill at ease to tell me the horrible truth.

When I returned to the boarding school, I kept asking the staff if my mother had come. I was repeatedly told that she had not. I felt something was wrong. I began to cry, and seemed unable to stop. Morning till night, my face awash with tears, I would walk up and down to the Metro in the hope of meeting my mother. Still she did not appear. I had an awful premonition.

When I returned from one such walk, I was called to the headmistress's office. There, I was informed that my mother had been arrested by the Gestapo, accompanied by Grand-Jean, who presumably had denounced her to them. (After the war, he was indeed executed as an informer and collaborator.) Had I stayed with my mother for the night, on the weekend she was taken, as I had begged her in vain to let me do, I would not be here to tell this story. She had forced me to return to safety.

After my mother's arrest, I was no longer able to eat or sleep, and I experienced what was probably my first nervous breakdown. Impetigo covered my body, and I became very sick. After this, I used to visit my cousins, my only remaining relatives, until they themselves also had to flee. So some non-Jewish friends of my parents took over my care and began looking for a safer hiding place for me. We tried a convent for one night, but when they found out the next day that I'd had to shower with a nightie on for fear of exposing my naked body, this did not seem to satisfy them.

Eventually, they took me to the Preventorium de la Motte Verte, a sort of Catholic orphanage at Dammartin-en-Goele, 60 kilometres outside of Paris. There I remained until the end of the war, and for some time afterwards.

Unknown to me, my brother Marcel had returned to France with General Leclerc, whose forces liberated Paris in August 1944.

Marcel came looking for me, but never found me. Sadly, he was killed only a few months later in the Ardennes, during the final German offensive in the West.

After the end of the war, while I was still in the Preventorium, we often used to look up at the planes coming back from Germany. Some of them were bringing home French soldiers who had been prisoners of war in Germany since 1940. I did a lot of plane-watching, and I was always hoping and wishing, 'Maybe Maman and Papa are on this plane.' But, sadly, this was not to be.

One day, my uncle came to fetch me. I didn't want to go, but I couldn't continue my education at the orphanage past the age of 14, so I had to leave. My uncle promised me that he would not put me into another boarding school. But he reneged on his promise a few weeks later; in fact, he returned me to La Pension Jeanne d'Arc to continue my education for another two years. After that, when I was 16, my uncle put me into a home for Jewish orphans run by the OSE (*Oeuvres de Secours aux Enfants*), where I continued to study for a secretarial course.

At the orphans' home, we were visited by representatives of the American Jewish Joint Distribution Committee ('the Joint'). They suggested that, if any of us wished, we could immigrate to Canada, Palestine, the United States, Australia, or New Zealand. I took a good look at the world map and, realising where New Zealand was located, I decided not to go so far away. Working under the mistaken belief that everyone in Canada spoke French, I chose Canada.

My uncle had threatened to send me to be a farmer's maid in the country if I failed my exams. However, I felt that it was futile to bother going to school when I was leaving for Canada and would not finish the year. So I wagged school a bit. And I was found out.

I was frightened of the future, and I was probably looking for an escape. As it turned out, all the visas to Canada had been revoked, so immigration to Canada was out of the question. I took another long look at the map of the world and decided that Australia might be more welcoming. I just had to go somewhere.

I left Paris for Australia in September 1948, sailing from Marseilles via Genoa aboard the *Napoli*. It was an exciting trip for a 17-year-old girl. I was part of a group of 18 young people, all orphans, and all of us eager to start a new life after the horrors of the war. In spite of the discomfort on the ship (dormitory beds, washing in salt water, and boring food, mostly noodles — I really felt the absence of fresh produce), the trip was so enjoyable that I would have been happy had the voyage gone on forever.

When we arrived in Sydney on 28 October 1948, I had no idea what town or family awaited me. To make matters worse, we were greeted by an official from the Jewish welfare society who spoke entirely in English. I had learned some English at school, but I couldn't understand a word he said.

I only wish that the Jewish welfare society had been more thoughtful and had employed an interpreter to explain to a frightened young girl where she was going and with whom. That might have avoided the hellish 90-minute ordeal that I went through next. This is what ensued: I was introduced to what seemed to me to be an old gentleman (he was actually 37) dressed in a drab brown suit and a brown hat. He tried, unsuccessfully, to explain things to me, but I could not understand him. At this stage I became apprehensive. Soon, increasingly overcome by fear, I started to sob uncontrollably. All I could think of was that I might be entering into a 'white slavery' racket. In France, this peril was much discussed, as we had colonies, such as Algeria, where it was known to have occurred.

I was terrified. I was sure that I was doomed to live alone with this man, Mr Brent. I felt that I had no other option. The prospect seriously distressed me, and I continued sobbing. During the trip from the ship to Strathfield, we travelled by taxi, train, and bus. The only words I understood from Mr Brent were 'my Studebaker car' and the number '380'. Since we were catching public transport, I felt sure he must be lying to me, for where was his car?

When we arrived in Bareena Street, a very short street, I looked around, and thought, 'There can't be 380 houses in this street! I'm certain he's deceiving me …' I hadn't stopped weeping once through the whole journey. But, finally, we reached our destination, a lovely new house, and my nightmare came to an end.

As we entered the house, Mrs Ellen Brent, wearing a lovely floral dressing gown and holding flowers in her hand, greeted me in perfect French and excused herself for not coming to meet me on the ship. She explained that she had just returned from a holiday. She gave me a hug and kissed me, and my smile returned. The Brent family were very good to me.

And so began my new life in Australia.

GRETA SILVERS

Chosen to live: the only survivor of a large family

I was born in 1932 in Košice, in what was then Czechoslovakia, to Teresa and Mayer Tabak. My father was a brushmaker who eked out a modest living. I had two younger brothers, Lazar and Sender; we attended school in the morning and religious activities in the afternoon. My happiest time was the Shabbat festivities. This is how we lived our lives, and we were a happy family.

In November 1938, Hungary annexed our part of Slovakia. After that, I attended Hungarian school. During the war, my father was taken to a labour camp, where he taught brushmaking to his fellow prisoners. Later, he was taken to the Russian Front as a trench digger. He died there, before the liberation.

In April 1944, my mother, my brothers, and I were taken to Auschwitz. When we got out of the transport, one way was for the living, and the other was for those who were to die. We didn't know that; but, before we went through the gate, a fellow called to my mother, 'Don't hold on to your daughter or she will go with you!' My mother managed to push me away, but my little brothers were holding on to her. So we were separated. I lost sight of them, and I assume they went to the gas chamber.

In Auschwitz, I survived because I stayed out of trouble. I hid under the bed so as not to be seen, as I wanted so badly to stay alive. I wanted to survive and go home. That kept me alive; it kept my hopes up.

After I had been in Auschwitz for three months, the female prisoners of Lager C were called for special selections. We had to walk past a committee of civilians with our hands held out in front of us. They were looking for young girls with 'nice hands and nice eyes' for work. Three hundred were found to be suitable, all of us from the Hungarian and Transylvanian territories. We were transported to Weisswasser.

Weisswasser was a small town near Dresden with a population of about 15,000. The town was known for its centuries-old glassworks which, during the war, were used to manufacture special globes for aircraft, submarines, and specialised military equipment. This is where the female labourers with 'nice hands and eyes' were needed. It is not quite clear why those were the criteria of selection.

The *lager*, or camp, was not quite finished when we arrived. Our work there was manual. In general, our treatment and accommodation were much better and more humane than they had been in Auschwitz, and the work was far easier. We marched to work at dawn, through the deserted streets of Weisswasser, and returned after dark. Only the patter of our wooden shoes could be heard. We spent five months there.

As the war neared its end, the Germans marched us to Hamburg, and then sent us by train to Bergen-Belsen. On our arrival, fresh bread was being baked with poison in it for quick annihilation of the whole camp. The British arrived just before the bread was distributed, so we were lucky indeed.

After the liberation, I contracted a severe case of typhus, and spent four months in hospital in Celle, the nearest town to the camp. After my recovery, I headed home to Košice, where the sad news awaited me that none of my family had survived. I was all alone in the world. This was the most horrific experience in all my young life.

The Jewish welfare society arranged for me to live with a family of a man known as 'the tutor'. On his return to Slovakia, the tutor had taken over a furniture-making factory in Liberec as compensation for his efforts during the war. So I was taken from Košice to Liberec. But this new departure did not turn out well. Once again, I was torn from my roots and, in my tutor's household, I was exploited as a housemaid for two years.

In the end, a good Samaritan who knew about my miserable existence 'kidnapped' me and took me back to Košice. There, I lived with my childhood friends and put my name down with 'the Joint', the American Jewish Joint Distribution Committee, to immigrate to Australia as an orphan.

When I arrived in Australia in February 1948, I was lucky enough to be picked up by lovely Australian families who became my mentors. And so I began a new life in Sydney.

Of all my vast family, I was the only one chosen to live.

SHULAMIT ULLMANN

Selma Rosentower's story

Campulung Bucovina, the town where I was born, was in a province of the Austro-Hungarian Empire until 1918, when it became part of Greater Romania. It was a beautiful town, situated in a valley surrounded by high mountains and forests.

My early childhood in Campulung Bucovina was happy. As an only child, I was pampered by everybody. I loved visiting my paternal grandmother, Toni Rosentower, who always gave me a glass of cold spring water with raspberry syrup, which is still my favourite drink, even today. My favourite playmates in kindergarten were German twin sisters and a Romanian girl, Lenuta Piticari. Most of the Jewish population spoke German and Romanian, so I grew up bilingual.

My first painful memory is the loss of my father, Sigmund Rosentower, when I was six years old. He went for a walk one afternoon, had a massive stroke, and never returned. My mother was devastated. Our home was filled with sadness, and my maternal grandmother, Fany Landau, came for a prolonged visit.

The local population consisted of Romanians, Germans, and Jews, who lived in harmony until 1940. It was then that our persecution began. By 1940, Romania had become an ally of Nazi Germany. The fascist Iron Guard government, copying the anti-Semitic measures of the Nazis, introduced a law that directly affected me. All Jewish pupils were to be expelled from the public schools.

I remember with gratitude my teacher, a Romanian lady, visiting my mother to warn her about the impending expulsion. She suggested that to save Jewish children from public humiliation, they should not be sent to school. Most Jewish children continued their education in groups tutored by private teachers. My mother insisted that I should have my lessons from a severe retired male schoolteacher. I may have learned more than the other children, but I was lonely.

At this same time, the Jewish population was ordered to wear the yellow Star of David. But the most devastating event came in

Shulamit Ullmann's parents, Jeanette and Sigmund Rosentower.

At the Campulung Bucovina swimming pool, in about 1936: Shulamit Ullmann holds a paper parasol. Left, her uncle Salomon; right, her parents.

October 1941, when the town crier, beating his drum, announced loudly and clearly that all Jews had to assemble at the railway station the following day for 'evacuation'. We were to bring only 15 kilograms of luggage, and had to deposit all valuables at the National Bank for safekeeping. The order also stated that Jews found with valuables would be punished by death. My mother gave most of her jewellery to a German family, who returned it after the war. I gave my friend Lenuta my silver chain and locket, together with my cat, Mitzy.

As ordered, the Jews of Campulung Bucovina assembled at the station. I was carrying a satchel with my schoolbooks. We were loaded into cattle wagons, which Romanian soldiers locked from the outside. Then our journey into the unknown began.

I don't remember much about the journey, except trying to peer out between cracks in the walls of the wagon. After about 60 hours, we arrived in Attaki, a small town on the banks of the River Niester, and were ordered out of the wagons. It was evening, it was raining and muddy, and we discovered that all the houses in Attaki had been destroyed. Taking shelter in one roofless house, to our horror, we found Yiddish inscriptions on the walls, written in charcoal and what looked like blood. One of them was: *Here were tortured and murdered many Jews, whoever reads this say Kaddish for us.*

The next day, we crossed the River Niester on barges to the Ukrainian town of Moghilev. This whole area of Ukraine between the rivers Niester and Bug was now under Romanian control and had been renamed Transnistria. When we were assembled, the frail and elderly, including my father's mother, were removed to an old people's home, where they all perished.

My mother and I had one piece of good fortune. Amongst our friends, it was known that my mother still had my father's silver Omega pocket watch. This she used as a bribe to secure a place for us all on a convoy to Shargorod, about 80 kilometres from Moghilev. Horse-drawn wagons carried our possessions, the adults marched on foot, and the children were allowed to take turns riding on the wagons. At night, we slept on straw in peasants' barns. One peasant woman offered to keep me till the end of the war, but my mother refused.

Shargorod was a miserable, primitive place, but we were the lucky ones. We had official permission to reside there. The local Jewish population was forced by the Romanian authorities to share their poor homes with us. Sanitation was non-existent, and we had to use a vacant lot as a toilet. There were no washing facilities. Everybody had lice, and I remember checking my clothes every night before going to sleep. I was always hungry, cold, and very much afraid.

We lived in a tiny narrow alcove off a larger room occupied by our landlady, Mrs Schmuklerman. In this alcove, my mother slept on a plank, her mother slept on a wooden box, and I slept between the two of them on three chairs pushed together. That was the full width of the alcove. We survived by selling our possessions for food. The first winter was terribly cold. When my mother caught typhoid fever and became very sick, I was sent out from the alcove to stay with Mrs Schmuklerman, while my grandmother nursed my mother. After Mrs Schmuklerman found out that I was afraid of primus lamps, she always lit the lamp as soon as I came into her room, and so I spent my days outside in the biting cold until my mother recovered.

In the second year of our enforced stay, we got financial help from our relatives in Romania and were able to afford about two meals a day. I also continued my education thanks to the books I had brought from home, and many other children also used them. When I got jaundice, the only treatment available was a dose of Epsom salts, taken every morning for two weeks.

As the war progressed and the German army fell back from the advancing Soviets, rumours began circulating about atrocities committed by the retreating soldiers. The adults spoke freely, within earshot of the children, and I was petrified.

In March 1944, we were liberated by the Red Army. Slowly, we made our way home. I resumed my education, sat for some exams, and joined the second-year high school class — my first time in a normal classroom since 1940. On my return to school, the first person who greeted me with hugs and kisses was my friend Lenuta, who was by then in third year.

The following summer, I studied hard and completed third year during the long school break. My best moment came when registering for the new school year. The teacher started to write 'Rosentower, third year', and I was able to correct her and say 'fourth year'. She looked up and said 'Bravo!' I was so happy, and my self-esteem was restored. After all that time, I had succeeded and rejoined my previous classmates. There were only three Jewish students in the class, but it made no difference to me. I was happy.

It was about this same time that I joined a Zionist youth group, Hanoar Hazioni, and I can truthfully say that this was the happiest time of my youth. I was at school and loved it, I had many friends — most of them returned from Transnistria, like me — and, best of all, my mother had remarried. Her new husband was a kind and gentle man who was like a father to me.

Towards the end of 1947, all kinds of rumours started circulating about the possibility of going on *aliya* (making ascent, or returning) to Palestine. Our Zionist group received ten places on the next ship sailing to Palestine, and we added an extra ten names to the list. I was embarrassed to leave my name off the list, and I became number 20. Unbeknown to us, someone pulled strings in Bucharest and all 20 names were approved. After much debate at home, my parents agreed to let me go on *aliya*. On 22 December 1947, I boarded a train, surrounded by friends but without my parents.

Winter in Campulung Bucovina: Shulamit Ullmann in 1947, shortly before emigrating.

We reached the town of Burgaz in Bulgaria, where we boarded the 'illegal' ship the *Pan Crescent*, which was bound for Palestine. We were intercepted by the British and interned on the island of Cyprus. I was very miserable there, and regretted what I had done. I missed my mother and I missed school. But, after three months, our turn came to go on to Palestine. The person who processed my identification said, 'You can't go to Eretz Israel with a name like Selma.' I remembered that my Hebrew name was Shulamit, and I have been known by that name ever since. And so, in March 1948, I reached Palestine, just two months before Israel's Declaration of Independence.

Our group was sent to an agricultural school in Magdiel for training to join a new settlement; but, by then, I knew that communal life was not for me. In 1949, I was accepted as a nursing student at the Assuta Hospital in Tel Aviv. I graduated in 1952 and nursed for over 50 years, retiring in 2006, age 75.

In 1954, I married John Ullmann in Tel Aviv, and Selma Rosentower became Shulamit Ullmann. Two years later, we immigrated to Australia where, in 1962, I was finally reunited with my parents. In 1965, John and I were blessed with twin daughters, Anita and Naomi. Today, we are blessed with four grandchildren — Hugo, Orli, Holly, and Lily — who have brought much joy into our lives.

Graduation: Shulamit Ullmann graduates as a nurse, 1952.

KATHY VALER GORDON
A very young breadwinner

I was not yet six years old when the Germans occupied Hungary in March 1944. Following the German occupation, the situation in Hungary deteriorated very rapidly, especially for us Jews. One of the first restrictions the Germans imposed was the compulsory wearing of the yellow star by all Jews over six years of age. My mother, Klara Hedvig, told me that, if asked, I was to say that I was still only five years old. It was very disappointing to me — at five, I was still a baby, whilst at six, I was a big girl, ready for school.

My mother must have had foresight, and this eventually helped save our lives. When we all had to cram into so-called 'Jewish houses', and the curfew restricted the movement of all Jews wearing the yellow star, I was free to move, and could go out at any time. From then on, I was the 'girl Friday'. I did the shopping, and acted as a messenger for the others who had to move in with us, when they needed to send a note to their families. When I look back on those fearful days, I realise how many small miracles helped me. I had to perform all these tasks when I was still at preschool age and could not read or write. Also, it is so strange that, although I was out on the streets most of the day, for weeks on end, nobody ever stopped me to ask what a little girl was doing on her own, without an accompanying adult.

My father, György Hedvig, was in a forced-labour camp in Budapest, where we lived. Occasionally, he could come home on day-leave. It was on one of those days that my parents decided that, if we were to survive, we had to go into hiding. Everything was prepared. It was agreed that when my father came home on his next day-leave, we would simply walk away and make our way to a hiding place on the outskirts of the city. The day came, but my father did not come home. My mother waited in vain, and then decided to go out and look for him. She was caught. Luckily, she was not shot dead on the spot, but she was imprisoned. Meanwhile, my grandparents were notified that my father had been shot and killed by members of the Arrow Cross, the Hungarian Nazi party.

The next dreadful time occurred when they came for us on a cold, windy autumn day, and herded us — my sister, my grandparents, and me, with many thousands of others — onto the local racecourse. We had to stand there, shivering for hours and hours, before we were taken to the ghetto. If living conditions in the 'Jewish houses' were bad, there was worse to come in the ghetto.

After we were taken away, my mother managed to escape from the prison and go home, only to find out that my father was dead. She was widowed at 33 years of age. She also learned from the neighbours that her mother and children had been taken away and locked up in the ghetto. Afraid of being caught again, as she was now the only Jew left in the neighbourhood, she quickly made her way to the hiding place that she had planned with my father. It was there that she organised our rescue from the ghetto. She knew full well that young children had little chance of surviving the ghetto's awful conditions.

My sister Panni, four years older than me, was rescued by a wonderful friend of my father's, József Nagy. He was a journalist and, as a Christian, had all the right papers, but he was risking his life and did not dare to offer to rescue both of us. My mother had to make the painful decision to decide which one of us he was to rescue — my sister, or me. He was a person of authority and had little trouble intimidating the guard in front of the ghetto, saying that he had all the right papers to take my sister. He succeeded. At least Panni was now safe.

In her desperation, my mother turned to Rózsi, an illiterate 17-year-old country girl who had lived with us as our maid until, under the Nazi laws, she had to leave us. 'Aryans' were not allowed to work for Jews, so the poor girl had to find herself a room and another job to support herself. While she was living with us she had been well provided for and had a much better life than she'd had in the village where she came from. So when my mother approached her, she knew the risks, but was willing to help save me.

I owe my life to Rózsi. As a teenage girl, her way of achieving her goal was to flirt with the guard at the ghetto gate. While she was promising him a date after duty, I snuck out of the ghetto, and met her around the corner. The most difficult task was accomplished, but we were still not out of danger: the two of us had to roam the streets during the cold winter days; and, after dark, we had to sneak, unseen, into her tiny room to spend the night in her single bed. If anybody had seen us, we would have been in danger, as many people reported Jews for the financial reward offered by the Nazis.

After a few days, my mother arranged to meet us, and I still remember clearly the joy of seeing her on the other side of the open square for the first time after what seemed like an eternity. Mum took me to our hiding place, a disused factory where a friend of my mother's had worked before the war. My sister was there, as well as my mother's friend with her daughter, her sister, and her son — seven of us altogether. We stayed there in hiding for many weeks.

It was January 1945, a cold winter's day, when I looked out of the window to see soldiers approaching. I became very frightened as, even at such a young age, I had learned that soldiers were always bad news. But this time the adults were joyful. They were Soviet soldiers, our liberators from the Nazis! Even then, I realised that these solders were a strange lot — a mixture of men, some 'older' women, and some very young boys. There were about 40 or 50 of them, and they stationed themselves with us, sleeping on the floor or wherever they could find a place. In the evenings, they would all sit around in one of the rooms, making music, eating, and drinking. Our mothers were still young women, and were afraid to show themselves during these times. But not me! I often joined them, going around and sitting on a soldier's lap till I was given a piece of bread or something else to eat. Then, I quickly jumped up, and took whatever food I was given to share with the others. This went on for hours and days on end. They probably realised what I was doing, but they did not seem to mind. The soldiers always welcomed me, probably because most of them remembered their daughters or their younger sisters left behind at home. Blonde little 'me' reminded them of home and of peacetime.

This is my story, of the way that I, a child of six living in those dreadful times, became the 'breadwinner' for our friends and family.

When the war ended, we left our hiding place and went back to our apartment, where we found that a lot of our movable belongings have been 'pilfered' by our neighbours. I guess they did not expected us to return. Though the adults did not tell me to, when I went around visiting our neighbours, I collected various items by just telling them they were ours, picking them up, and taking them home. Nobody would argue with a child so, in this way, I managed to collect some of our things.

I started school soon after, in a very good, strict private Scottish school, and completed my first year in three months. When I completed my fourth year of primary, the school was nationalised, and I continued my studies in the local public school.

While I was still in primary school, Hungary became a

communist country, and life became very, very difficult for us. My mother never had to work before the war, but had to become our main breadwinner after my father was killed. For many years, there was a shortage of food. Clothing and shoes was also a problem for us, as we grew out of our old ones before mum could save enough money to buy new ones. So the years went by.

I continued with my studies, and received my mechanical-engineering diploma a few months before the Hungarian uprising. My mother, sister, and I left the old country separately — among 200,000 political refugees — and illegally crossed the border into neighbouring Austria. Most people managed to cross in a day or two, but it took me 17 days. At my first attempt, I was caught by the border guards and ended up with the notorious secret police, where I was held and interrogated for some days, before I was returned to Budapest. Soon after, I left again, and that time successfully managed to reach Austria, where I was reunited with my mother and sister, who had left before me.

With my mother, we had to wait for a few months in various refugee camps until we received our Australian visa. My sister decided not to come, but my mother and I sailed from Italy to Melbourne. We ended up in the Bonegilla refugee camp where, to the best of my knowledge, we were the only Jews at that time; it was not a safe place for Jews.

I had given up working in my engineering profession, as it was very strictly a men's profession in 1950s Australia; however, through a set of interesting circumstances, I was able to start at the bottom of the ladder — without any English knowledge — and work my way up, and I spent 40 years in consulting engineering, until my retirement.

After retirement from my professional life, I still felt that I could do something useful, and I volunteered with Courage to Care, a travelling exhibition and educational program about respect and acceptance of all peoples. Until then, I had not considered myself a 'child survivor', only a child who had somehow survived the war.

I am very grateful that I was allowed to live in Australia, my adopted country. Travelling to various regional centres with Courage to Care's anti-discrimination education program, I feel I can give something back to the future generations.

My past was left behind. Life was not easy for me, and I had to learn to make decisions early in life. These experiences were probably character forming. The Nazis took away my childhood, the communists my youth, but I have learned one thing in life: to always be positive. Don't live in the past — always look ahead.

JUDY BAHAR
I don't remember

I don't remember when the soldiers took my father away. But, a few years ago, when I accompanied my mother back to Debrecen, the town in Hungary where I was born, she took me to the building where we lived, and she pointed to the corner balcony on the first floor. She said that was where she stood, with me in her arms, when my father, flanked by the uniformed boys, turned around, waved to us, and walked through the vaulted entrance to disappear forever … *I was five months old.*

I don't remember the journey in the cattle wagon. But I have been told that I was fed biscuit crumbs, which my mother grabbed at the last minute as we were leaving the ghetto. Although I can't remember, I can see in my mind's eye how my mother looked then: young, fit, healthy, dressed in a sensible ski suit, with a stuffed rucksack on her back, from which dangled a glass potty. My practical mother with that incongruous glass vessel … *I was eight months old.*

I don't remember when my mother, risking her life, crossed that foreign town to get to the hospital, while the other women back in the labour camp covered for her absence. I don't remember her bursting into tears at the sight of me, a dying, emaciated child with a hollow face dominated by the huge eyes of the malnourished. I don't remember her stealing me from the hospital, back to the camp, from which all the inmates were sent on a death march the very next day. I don't remember all the 'kind' souls trying to get my mother to see the pointlessness of carrying that dying child ... *I was 16 months old.*

I don't remember the old couple who gave us shelter in their house in that foreign land one night, after my mother escaped into the forest from the thinning line of marchers which left corpses in its wake, like a nightmare version of Hansel and Gretel's pebbles. I don't remember how the other villagers brought scraps of food 'for the baby'. I don't remember being in my mother's arms as she greeted the liberators ... *I was still barely one-and-a-half years old.*

I don't remember ... but I do. I see every one of those scenes, vividly, embroidering the details, being in awe of what my mother went through, being overwhelmed by the miracle of survival.

Acknowledgements

The Sydney Child Holocaust Survivors group owes its strength and longevity to its hardworking committee, especially to Lexie Keston, whose organisational skills and dedication to the group is invaluable.

Credit must also be given to Ruth Leiser, who meticulously looks after the group's finances, and to Hannah Meyer, who helps wherever she can, especially in sending out the group's newsletters.

Special acknowledgement is given to Naomi Goldrei, who devoted so much time, initially, to this book, until illness stopped her.

The support and loyalty of all our members, and the need for us to finally tell our stories to others rather than to each other, has culminated in the publishing of this book.

We also wish to acknowledge Keith McLennan's contribution to this book. In his early editorial work, Keith encouraged us, the storytellers, to tell more, often visiting people who were not computer literate, taking notes, thoroughly checking and rechecking historical backgrounds and facts, and being very patient in accepting late changes and additions.

Lastly, our group owes an immeasurable debt of gratitude and thanks to our member, patron, and sponsor, Paul Kornmehl.